D1127512

Church-State Relations in Ecumenical Perspective

CHURCH-STATE RELATIONS IN ECUMENICAL PERSPECTIVE

edited by

ELWYN A. SMITH

DUQUESNE UNIVERSITY PRESS
Editions E. Nauwelaerts, Louvain
1966

DUQUESNE BOOKS OF ECUMENICAL INTEREST

THE ECUMENICAL VANGUARD: *The History of the Una Sancta Movement,* Swidler

ANGLICANISM IN ECUMENICAL PERSPECTIVE, van de Pol

SCRIPTURE AND ECUMENISM, Swidler, editor

THE CHANGING CHURCH, van Bilsen

FAITH AND THE WORLD, Dondeyne

Library of Congress Catalog Card Number 66–18450

Printed in the United States of America

Contents

INTRODUCTION

SINCE the coming of religious toleration, Western political thought has been struggling to define the secular state in such a way as to secure the integrity of religion, the independence of the state in its own sphere, civil and religious liberty for all citizens, and the spiritual health of society. The evolution of the relations of church and state in the United States is an eminent chapter in that history; but the contribution of the American churches has consisted more in the excitement of their disagreements and a literature of controversy than joint inquiry into the civil conditions which answer to the character, purposes, and needs of religion itself.

In the United States, religious groups take form at the will of individuals and groups, not the state, and exist in competition with one another and other voluntary societies. While the state has become ever more fully rationalized, churches are gathered only in non-authoritative bodies such as the National Council of the Churches of Christ and smaller ad hoc committees. From that Council, the most comprehensive body of that kind, the Roman Catholic Church stands aside, as do large groups such as the Southern Baptists, Missouri Synod Lutherans, most sects, and other bodies gathered in the National Association of Evangelicals.

Typical of the performance of religious groups in relation to the law was the struggle of the Congress to formulate the Education Act of 1965. The lawmakers confronted a succession of witnesses from religious bodies expressing conflicting views and pressing different interests. The Congress as representative of civil authority was, of course, highly organized and fully capable of arriving at its decision; but not the spokesmen of religion. Some felt that the proposed law would intrude on religious freedom; others did not. The Congress decided. In such circumstances, some see danger to religious liberty and damage to the integrity of religion.

No super-church is needed to state the concerns of religion in American society; only the congress of scholars and churchmen of different religious persuasions. From the point of view of some American founders, a level distribution of the populace among a large number of different religions was a guarantee of religious freedom. What could a congeries of contending sects better agree to support than state neutrality toward religion? Yet the peace of this country has also been disturbed by religious conflicts, most painfully the anti-Catholic politics of the nineteenth and twentieth centuries. Had Protestants and Catholics been on speaking terms between 1835 and the election of John F. Kennedy, American political history might have been more tranquil and the reputation of religion less blemished.

The coming of ecumenism presents important new possibilities—and dangers. Will Catholic-Protestant solidarity create a Christian bloc that threatens the Jewish community? Does it imply the development of "Christian" politics instead of a religiously neutral secularity? Will Christian churches consent to programs of cooperation with government and by majority power silence critics of the intermixing of religion and public authority?

There is also promise. Protestantism has been nowhere more individualistic than in the United States; in dialogue with Catholics and Jews it may rediscover its earlier communal self-understanding. Catholicism achieved its fullest development in medieval society, which exalted community at the expense of freedom and the individual; but there is evidence in the Decree on Religious Liberty of the recent Council that its American experience in a Protestant environment has helped it recover and expand its ancient respect for conscience. Ecumenism need not threaten Jews but may lead to a better grasp of the Jewish situation and even recover important common foundations in faith.

How shall Christians understand civil power itself? Is it secular or sacred? Is it of God or natural?

These are some of the questions touched in this book. Ecumenical dialogue has passed through its first moment of blossoming congeniality and plunged into discussion of basic historical and theological themes such as church authority, Scripture and tradition, and Christology. But discussion of the vexing ethical problems of modern life is only beginning. On some of these, internal debate is heated, as with the Roman Catholic search for a contemporary morality of birth control. Some will judge that it is not yet opportune to attempt discussion of such problems on an ecumenical basis. But it is high time that Catholics and Protestants, together with Jews, got down to business with church-state relations. The issue has been public for over three generations and has persistently divided the three communities. Internal debate within each is animated but not threatening, nor does lack of common concepts condemn intergroup discussion to misunderstanding. A decided easing of tension occurred during the period of the Second Vatican Council, which corresponded with the Kennedy-Johnson administrations. Discussion of fundamentals has already waited on politics a long time. The public may be grateful for some respite from religious conflict; but the churches have little reason to congratulate themselves upon achievement of new insight through common study. It is now apparent that America's historic "religious" divisions have been principally produced by sociological power clashes. The new climate invites churches to bring theological and ethical unities to bear in an area neglected by theologians.

The eleven essays that compose this book touch four areas. A first group studies the relation of ecumenism to recent social change: ecumenism and the secularization of modern life (Daniel Callahan); the impact of ecumenism on Roman Catholic attitudes toward church-state relations (Leonard Swidler); changing Jewish attitudes toward the stake of Jews in a free society (Arthur Gilbert).

The second group consists of two studies of the religious meaning of community for civil life. The first concerns Biblical concepts of community and state (John L. McKenzie); the second examines the community, as opposed to the individual, as the referent of ethics itself (Michael Novak).

The third section contains three studies of natural law: the problem in the writings of St. Paul (Markus Barth); of St. Thomas Aquinas (Michael Strasser); and in the thought of John Calvin (Arthur C. Cochrane).

The last section is composed of three studies in American law: the relation of status and contract in religion and law (Leo Pfeffer); the concept of subsidiarity and its practice among churches disposed to cooperate with the state (Dean M. Kelley); and the steady evolution of the concept of religion in American constitutional thought in the direction of conscientiousness (Elwyn A. Smith).

With one exception, these essays were delivered during the academic year 1965–66 to the graduate Seminar in Ecumenics jointly conducted by Duquesne University (Pittsburgh) and the Pittsburgh Theological Seminary (United Presbyterian).

We wish to acknowledge our debt to the Howard Heinz Endowment for its assistance in aiding the Seminar on Ecumenism. An earlier volume, also made possible by the Heinz Endowment, has been published in the *Duquesne Studies,*

Theological Series: SCRIPTURE AND ECUMENISM—*Protestant, Catholic, Orthodox and Jewish,* edited by Leonard J. Swidler (Duquesne University Press, Pittsburgh, 1965). The Ecumenics Seminar has been operative for five years and represents the practice of ecumenism in academic life. It is hoped that its example and written product may cultivate ecumenical understandings of the problems which come before it year by year.

Elwyn A. Smith

April, 1966

SECULARITY AND ECUMENISM

by

Daniel Callahan

LIKE people, historical movements are sometimes forced to live down the gossip that their birth was illegitimate. "Secularization" and "ecumenism" have had this problem. Only recently have they gained a certain respectability in polite company. For decades, secularization was understood to mean "secularism," a God-denying, materialistic outlook which spelled doom to "spiritual values." Ecumenism was taken to mean "indifferentism," a frame of mind apt to reduce all theological differences to personal taste and to betray truth for the sake of a simpering "spirit of brotherhood."

Yet though "secularization" and "ecumenism" shared a common initial fate in the popular religious mind, their rise to respectability followed different lines. After beginning more as moods than movements, each was given a retroactive birth certificate, attesting to its lineage, and each was taken up as the object of study, discussion and enthusiasm. On the surface, the main impetus behind the ecumenical movement seemed to be the patient work of a handful of scattered theologians and journals. They argued, successfully enough, that ecumenism does not mean a compromise with truth, nor that theological and ecclesiastical convictions are unimportant. Similarly, secularization engendered an attempt to show how and why it was possible for Christians to affirm the turn taken by Western history away from sacralism and an other-worldly orientation. The secularity movement (if I may so call that attempt) apparently took its rise especially from the effort of various social thinkers to convince the churches and the world that Christians could take man's terrestrial existence and welfare with full seriousness.

So far as they go, these casual explanations are plausible enough. But in the broad view they are actually somewhat misleading. Do these movements, for instance, really spring from different sources? This becomes extremely doubtful as soon as one considers the very deep cultural currents which have been stirring Western society since the end of World War II: the inclination toward world unity, the growing dominance of science and technology, the evidence of a diminishing spirit of nationalism in some parts of the West, and a growing skepticism about ideologies of any kind. Since this is the context in which most of Christianity exists, it would be amazing if the churches did not reflect some of these same attitudes in their theologies; and of course they do. Ecumenism can be seen as a reverberation within the churches of the trend toward world unity in the political sphere. Equivalently, Christian secular theology can be looked upon as an osmotic response by the churches to the acceptance of urban life and technology by society at large. The parallels between anti-nationalism and anti-denominationalism hardly need spelling out.

Historical observations of this kind need not minimize the contributions made by particular thinkers and specific theological schools. They only help emphasize that theological changes often have roots which are as often cultural as intellectual, as often a product of the *Zeitgeist* as of dedicated men.

That said, let us go a step further. Not only should ecumenism and Christian secular theologies be thought of as springing from similar origins, but they are also areas of concern and speculation which should be treated together in a conscious manner. In a way, this is already being done, at least if one heeds the common advice that, whatever their differences, Christians can and should join hands to combat the ills of racial discrimination, slums, poverty, and so on. That is good advice, but still a long way from recognizing that secularity and ecumenism are problems intimately related.

What, exactly, is the relationship? The first place worth looking for an answer is in modern history. If we grant that Western society has in the past four-hundred years or so undergone a process of secularization, then it is worth recalling the part played by the Reformation, the Counter Reformation and the legacy of disunity. I use the word "recalling" advisedly. Men have been arguing for centuries just what, if any, responsibility Christian disunity has had for the way the modern world has turned out. To avoid getting myself embroiled in these wrangles, let me simply cite the words of a diverse sampling of commentators.

Harold J. Laski has written of the Reformation that "Because it was a grave blow at authority, it loosened the hold of tradition on men's lives. Because it called into question ideas which had long held sway, it gave a deep impetus to the temper of rationalism. Both its doctrines and its social results were emancipating to the individual."[1] For Christopher Dawson, "The secularization of Western Christendom . . . involved first the loss of Christian unity, which was itself due not to secularism but to the violence of religious passion and the conflict of rival doctrines."[2] As for the impact of the Reformation on political thought, the views of Karl Holl are representative of a major school of thought: "In Lutheran territories the Reformation helped that view triumph which saw in the state something superior to the individual will, an institution which served to direct all the efforts of the people. . . . At the same time it was the Reformation that first set a rigid limit to the absolute power of the state."[3] Or we may listen to Ernst Troeltsch: "the social influence of ascetic Protestantism upon the history of civilization has been penetrating and comprehensive. Through its ecclesiastical ideal, which merges into the ideal of the Free Churches, the democratic constitution of its individual congregations, as well as of its general ecclesiastical structure, its autonomous individualism, based upon the Will of God and the fact of Redemption, and its systematic and positive industry, it has become one of the basic causes of the immense changes in modern society."[4] One hardly needs to mention the work of Max Weber on the economic impact of the Protestant ethos.[5]

Considerably less speculation has been lavished upon the Roman Catholic responsibility for secularization. John Courtney Murray, S.J., first became famous for his argument that Roman Catholics could accept what he called "the American proposition" because they had a long tradition which recognized the autonomy of the state, its properly secular nature and end.[6] From a different perspective, a host of Catholic writers has blamed the Church's fawning upon civil authority during the seventeenth and eighteenth centuries for the sake of privileges and protection as one source of an overweening pride on the part of the modern state. But examples of Catholic contributions to secularization are hard to come by; on the whole, Roman Catholicism set its face for centuries against the demise of the "sacral age" which had been a mark of its pre-Reformation hegemony. One might guess that its main contribution was its tendency to tolerate, then to accept and finally to praise (with necessary distinctions) what modern civilization produced—though it usually did so long after the fact.[7]

There seems little doubt, however, that the continuing friction between Protestants and Catholics, did much to strengthen secularization. These conflicts helped to assure the disappearance of established churches, to necessitate state neutrality toward the competing claims of the churches, to stimulate the development of secular theories of human freedom, and to allow cultural leadership to pass from religious to secular hands. I am not suggesting, in any sense, that one can explain secularization solely in these terms; at most, they were contributing causes, sometimes by commission, sometimes by omission. But taken together with industrialization, urbanization, scientific and technological progress, they played a key role. At the very least it becomes ridiculous to look upon secularization as something which came upon the churches wholly from the outside, as if it was a stranger for whose presence Christianity bore no responsibility.

If it is true, then, that Christian disunity has had much to do with the shaping of a secular world, it seems no less true to say that secularization has, in its turn, profoundly affected the relationship of the churches to each other. This was not true at first. As the industrial age and the nation-state came upon Western society, most forcefully in the nineteenth century, the churches were still sharply divided. Where they could, they resisted pluralism, trying with all their remaining resources to hold on to traditional prerogatives and dominance; hence in America Protestants resisted the coming of the Catholic immigrant, in England the established church fought a (losing) battle against the Emancipation Act, in Spain and Latin America Protestants got short shrift, and so on. Though industrialism was beginning to leave its mark, it had yet to create what Brian Wicker has aptly called "an overwhelming force towards common ideals and experience, even between the most disparate societies."[8] Though science and empiricism were coming into their own, they had not yet become man's primary tool for mastering the world in which he lived. Nor had what Harvey Cox has called the "pragmatic" and "profane" style of contemporary man yet replaced the older ways of tribal and town man, much less his proclivity for metaphysical questions.[9] By and large, religion still held a lofty place. The colossus of technology cast a relatively small shadow in the beginning and only a few acute observers noticed that here and there industrialization was taking its toll among the working classes.[10]

The shadow was destined to lengthen. Whatever one can say about the vitality of the churches, the quantity of the faithful, or the creativity of theology, only a rash person would claim that institutional religion still occupies the center of the human social drama. If it is not quite proper to say that the technological mentality represents a formulated ideology, it nonetheless has created an ethos as all-encompassing as anything ever dreamed of by deliberate social planners. However much the churches might have shouted imprecations in the face of this change from a sacral, then to a religiously pluralistic, then to a secular culture, the change came. One of the most common themes of the religious artist today is that of the small, usually gothic church surrounded by towering skyscrapers; though overdone, the image is apt enough.

What did this mean for the churches? Most notably, it meant that their own disputes, their debates over creeds and orthodoxy, their nasty disunities, became exceedingly minor struggles on the world stage. Those with a particularly religious bent of mind, or those involved in religion professionally, could lavish great passion on these matters; for the great mass of men fewer and fewer had any interest at all. Though Christians today deplore the bloody religious wars of the sixteenth century, it has at least to be said that men then took their belief as a matter of life and death. It is almost unthinkable that Christians today, whether practicing or nominal, would defend or promote their religious commitments by means of warfare. We will fight about race or borders or political methods or secular ideologies; we will not fight about religion. The optimist might credit this shift to the intrinsic good sense and charity of contemporary Christians; the realist could make a better case that ecclesiastical loyalties just don't count for that much anymore. Perhaps I should modify this last statement and just say that, although such loyalties may count, they have lost much of their old tenacity.

The net result of this shift seems clear enough. Where the churches once fought to divide the world among themselves, they have now been forced to work for their very survival as culturally influential bodies. In the face of secularization, the struggle of one has become the struggle of all. Whether they like it or not, the Christian churches have been downgraded together to a secondary position in society. In the early days of ecumenism, one could often hear pleas that the churches patch up their quarrels for the sake of offering a common front against mutual enemies: Communism, materialism, secularism, or what have you. Nowadays one can hear a more sophisticated version of the same line of thought: that the churches have to unite better to meet the social problems of the world. Thankfully, neither the crude nor the sophisticated version has had much influence in serious ecumenical circles, but the very fact that such arguments could be put forward is adequate testimony to the displacement of Christianity as a decisive determinant of the shape of the world. One way or another, it was altogether natural for divided Christians to begin noticing that they shared an embarrassing common lot. One observer has suggested that, faced with increased external competition, it was hardly surprising that the churches should begin banding together, that a process of religious "cartelization" should make its appearance.[11]

No less important, the impact of pluralism has been decisive for ecumenism; and pluralism is one direct consequence of Christian disunity. In the centuries immediately following the Reformation Europe was split roughly into two spheres: Protestantism dominated the North and Catholicism the South. To theological divisions were added geographical and cultural divisions; the likelihood of any ecumenical drive surmounting this many obstacles was slight. Only in the late nineteenth and in the twentieth centuries did these separations begin to diminish. The Catholic immigration to America, the coming of the Irish to Great Britain, the effect of World War II in Germany—to cite only the most prominent examples—all had the effect of placing Protestants and Catholics in physical proximity to each other. Eventually they had to find ways of living and working together, of creating a culture in which both could live in some productive way, and of theologically justifying the new relationship forced upon them.

At first it was exceedingly difficult to do these things, but with time, experience and a gradual acceptance of the reality of pluralism the sharper edges of conflict were honed away. There still exist many Protestant-Catholic conflicts over issues of Church and State, but they are now remarkably mild when compared with past decades. The reduction of earlier political tensions has, in its turn, created a favorable environment for a reduction of theological differences. Indeed, since Protestants and Catholics increasingly share a common cultural, social, and political life in most Western nations, their only significant divisions are coming to be theological. One might say that the upheaval of the sixteenth century has now come full circle. What began as a theological dispute and then degenerated into a religio-political cold (and sometimes hot) war has once again become theological. The great success of recent Protestant-Catholic dialogue would indicate that theological oppositions are far easier to handle and overcome than cultural and political divisions. That should be a valuable lesson for the future as well as a major vindication of the value of pluralism for Christian life.[12]

Yet to point to some of the valuable offshoots of secularization for the progress of ecumenism by no means exhausts the complexity of their relationship. If nothing else, these offshoots have usually been accidental, often resisted by the churches and rarely appropriated in a creative way at the outset. It is easy enough to concede after the fact that secularization has not been the disaster the churches imagined it might be. It will be far more difficult to take the next steps: to anticipate the changes that secularization will undoubtedly continue to bring, to shape a viable, flexible and continuing Christian response, and—hopefully—to make some difference to the possible directions which secularization can take.

That many such attempts are now being made should be apparent to anyone even vaguely familiar with recent Christian thought. Not all of these attempts are favorable to the emergence of secularization. The work of Christopher Dawson and T. S. Eliot[13] provides an example of two sensitive writers intent on showing the necessity of recreating some form (however updated) of Christian civilization. The ideology of the conservative thinkers grouped around the *National Review* and *Modern Age* heavily emphasizes the enduring validity of the idea of "the Christian West." On a more popular level, the outcries directed against recent Supreme Court decisions on prayer and Bible-reading lay major stress on the evils of a "Godless" and "secularistic" society. And as one articulate writer put it, "The harmony . . . between religion, military courage and science, is responsible for the noble character which all nations have hailed with universal acclamation. . . . Take the first element away from it, and the unity, or in other words, the whole beauty of it, disappears." These last words were not written, as one might reasonably guess, by a God-fearing patriot urging the United States to stem the tide of atheistic Communism, but by a spiritual ancestor of that breed, Joseph DeMaistre.[14] A contemporary of DeMaistre expressed the ultimate fear: "The day when the atheistic dogma of the sovereignty of the people replaces in politics the sacred dogma of the sovereignty of God; the day when Europe ceases to be Christian and monarchical, she will perish, and the sceptre of the world will pass to other hands."[15] As it happened, Europe did not perish, but "the sceptre of the world" did "pass to other hands"—to the increasingly world-wide dominion of technology and (almost to) the newly emergent Afro-Asian lands (however odd this juxtaposition may seem). A constant premise of contemporary conservative thought is that a spiritual disaster is at hand if this movement is not reversed—by spiritual means, if possible; by force, if necessary.

The positive response to secularization has been equally varied, though it too shares some common premises. These are roughly: a) that technology and material progress are to be welcomed and fostered; b) that the demise of monarchical Europe and its attendant assumption of a well-merited Christian spiritual hegemony has proved to be a source of human liberation; c) that political, psychological, cultural and religious freedom are necessary conditions for human development; and d) that Christianity will be faithful to its essential nature only insofar as it affirms the dignity of the material world and contributes to humanity's temporal well-being. Other premises might well be detected, but I think there would be some general agreement on those suggested. All would not be rejected by conservative thinkers, but some probably would; and those accepted might be seen in a very different light than is common to Christian secular thought.

As could be expected, the strategies which have been devised from these premises vary to a considerable degree. Some, like Harvey Cox in *The Secular City,* are apt to seek a rich Christian appropriation of just those aspects of contemporary secularization most despised: mobility, anonymity, pragmatism, organization-life, a love of the profane. Others are more prone to stress the alienation, rootlessness and demonic side of present-day life, pressing all the while toward the vision of a new society which transcends both the *ancien régime* (in its rigid and modified forms) and the crushing embrace of a technocratic world. Still others, like Teilhard de Chardin and many of his followers, seem to believe that in the very nature of things man and matter are moving inexorably toward the Omega point; it is less a matter of strategy than of acceptance and perception. Some, like Karl Rahner, welcome the advent of secularization but emphasize less the creation of a new man and a new society than the necessity for the Christians' acceptance of their "diaspora situation" and the establishment of a qualitative rather than quantitative witness to salvific truths.[16] And then there are a few who believe, with Paul Van Buren, that the main job at hand is to find "the secular meaning of the Gospel."

Whatever the different strategies, however, and whatever the common premises, our attention is being called to certain facts. One of these facts—though it is boring by now to use the word—is the lack of Christian "relevance" to the complex, urbane, confusing human situation of the second half of the twentieth century. Another is that man seems to be making a decent go of a life where religion may still capture his nominal allegiance but does not grip and animate his imagination. Another is that where religion is not irrelevant it too often falls into an equally bad pit, that of providing transcendent sanction and legitimation for the political status quo. Another is that technology and urbanization are here to stay and that religion had better make the most of it. Finally—and here I will add my own assertion of what is a "fact"—that nothing could matter much less to contemporary man than the truth about justification, papal infallibility, *agape,* Mary's heavenly titles, the relationship of Scripture and tradition and much else that the most serious and dedicated ecumenical scholars would find worthy of a life's work.

This last fact, if it can be accepted as such, points to a sobering conclusion. Even if the most exalted dream of total Christian reunion could be achieved, there is no longer any certainty that it would have a decisive influence on the future of the world. Despite all the progress which ecumenism has made, it would be difficult to argue that this has significantly changed the relationship of nations, affected the quality of most human encounters, altered the character of urban or rural life, or has solved in any way whatsoever the problems posed by automation, cybernation, nuclear power and the imbalance of rich and poor nations. If my earlier assumption is correct—that ecumenism is as much the result of social change as of theological illumination—then one could almost say that what happens in the world will make far more difference to the churches than the converse.

One might reply to this that ecumenism is still so new and tentative that to expect any immediate decisive influence on the world would be precipitous; it is enough to hope and work for this influence and leave the rest in the hands of God. This is a good retort and for that matter, very disarming. But one would at least like to see some preliminary hints that this hope has some foundation in reality. If there are such hints, they are surely "preliminary" in the extreme: the effectiveness of an ecumenical witness in the area of American race relations (an effectiveness, however, which has presupposed and built upon a prior legal and political consensus whose origin is heavily secular); the effectiveness of an ecumenical witness against the horrors of nuclear warfare (but an effectiveness, again, whose roots are the very human fears and anxieties about physical destruction); the symbolic value for mankind as a whole of two antagonistic forces beginning to patch up their differences after four hundred years of tension and suspicion (but a symbol whose value is diminished when one realizes that historical and sociological changes have been as important as prayer, charity and understanding).

Nonetheless, however much one may be able to qualify the various contributions of ecumenism to the general problems which torment, divide and hinder the human race, they may be the only kind which ecumenism can offer. More specifically, ecumenism can provide mankind with little in the way of direct help, but may be able to make many indirect contributions, the sum total of which could be significant. There are three ways (minimally) this could be done: 1. by stimulating the inner renewal of the churches, thus fortifying and enriching their perception, appropriation and witness of Christ; 2. by making possible the formation of broad Christian pressure groups whose strength can be brought to bear, together with other groups, in the formation of political and social policy; 3. by providing the world with a model of the ways in which men whose divisions are deep can go about achieving reconciliation.

The value of each of these contributions can be spelled out very briefly. It is a principle common to all Christians that Christ came to redeem the world, but that this redemption must be carried on and extended by the Church; hence the need for inner renewal if this work is to be done. There is now a general agreement that in highly organized yet socially fragmented societies political and social developments require the kinds of pressure which strong individual groups, or coalition groups, can bring to bear on the body politic; hence, the need for Christian "pressure groups," in the non-pejorative sense of working in alliance with others. Finally, it should be clear that mankind has made only small progress in the direction of developing techniques for the reduction of nationalistic antagonisms, ideological confrontations, racial, ethnic and class hostilities; hence, the great need for some useful models or examples of communities which have devised methods of overcoming long-standing hostilities. Expressed in the most primitive terms possible, ecumenism would have much to give the world if mankind could point to divided Christians and say: see how they love each other despite their differences; see how they work together for the good of mankind; see how they each strive to live up to the highest ideals of their respective traditions; see how they are able, in peace, to work through their disputes.

To the extent that the process of secularization continues, to that extent will the world require the particular gifts which an ecumenical Christianity can offer. While there are many indications of a trend toward world unity, they are indications only. Practically speaking, the spirit of nationalism has been one consequence of secularization; national groupings have come in great measure to replace religious groupings. The realization of world unity will necessitate that the nations learn to get along with each and to find the means whereby their narrower allegiances can be transmuted into broader, more universal bonds. Again, secularization has done its part in the movement toward urbanization. Yet for all its worth, urbanization poses serious dangers to personal identity, to a sense of human community, and to the possibility of man dominating his environment. Still again, secularization has often meant a diminishing of man's search for some abiding realities, for some ultimate meaning behind human life. By enlarging and deepening the contributions which an ecumenical Christianity can make to man's quest for his own significance, it is possible to hope that the dangers of secularization can be lessened.

More importantly, it is possible to hope that an ecumenical Christianity can help mankind to realize the inherent strengths and possibilities of secularization. To my mind, one of the most useful sketches of the characteristics of secularization has been presented by D. L. Munby in *The Idea of a Secular Society.*[17] Let me simply quote Munby on "the marks of a secular society" and add some suggestions of my own about appropriate ecumenical responses.

"(a) A secular society is one which explicitly refuses to commit itself as a whole to any particular view of the nature of the universe and the place of man in it."[18] This should pose no special problems for Christians. They, above all, should know from their own history how much mischief was done by the attempts of the churches to impose their pattern of belief and practice at the expense of religious liberty. At the same time, ecumenical Christianity should point out to mankind that truth matters and that the individual has the human duty to try and discover what the universe means and who he, as man, is. It should also resist, as part of its prophetic task, the attempt by any church, ideology or faction to impose its own world-view on everyone.

"(b) Such a society is unlikely to be homogeneous, and we do not find homogeneity."[19] Ecumenical Christians should welcome this lack of homogeneity. It will be a reflection, at one level, of the diversity of human gifts, temperaments, personal experience and different assimilations of the truth. At another level, it will reflect the actual freedom open to persons to seek, express and witness their own reading of the universe and what it requires of them. Given a natural human diversity, the presence of homogeneity in a society may be taken as *prima facie* evidence that freedom is lacking. It would, however, be very curious for ecumenical Christians to assert in some dogmatic fashion that no common values should be sought or desired; they would thereby be denying that their own beliefs have anything more than local, subjective and idiosyncratic value.

"(c) A secular society is a tolerant society. It makes no attempt to enforce beliefs or to limit the expression of belief. . . . [It] expressly tries to draw boundaries between public and private morality, and to widen the sphere of private decision and private choice."[20] My comments on (a) and (b) are pertinent here as well, but an additional point is also in order. If ecumenical Christians are serious about the centrality of religious liberty, both for the good of individuals and the integrity of the churches, then they have equally to realize that such liberty demands the presence of as many serious options as possible. Spain and the Soviet Union have a theoretical religious liberty; but the practical choices available to individuals makes this liberty null and void. Protestants and Catholics should not work only for the freedom of choosing between Protestantism and Catholicism but also for the freedom of choosing between secular humanism and Christianity, atheism and belief, and so forth.

"(d) Any society must have some common aims, in the sense that people are doing things together to produce certain effects. . . . In order to produce these effects there must be organization, an agreed method of solving problems, and a common framework of law. There must be political institutions, a legal system, and an economic organization . . . in a secular society these organizations and institutions have limited aims—at least in principle."[21] Among other things, Mr. Munby is here saying that politicians, legislators and judges should not be allowed to function as the "architects of manners and morals" or as "prophet-priests of the national conscience."[22] This is an astute observation and one which should be appreciated by ecumenical Christians aware of the way in which sacral Christianity (whether of the medieval or post-Reformation variety) endowed law-givers and magistrates with the power to coerce consciences and to shape society in ways determined by the churches. People will be free in so far as political leaders do not attempt to impose an over-arching value system. Whether this is done in the name of Christian values or anti-Christian values is irrelevant; in either case human dignity will be lessened. Still, it must be said that some degree of unity and shared values is necessary for a stable and viable society. The Christian contribution should be that of keeping before the eye of the public basic human needs: the need for liberty, peace, food, jobs, family stability, social justice, adequate clothes and housing. Ecumenical Christianity can also serve the unity of society by exercising its power of reconciliation, its ability to cut across class lines, and its potentiality of perceiving where men differ and where they agree.

"(e) In such a world we have discovered how various are the problems that can be solved by examination of the facts."[23] If nothing else, the ecumenical movement has demonstrated the value of hard, impartial investigation of Christian disunity; one need mention only the profound effect upon Catholicism of recent Roman Catholic studies of the Reformation. Beyond this parochial matter, empirical examination has established its validity in every domain. Christianity has a special stake in promoting its wider use: it helps to destroy harmful myths about man, religion and society and it helps to locate the genuine problems.[24] Yet it would not be impertinent for ecumenical Christianity to remind those overly enamored with data and statistics that man has secret recesses in his heart which cannot be charted on graphs; that despite all the predictions which can be made about his behavior, man remains a mystery.

"(f) A secular society is a society without official images. If there are no common aims, there cannot be a common set of images reflecting the common ideals and emotions of everyone. Nor can there be any common ideal types of behavior for universal application."[25] This particular mark of a secular society presents some difficulties. To say that a secular society requires that there be no official images makes considerable practical sense; images can dominate men almost as effectively as dogmas and rituals. But it seems to me something else again to accept passively the absence of any common aims. If human beings do have the needs I suggested above, and some right to expect society to help them to satisfy these needs, then there must be a minimal set of common aims. A society where people did not seek justice for all and did not maintain the ideal of justice would be an unhealthy society; it could be positively barbarian. So, too, for a society in which people did not hold to the ideal of human beings taking concern for each other's welfare. Beyond considerations of that kind, it is almost inconceivable that a society could long exist in which those who made it up shared no ideals at all. How could one, for instance, hope to maintain a legal system in the absence of a shared view that a certain degree of lawfulness is essential for the sake of civic peace? The question, really, is how far Christians should press for some common civic and social ideals, and what kind they should press for, and how far they should promote the establishment of private visions of the good life and the good society. Out of respect for the common ideal of decent brevity, I will not try to answer that question here.

Mr. Munby concludes his description by saying that "The positive ideals that lie behind the idea of the secular society are firstly a deep respect for the individual man and the small groups of which society is made up."[26] This seems to me as good a thumbnail sketch as any. Just how closely this ideal accords with a major impetus of the ecumenical movement should require no special elucidation.

What will the future bring? Historically, the roots of secularization appear to be deeper and more extensive than those of ecumenism. It is conceivable, though highly unlikely, that ecumenism could lose its present drive and become once again only the concern of a few specialists. But it is almost inconceivable that the movement toward secularization could reverse itself; and that because it is so much a result of urban and technological changes which now seem permanent. In any case, at the moment ecumenism and secularization are solidly entrenched. Sociologically and culturally, the latter provides the human context for the former. Just as the turns taken by society in the past were crucial for Christian relations, so they are likely to remain in the future. The main difference now, however, is that Christians are in a position to profit from, rather than instinctively resist, these turns. This can only be done in the present situation by recognizing the impact which ecumenism and secularization can have on each other. To think that ecumenism can be carried on independently of contemporary culture would be naïve. To think that ecumenism has no special duties toward broader human concerns would be irresponsible.

NOTES

[1] *The Rise of European Liberalism* (New York: Unwin Books, Barnes and Noble, 1962), p. 33.

[2] *The Historic Reality of Christian Culture* (London: Routledge and Kegan Paul, 1960), p. 19. Notice how Dawson uses the words "secularism" and "secularization" interchangeably.

[3] *The Cultural Significance of the Reformation,* trans. by Karl and Barbara Hertz and John H. Lichtblau (Cleveland: World Publishing Co., Meridian Books, 1959), p. 53.

[4] *The Social Teachings of the Christian Churches,* trans. by Olive Wyon (New York: Harper Torchbook, 1960), Vol. II, p. 818.

[5] *The Protestant Ethic and the Spirit of Capitalism,* trans. by Talcott Parsons (New York: Scribner's, 1958).

[6] cf. *We Hold These Truths* (New York: Sheed & Ward, 1960).

[7] See especially Jacques Maritain, *Man and the State* (Chicago: University of Chicago Press, 1951), p. 159; cf. John Courtney Murray, "The Problem of Religious Freedom," *Theological Studies* XXV (December, 1964). One need only compare the *Syllabus of Errors* of Pope Pius IX with contemporary Roman Catholic writings to see how much of what was once condemned is now praised by Roman Catholicism.

[8] *Culture and Liturgy* (New York: Sheed & Ward, 1963), p. 29.

[9] See in particular *The Secular City* (New York: Macmillan, 1965), Chapter 3.

[10] For an acute analysis of how and why this happened in one English city see E. R. Wickham, *Church and People in an Industrial City* (London: Lutterworth Press, 1957), esp. Chapter 6.

[11] I am indebted to Professor Peter Berger of the New School for this intriguing idea.

[12] Cf. H. Richard Niebuhr, *The Social Sources of Denominationalism* (Cleveland: World Publishing Co.; Meridian Books, 1957), p. 270.

[13] Dawson, *Historic Reality of Christian Culture, op. cit.,* and T. S. Eliot, *The Idea of a Christian Society* (London: Faber and Faber, 1939).

[14] "War, Peace, and Social Order" (1852), in *Catholic Political Thought: 1789–1848,* edited by Bela Menczer (Notre Dame, Ind.: University of Notre Dame Press, 1962), p. 62.

[15] Vicomte De Bonald, "The Unity of Europe" (1799), in Menczer, *op. cit.,* pp. 88–89.

[16] *The Christian Commitment,* trans. by Cecily Hastings (New York: Sheed & Ward, 1963), esp. chapter 1.

[17] (London: Oxford University Press, 1963).

[18] *Ibid.,* p. 14.

[19] *Ibid.,* p. 17.

[20] *Ibid.,* p. 20.

[21] *Ibid.,* p. 23.

[22] *Ibid.,* p. 25.

[23] *Ibid.,* p. 25.

[24] " 'Don't think, but look!' was Wittgenstein's repeated advice to his students. It should be taken to heart by all expositors of religion. As applied to Christianity in particular, no amount of laborious excogitation can answer the basic question: What is the evidence? And what is its value?" Dom Aelred Graham, "The Pathos of Vatican II," *Encounter* XXV (December, 1965), p. 19.

[25] Munby, *op. cit.,* pp. 30–31. It is worth noting a comment made by Anson Phelps Stokes on the origin of the expression "In God We Trust": ". . . this familiar motto on our coins was the direct result of the crisis through which the country was passing during the Civil War, and was an evidence of the feeling that the nation needed to cultivate the spirit of religion." *Church and State in the United States,* revised edition by Anson Phelps Stokes and Leo Pfeffer (New York: Harper & Row, 1964), pp. 568–569.

[26] Munby, *op. cit.,* p. 33.

THE IMPACT OF ECUMENISM ON CATHOLIC CHURCH-STATE RELATIONS

by

Leonard Swidler

IF PRESENT U.S. Church-state relations are to be viewed in correct perspective, they must be seen as products of past persons and forces in this country and abroad. The same must be said, with even more emphasis, about the development of ecumenism. Furthermore, since ecumenism (in the sense of Roman Catholic involvement in religious conversations with non-Catholics) has had a longer history in some European countries and has had some obvious effects in the political arena, a brief look in that direction will also cast some additional light on the possibilities inherent in the forces present in the American scene. Consequently, I will attempt to present some of the major positions taken by the Catholic Church concerning Church-state relations, singling out those particularly which have played a significant role in American history—either as positions held and implemented by Catholics when possible, or as images of Catholic positions that *existed* in Protestant American minds. Then I will describe the effects that ecumenism and its necessary forerunners and concomitants, pluralism and renewal, have had in some areas of Europe and America.

As is known by all, the Christian religion began with no recognition whatsoever by the state; in its first years it was viewed merely as a Jewish sect. After it was distinguished from Judaism, it led a checkered career in its relations to the state, sometimes tolerated, sometimes persecuted. But by the end of the fourth century the Christian Church had become the established religion of Rome. In the Eastern Empire there developed a caesaro-papism, while in the West the situation—much more anarchic than in the East—evolved toward a papal-caesarism.

The apogee along this line of Church-state relations was reached with the infamous two-sword theory, put forth in its greatest clarity and vigor by Pope Boniface VIII in his Bull *Unam Sanctam* (1302) directed against Philip the Fair of France.

> The Gospel teaches us that there are two swords in the hands of this shepherd (namely, Christ and His vicar the Pope): the spiritual and the temporal sword. For indeed, when the apostles said, "Behold there are two swords here" (Luke 22, 38), that is, in the Church, the Lord did not reply, "It is too much" but on the contrary, "It is enough." He who would dare to deny that the temporal sword is in the hands of Peter would pay little attention to the words, "put your sword into its scabbard" (Matt. 26, 52). The two swords, the spiritual and the temporal sword, then, are in the power of the Church; the first is used by the Church, the second for the Church; the first by the priests, the second by kings and soldiers, but only for as long as the priest wills and suffers it (*ad nutum et patientiam sacerdotis*). Therefore, one of those swords must be subject to the other, the temporal power must bow before the spiritual power.[1]

This position was not an extraordinary one at the time; Boniface was merely using arguments long familiar in medieval Christendom. For example, the same line of reasoning was expanded and ramified by the contemporary papalist, Giles of Rome, in his work *De Ecclesiastica Potestate,* and James of Viterbo and Henry of Cremona in their parallel writings. Naturally not everyone accepted these claims, even though the popes made them triumph *de facto* over the empire in the latter part of the thirteenth century. Among other demurrers, there were the moderates John of Paris, O.P., who wrote his *Tractatus de potestate regia et papali* in 1302 (John Courtney Murray, S.J., has said that John found a genuine middle way that is "indeed 'the great Catholic tradition' and, . . . if developed *in eodem sensu,* it may show the way to the solution of the contemporary problem."[2]), and Dante, who wrote his work *De Monarchia* within a decade of Boniface's death. Before another quarter of a century passed much more radical tracts were written by William of Occam, and, most of all, Marsilius of Padua and John of Jandun, who wrote the treatise *Defensor Pacis,* which eliminated *all* clerical power over temporalities, even the clothes the clerics wore and the food they ate. Needless to say, these latter positions were execrated by the popes and never received the laurel of orthodoxy.

While not all the positions of Giles of Rome and like-minded thinkers received approbation by a pope, one must never make the mistake of thinking that the papalist's assumptions and doctrines existed only on the fringe of medieval reality: the writings and actions of Boniface VIII and John XXII, among others, give the lie to this thought. One need look no further than the now accepted bulwark of orthodoxy, Thomas Aquinas, to see how far the prevalent assumptions about the compenetration of religion and politics, with the presumed supremacy of the former, extended at that time. In treating of heretics he views them as common criminals. Their crime is even greater than that of counterfeiters, for "it is much more grievous to corrupt the faith . . . than to falsify money." Therefore, heretics "may not only be excommunicated, but may justly be killed." The Church should properly tolerate his existence for a while, so long as there is some reasonable hope of conversion, but when that is gone then the heretic "must be cut out like rotten flesh, as Jerome says." He should be handed over "to the secular judge to be exterminated from the world through death."[3]

Though the overweening power ambitions of the popes and

their supporters called forth violent reactions that greatly weakened the papacy and rent the Church asunder in the fourteenth and fifteenth centuries—most dramatically exemplified in the succession of the Avignon papacy, the Western Schism, Conciliarism, and culminating in the sixteenth century Reformation—the main line of claims receiving papal support, at least in practice wherever possible, was the ideal of an intimate union of Church and state with the Church always ultimately supreme, even though its power over temporalities might be, allegedly, *indirect* rather than direct. St. Robert Bellarmine, S.J., of the seventeenth century is perhaps the most renowned and profound proclaimer of this latter position. Yet the net result of Bellarmine's revolutionary new approach—that the pope's power over temporalities is indirect (ironically, his work was almost placed on the index by Pope Sixtus V[4])—was that the pope could depose and appoint kings as well as annul and make laws for civil society. Although Bellarmine said that the pope could use his powers only when absolutely necessary for the salvation of souls, he was also clear that the pope alone was the judge of such necessities.[5]

Although there were many eddies in the mainstream of Church-state relations in "Catholic" countries through the Counter Reformation and into the eighteenth century, the flow was constantly in the direction of the union of Church and state. Although the Church was ever more chastened in its practical demands of superiority in the temporal area, still the theory and ideal never changed. It was challenged vigorously, even viciously, by the French revolution; the theory was only reinforced. Chief lay expositor of the absolute supremacy of the papacy was Count de Maistre who after 1815 wrote of those two pillars of society, the pope and the executioner.

In the nineteenth century there finally appeared Catholics who urged that Church and state should be separate, that there should be "a free church in a free state"—this was said first by

Montalembert and his friend Abbé Lamennais in the early 1830's, long before Cavour ever used it in a somewhat vitiated fashion as a weapon in the battle of the *risorgimento.* Unfortunately their position was rejected out of hand by Pope Gregory XVI in his encyclical *Mirari vos.* The idea that liberty of conscience ought to be assured was there called sheer madness; whoever says that religion has something to gain from this pernicious error is said to be extremely impudent. Freedom of the press is called execrable and detestable. Separation of Church and state is disapproved and the princes, "Our dearest sons in Jesus Christ," are said to have been given their authority not only for temporal government but chiefly for the defense of the Church.[6]

The following are the pertinent portions of the encyclical.

We come now to a source which is, alas! all too productive of the deplorable evils afflicting the Church today. We have in mind *indifferentism,* that is, the fatal opinion everywhere spread abroad by the deceit of wicked men, that the eternal salvation of the soul can be won by the profession of any faith at all, provided that conduct conforms to the norms of justice and probity. . . .

From this poisonous spring of indifferentism flows the false and absurd, or rather the mad principle that we must secure and guarantee to each one liberty of conscience; this is one of the most contagious of errors; it smooths the way for that absolute and unbridled freedom of thought, which, to the ruin of Church and State, is now spreading everywhere, and which certain men, with outrageous impudence, do not fear to represent as advantageous to religion. But what more fatal blow to the life of the soul than freedom of error, says St. Augustine. As we thus see lifted from the shoulders of men the reins that alone can keep them in the way of truth, dragged as they already are by their natural inclination to evil to the very brink of eternal loss, it is in truth that we say that there now lie open before them the jaws of the abyss, of which St. John spoke. . . .

To this [error] is attached liberty of the press, the most dangerous liberty, an execrable liberty, which can never inspire sufficient horror, and which some men [nevertheless] very noisily and insistently demand [and attempt] to spread everywhere. . . .

We cannot foresee any happier results for religion and the civil power from the desires of those who so warmly advocate the separation of Church and State and the rupture of the agreement between clergy and Empire. For it is a well-known fact that all the most ardent lovers of liberty fear more than anything else this concord that has always been as salutary and as fortunate for the Church as it has been for the State. . . .[7]

Montalembert and Lacordaire submitted and remained within the Roman Catholic Church, promoting their liberalism as well as they could in those unfavorable times. Lamennais became perhaps the greatest loss to Catholicism in the nineteenth century —one might almost say perhaps the greatest loss to European civilization, for his fertile and penetrating mind seemed to fly off at a tangent once loosed from its natural roots. In absolute terror of the break-up of the papal states under the impact of the modern ideas of liberty, the papacy[8] clamped Catholics in the vice of the union of Church and state wherever it could. Where it could not, it merely tolerated the inevitable.

In 1846 when Pius IX came to the papal throne (this term, a reflection of the medieval and baroque papacy, gives some insight into the conception of the role of the pope prevalent until John XXIII refurbished the ancient papal title, the "servant of the servants of God") he determined to do something about improving the government of the Papal States, which had been described at that time as an open scandal to all Europe. The great powers had earlier insisted that the pope clean up his corrupt and incredibly inefficient government and threatened to do it for him, since his lands were a breeding ground of discontent and rebellion. Pius IX vigorously undertook this task, but he had come to the papacy too late. Before anything substantive could be accomplished he was caught up in the maelstrom of the Europe-wide revolutions of 1848. His minister Rossi, who was quite able, was assassinated and Pius himself had to flee from the insurgents, returning only behind French bayonets. Needless to say, any "liberal" ideas Pius IX may have had[9] passed from his mind after his experience in 1848 with Mazzini and Garibaldi.

Before discussing the strong imprint that Pius IX put on Catholic Church-state theory, further note should be taken of the ideas and activity of Montalembert, who never lost his love for the principles of '89 nor his dream of reconciling Catholic thought and practice to them. He gained further supporters after the century passed the half-way mark, finding his staunchest and most brilliant aide in Bishop Dupanloup, bishop of Orleans.

In 1863 Montalembert was invited to address a great Catholic conference held at Malines, Belgium. He was a magnificent orator and took this occasion to present his principles in a unified and effective fashion before a world audience. He quoted Bishop Dupanloup: "We accept, we invoke the principles and liberties proclaimed in '89. . . . You made the Revolution of 1789 without us and against us but *for us,* God wishing it in spite of you." The great purpose, said Montalembert, was to christianize democracy. "The more one is a democrat the more it is necessary to be a Christian, the fervent practical cult of God made Man is the indispensable counter-balance to that perpetual tendency of democracy to establish the cult of Man believing himself God." Nowhere, he argued, was true Catholicism less practiced than in so-called wholly Catholic countries. Naples and Spain, "those paradises of religious absolutism," had become "the scandal and despair of all Catholic hearts."[10]

Montalembert's speeches were enthusiastically received at Malines—but not at Rome. He was sent a private message from Rome ominously reminding him of the condemnation of Lamennais. Similar and even more vigorous repressive measures were taken about the same time against Ignaz Döllinger, a Catholic Church historian at the University of Munich. Döllinger also delivered an address at a great Catholic conference held that same year, 1863. His plea was not for a political liberalism on the part of the Church, but rather for freedom for Catholic scholars to pursue their disciplines without having to check with ecclesiastical authorities, except where matters of defined faith were involved—a pedestrian enough thought for non-Catholic Westerners a century ago. However, Pius IX was not of a mind to allow this. He issued a letter to the bishop of Munich in which he insisted that Catholic scholars were bound to subordinate all their work to the ecclesiastical authorities. It was, incidentally, also because of this letter that Döllinger's avid follower, Lord Acton, discontinued publishing his English Catholic quarterly, the *Rambler.* The following year, 1864, the encyclical *Quanta cura* and the "infamous" syllabus of errors was issued by Pius IX.[11]

Almost one hundred years later John XXIII wrote on the first page of his encyclical *Pacem in Terris:* "But what emerges first and foremost from the progress of science and the inventions of technology is the infinite greatness of God himself, who created both man and the universe."[12] In language somewhat less conciliatory toward the world Pius IX wrote on the first page of his encyclical:

> Wherefore those our predecessors have with apostolic fortitude continually resisted the nefarious attempts of unjust men, of those who, like raging waves of the sea, foaming forth their own confusion and promising liberty while they are the slaves of corruption, endeavoured by their false opinions and most pernicious writings to overthrow the foundations of the Catholic religion and of civil society, to abolish all virtue and justice, to deprave the souls and minds of all men, and especially to pervert inexperienced youth from uprightness of morals, to corrupt them miserably, to lead them into snares of error, and finally to tear them from the bosom of the Catholic Church.[13]

He then referred to the chief errors of the time which he had enumerated to some extent in earlier writings. The first error he then specifically mentioned was that of a separation of Church and state and then went on to abominate freedom of conscience.

> These false and perverse opinions are so much the more detestable by how much they have chiefly for their object to hinder and banish that salutary influence which the Catholic Church, by the institution and command of her divine Author, ought freely to exercise, even to the consummation of the world—not only over individual men, but over nations and sovereigns—and to abolish that mutual cooperation and agreement of counsels between the priesthood and governments which has always been propitious and conducive to the welfare both of Church and State. (*Gregory* XVI Encyclical, August 13th, 1832). . . . Contrary to the teaching of the holy Scriptures, of the Church, and of the holy Fathers, these persons do not hesitate to assert, that "the best condition of human society is that wherein no duty is recognized by the Government of correcting by enacted penalties the violators of the Catholic religion, except when the maintenance of the public peace requires it." From this totally false notion of social government, they fear not to uphold that erroneous opinion most pernicious to the Catholic Church, and to the salvation of souls, which was called by our predecessor Gregory XVI (lately quoted) the *insanity* (Encycl. August 13th, 1832) (*deliramentum*), namely, that "liberty of conscience and of worship is the right of every man; and that this right ought, in every well governed State, to be proclaimed and asserted by the law. . . .[14]

Toward the end of the encyclical Pius IX quoted two previous popes' statements on Church-state relations with approval.

> And do not omit to teach "that the royal power has been established not only to exercise the government of the world, but, above all, for the protection of the Church" (*St. Leo, Epist.,* 156), . . . as our most wise and courageous predecessor, *St. Felix,* wrote to the Emperor Zeno. "It is certain that it is advantageous for Sovereigns, when the cause of God is in question, to submit their royal will according to his ordinance, to the priests of Jesus Christ, and not to prefer it before them" (Pius VII. Epist, Encycl., *Diu satis,* May 15th, 1800).[15]

There then followed a list of eighty of the most prominent errors of the time, statements culled from the earlier writings of Pius IX. Many were strictly theological and caused no surprise, as, for example, the condemnation of pantheism. Several were very clumsily phrased so that confusion about their meaning abounded. But the last few appeared to have an incredibly general sweep. The Pope condemned the following statements as erroneous:

> 77. In the present day it is no longer necessary that the Catholic religion shall be held as the only religion of the State, to the exclusion of all other modes of worship.
>
> 78. Whence it has been wisely provided by the law, in some countries called Catholic, that persons coming to reside therein shall enjoy the free exercise of their own worship.
>
> 79. Moreover it is false that the civil liberty of every mode of worship and the full power given to all of overtly and publicly manifesting their opinions and their ideas conduce more easily to corrupt the morals and minds of the people, and to the propagation of the pest of indifferentism.
>
> 80. The Roman Pontiff can, and ought to, reconcile himself to, and agree with, progress, liberalism, and modern civilization.[16]

The root of the whole reactionary regime of Pius IX can no doubt be detected in the two previous statements that were declared false:

> 75. The children of the Christian and Catholic Church are not agreed upon the compatibility of the temporal with the spiritual power.
>
> 76. The abolition of the temporal power of which the Apostolic See is possessed would contribute in the greatest degree to the liberty and prosperity of the Church.
>
> Besides these errors, explicitly noted, very many others are rebuked by the certain doctrine which all Catholics are bound most firmly to hold touching the temporal sovereignty of the Roman Pontiff. These doctrines are clearly stated in the Allocutions *Quantis quanetumque,* April 20th, 1859, and *Si semper antea,* May 20th, 1850; Letters Apost. *Quam Catholica Ecclesia,* March 26th, 1860; Allocutions *Novas,* September 28th, 1860; *Jamdudum,* March 18th, 1861, and *Maxima quidem,* June 9th, 1862.[17]

The non-Catholic and most of the Catholic world was stunned. It looked as though the pope had set himself and all Catholicism four-square against all progress and civilization and was insisting that all Catholics everywhere work ceaselessly for the state establishment of Roman Catholicism and the subsequent abrogation of freedom of conscience. In fact, this impression was somewhat of an illusion fostered by the incredible ineptness of the pope and his advisers. First of all, the list of errors, as mentioned, were all taken from earlier documents and could be understood only in the original context. For example, the final statement about the pope being unreconcilable with progress, liberalism, and modern civilization was taken from the allocution *Jamdudum cernimus,* March 18, 1861. This document had been directed against the confiscatory actions of the Piedmontese government, which had justified its actions by saying that the pope would just have to accept these confiscations of the Church's property and reconcile himself to progress, liberalism and modern civilization. In this context the statement was simply a refusal to accept the high-handed actions of the Cavour government. But it is evidence of the isolated, ghettoized life of the Vatican that it could simply lift that phrase as it was and place it before the world for reflective meditation. Public relations sensitivity had not yet invaded the Vatican.

But what about the insistence on the union of Church and state and elimination of the freedom conscience? Was the position of the Ultramontanists, whom Pius IX greatly favored, the one the pope really meant to espouse? The organ of the Spanish Traditionalists, echoed by the principal journal of the French Ultramontanists, *Le Monde,* wrote: "Our unique faith is henceforth to stigmatize liberalism, progress and modern civilization as anti-Catholic. We condemn as anti-Catholic these abortions of hell."[18] If that were the position of the Pope, anarchy, apostacy and bloodshed would surely result. At this moment Bishop Dupanloup leapt into the breach with an *explication du texte* that brought sighs of relief all around the world. In fact Pius himself, who was stunned and horror stricken at the violent reaction of the whole world to the syllabus, wrote

Dupanloup that he had given the "true explanation" and told him "you have understood well."[19]

Dupanloup issued a pamphlet in which he explained the syllabus in terms of thesis and hypothesis. The thesis which was condemned was the notion that a variety of religious beliefs was ultimately and ideally desirable. But there could not be fairly deduced from this any "hypothesis" that it was undesirable to allow a variety of religious practices or even in certain cases a separation of Church and State here and now. The pope was not concerned to denounce such varieties as might happen to exist in various countries. He was only concerned to assert that such varieties should not be introduced everywhere else. He did not anathematize, he merely bade people reflect. *Notantur* was the word that he used.[20]

Which meaning did Pius really intend? One cannot be completely certain, but his inclinations were certainly in the direction of Louis Veuillot the French leader of the Ultramontanists, who said "in no sense can a Catholic be or call himself a liberal."[21] Nevertheless the interpretation given by Dupanloup was given approbation and hence "saved" many Catholics. Some liberal Catholics later accused Dupanloup of emptying the pope's words of their intended meaning. Perhaps so, but his intervention was a desperately needed political move. After all, the syllabus was *not* a matter of infallible statements. This is acknowledged by the vast majority of Catholic theologians today, as it was by the best, such as Newman, at that time. Doubtless many, perhaps most, ordinary Catholics then thought they were irrevocably bound by the statements. Indeed, such a sophisticated contemporary scholar as James Hastings Nichols (Presbyterian) wrote in 1956 ". . . but, infallible or not, the *Syllabus* is binding on all Roman Catholics and requires their internal assent."[22] It is true that this is what many ultramontane theologians put into the theology manuals since 1870, but that is *not* what Vatican I said.[23]

Since 1864 the thesis-hypothesis interpretation has been the main line of Catholic thought. Leo XIII was much more flexible in his diplomacy than his predecessor. But he still held to the theoretical position that the ideal state is the Catholic state, one where the state protects and fosters the Catholic religion alone.

A later example of this position can be found in the article on Church and State in the *Catholic Encyclopedia,* published in 1912 in America. Although granting the need to live peaceably in a mixed society, the author insists that the desirability of separation of Church from state in a Catholic state does not exist. "Such a separation for a Catholic State would be criminal, as ignoring the sacred obligations of the State." And in speaking of alternate theories of Church-state relations, none of which are acceptable to Catholics, he insists, he speaks only of an extreme, aggressive, atheistic regime; a caesaro-papist regime; and the "moderate liberalism" of the new Italian state. No mention is made of Montalembert's position or that of any other liberal Catholic. Of "moderate liberalism" he says: "The axiom of this newer Liberalism is 'a free Church in a free State,' which in point of fact means an emasculated Church with no more freedom than the shifting politics, internal and external, of a state chose to give, which in the event, as was to be foreseen, amounted to servitude."

In America there was hardly much possibility of opposition to the ultramontane position in the time of Pius IX since the Church was relatively so small and indigent. By the end of the century liberal and democratic thought began to show itself vigorously in the actions of Archbishop Ireland and others who saw a great advantage in the American system of separation of Church and state. They even preached its efficacy abroad. However, the condemnation of the so-called heresy of Americanism at the end of the century and the reign of terror during the Modernist heresy hunt in the years just before World War I scotched that development.

The tradition of insisting on the medieval ideal as *the* ideal state was continued by a group of conservative theologians centered at the Catholic University of America in Washington D.C. and persisted to this very decade. They have been referred to by one Catholic scholar as "the canonists," which is not inapt. They insisted that in a pluralist society one would have to have separation of Church and state, but when a vast Catholic majority was reached, as in Spain, the state had an obligation to render God public homage as state: i.e., it would have to promote the Catholic liturgy and forbid public (but not private) worship of all other citizens.[24]

This was challenged by Fr. John Courtney Murray, S.J., who in the 1940's began to argue that this was not the only possible Catholic position, that in fact a truer line could be found in John of Paris, among others, and that this truer line would hold that liberty of conscience was a right of man which could not be invaded. He also argued that when Leo XIII and other popes wrote in favor of Church-state union they were naturally writing against the background of the conditions of their time. Conditions have changed, and the same rules cannot be univocally applied. Separation of Church and state can be seen as being a positive good for our time, though it may not have been so in the past.

In 1953 Cardinal Ottaviani of the Holy Office entered the fight with an article in the *American Ecclesiastical Review* upholding the position of the "canonists."[25] After that Murray fell silent for many years. One Catholic scholar wrote that it is rumored that Murray had been silenced.[26] I would rather say that it is an open secret that he was silenced.

Another Catholic thinker in this area, Fr. Albert Dondeyne, a Belgian scholar, has recently maintained a similar historical position in his book *Faith in the World.* He says:

> We have already remarked that the concept "ideal" is something relative and that it leads to useless misunderstanding when it is used in

season or out of season. What may have been useful for Church and State in the Middle Ages would be a calamity for both in modern society. Moreover, one and the same juridical relationship can have various meanings according to the society in which it is adopted. Thus Catholics as well as non-Catholics in the U.S.A. consider, and not without reason, the complete separation of Church and State the best guarantee for a sound life of the State and a free Church. The same separation also exists behind the Iron Curtain, but there it has a totally different meaning.[27]

I wish to make two comments on the positions taken by Murray and Dondeyne. I would agree largely with the statement of Dondeyne above, but I would wish to add that the medieval Church-state strutcure *may* have been the ideal for the time, but just because it so existed doesn't mean it *necessarily* was the best.

Also, concerning the ultimate ideal, I believe a distinction has to be drawn between the Church and the state that usually has not been made and which is vitally important. The Church is, as far as man is concerned, essentially a voluntary institution. He belongs because he chooses to. For practically all men this is *not* so with the state. Man must for all practical purposes live in a state. He can move from one state to another but he can not secede from all states and still live a human life. Therefore the state, which men *must* belong to, may not perform, as state, acts which are essentially voluntary for man. Even if all citizens at one moment happen to be believing Catholics, the state as state should not perform religious liturgies, since this would tend to *force* all the citizens to remain Catholics, which they should do only voluntarily. Thus, I would suggest that all union of Church and state is basically inimical to human nature and the nature of religion, and therefore also basically anti-Christian. If we *must* use the terms "thesis and hypothesis"—which we need not—then separation of Church and state is the thesis, and their union is the hypothesis, the evil to be tolerated under some circumstances, e.g., the medieval.

Perhaps it should be noted at this point that there is no problem in asserting that the Church has seen and proclaimed less than the full truth on this matter in the past. *Perhaps* she could not have done better, given the state of knowledge and experience of men. We have learned more with the passage of time and hence are better able now in this situation to give a better description of what the Christian position in this problem should be.

This is exactly what happened most recently when two huge steps were taken vindicating the position of Fathers Murray and Dondeyne, and my further extension of their position. Pope John XXIII in his encyclical *Pacem in Terris* stated flatly that although error itself had no right to exist, men who might be erroneous were the bearers of rights. No reason whatsoever justifies forcing a conscience.

The second step, of course, was the Declaration on Religious Freedom, which had such a tortuous history at Vatican II. The Council Fathers declared that "the exercise of religion, of its very nature, consists before all else in those internal, voluntary, and free acts whereby man sets the course of his life directly toward God. *No merely human power can either command or prohibit acts of this kind.* [Italics added.] . . . Government . . . would clearly transgress the limits set to its power, were it to presume to *command or inhibit acts that are religious.*" [Italics added.] Thus the Constantinian age and concomitant Catholic Church-state theories have finally been sloughed off.

What has ecumenism had to do with all this? First of all, it should be recalled that Catholic ecumenism was preceded by the emergence of pluralistic society and the rise of a renewal movement within the Catholic Church. Which countries have taken the lead in ecumenism? Germany, Holland, France, and now most lately—because of the usual cultural lag—the United States. These also are countries with a pluralistic society. If it is objected that France is really a Catholic country it should be pointed out that Catholics are really a minority in an unbelieving society.

A survey of the history of Western Civilization since the Enlightenment indicates that it has been largely in those areas which have had a pluralistic society that a vigorous movement of renewal within the Church has also grown up.[28] The psychological reasons for this, I believe, are obvious. One of the great spurs to renewal in modern times has been the presence of believers of other commitments who have put serious questions to contemporary Catholics. This questioning has led to an even further and deeper renewal within Catholicism—and also incidentally within the faiths of the other discussants. As a result of this mutual beneficial interchange there has developed a new respect between Catholics and non-Catholics, and a joint search for truth in an ever-increasing number of areas. This attitude and mutual activity is, perhaps without having the name, ecumenism in the deepest sense. In its conscious form it is a common search for the truth in the hope and trust that this search will ultimately lead to the essential unity of the Christian Church, while keeping at the same time a maximum of accidental differentiating characteristics.

As this situation of pluralism, renewal, and ultimately ecumenism progressed, it was inevitable that the spirit of mutual trust and respect would diminish antipathies in the whole area of Church-state relations. The most spectular example of this perhaps is the extraordinary change of position on the part of many, many Protestants in this country concerning federal aid to education which is in some fashion church-oriented—for the most part Catholic schools. When the recently passed bill for federal aid to education was sent to Congress early in 1962—just before Vatican II began—Protestants of all kinds resisted the attempt of Catholic bishops to encompass Catholic schools within the benefits of the bill. Three years later—after Vatican II had revolutionized the situation between Protestants and Catholics, and after the ecumenical movement exploded in this country —a comparable bill was passed.

On the other hand, the movement has not been all in one direction. Many "renewed" Catholics have recently been raising very serious questions about the desirability of Catholic schools on all or any level. I am quite certain that this questioning has only begun. Without renewal and ecumenism it never would have taken place. The same can also be said of the dramatic changes in the position of the Catholic Church on Church-state relations that have been exhibited in John XXIII's encyclical *Pacem in Terris* and the conciliar declaration on religious freedom.

Renewal and ecumenism, only barely started, have already had a spectacular effect on Church-state relations, the future is pregnant with changes. I believe the progeny of the future will be felicitous.

NOTES

[1] Quoted in: Albert Dondeyne, *Faith and the World* (Pittsburgh: Duquesne University Press, 1963), p. 257.

[2] John Courtney Murray, S.J., "Contemporary Orientations of Catholic Thought on Church and State in the Light of History," *Cross Currents,* 5 (Fall, 1951), p. 24.

[3] *Summa Theol.,* IIª IIªᵉ, q. 11, art. 3.

[4] Luigi Sturzo, *Church and State* (Notre Dame: University of Notre Dame Press, 1962), p. 251.

[5] E. A. Goerner, *Peter and Caesar* (New York: Herder and Herder), p. 148.

[6] Cf. Alec R. Vidler, *Prophecy and Papacy* (New York: Charles Scribner's Sons, 1954), pp. 213 ff.

[7] Quoted in: Roger Aubert, "Religious Liberty from 'Mirari Vos' to the 'Syllabus,'" in: *Historical Problems of Church Renewal,* Concilium, Vol. 7 (Glen Rock, N.J.: Paulist Press, 1965), pp. 91–92.

[8] A. Simon, "Vues nouvelles sur Grégoire XVI," *Revue Générale Belge* (January, 1951), pp. 399 ff.

[9] Roger Aubert, *Le Pontificat de Pie IX* (Paris, 1963), pp. 14–29, 505–6.

[10] Quoted in Christopher Hollis, "The Syllabus of Errors," in: *Twentieth*

Century Catholicism (No. 1 supplement to *The Twentieth Century Encyclopedia of Catholicism*), ed. by Lancelot Sheppard (New York: Hawthorn, 1965), pp. 38–39.

[11] Cf. Leonard Swidler, "The Catholic Historian," in: *The Christian Intellectual,* ed. by Samuel Hazo (Pittsburgh, Duquesne University Press, 1963), pp. 134 f.

[12] Quoted in: Sheppard, *Twentieth Century Catholicism,* p. 165.

[13] Quoted in *ibid.,* pp. 143 f.

[14] *Ibid.,* pp. 145 f.

[15] *Ibid.,* pp. 151 f.

[15] *Ibid.,* pp. 151 f.

[16] *Ibid.,* pp. 77–80.

[17] *Ibid.,* pp. 163 f.

[18] Quoted in: Aubert, "Religious Liberty," p. 103.

[19] Quoted in Hollis, "Syllabus," p. 40.

[20] Cf. *ibid.,* pp. 39 f.

[21] Quoted in *ibid.,* p. 41.

[22] James Hasting Nichols, *History of Christianity 1650–1950* (New York: The Ronald Press, 1956), p. 214.

[23] Cf. Gregory Baum, "Doctrinal Renewal," *Journal of Ecumenical Studies* II, 3 (Fall, 1965), pp. 365–381.

[24] Cf. Goerner, *Peter and Caesar,* pp. 153–172 for a thorough investigation of the writings of the three major "canonists," Fathers Joseph C. Fenton, Francis J. Connell and George W. Shea.

[25] Alfredo Ottaviani, "Church and State: Some Present Problems in the Light of the Teaching of Pope Pius XII," *American Ecclesiastical Review,* CXXVIII (May, 1953), pp. 321–334.

[26] Goerner, *Peter and Caesar,* pp. 175–176.

[27] Dondeyne, *Faith and the World,* p. 258.

[28] Cf. Leonard Swidler, *The Ecumenical Vanguard* (Pittsburgh: Duquesne University Press, 1966).

[29] Cf. among others: Mary Perkins Ryan, *Are Parochial Schools the Answer?* (New York: Holt, Rinehart, and Winston, 1964); Leonard Swidler, "Catholic Colleges: A Modest Proposal," *Commonweal* (January 29, 1965).

JEWISH COMMITMENTS IN RELATIONS OF CHURCH AND STATE

by

Arthur Gilbert

IT IS not unknown to American Christendom that Jews have been in the forefront of the effort to maintain as absolute a separation as possible between church and state. Jews were litigants in the cases that resulted in Supreme Court decisions barring devotional Bible reading and the recitation of the Lord's Prayer as public school exercises. Jewish organizations and lawyers have called for judicial review of the church-state aspects of the Poverty and Education Acts. Throughout the United States, Jews have opposed religion in the public school, the use of public funds in aid to parochial school education and the legislation of sectarian morality. In some communities controversy over these issues has been accompanied by cross-burnings and the distribution of anti-Semitic hate literature.

There would be no need at all to discourse on Jewish commitments in relations of church and state—they seem so obvious—were it not for the fact that division has now appeared in Jewish ranks. Dissenting voices calling for a revision of policy have been raised. Orthodox Jewish leaders have applauded President Johnson's child-benefit formula for getting poverty and education money to church-related school children. And rumblings in Israel are indicative of the fact that many Jews there believe that the Jewish State fulfills its highest ideals when it aids, supports and encourages religion.

It would be helpful for the Christian, then, and for the Jew, too, were we to explain why and how Jews have come to their differing positions and consider the implications of this explanation for Jewish-Christian relations.

Traditional Judaism is distinguished by its affirmation that God is Lord over all life and that all men and institutions are subject to His will. "The earth is the Lord's and the fulness thereof, the world and those who dwell therein." (Psalm 24). "For the Lord is our Judge, the Lord is our Ruler, the Lord is our King; He will save us." (Isaiah 33:22)

There was never in the history of Judaism, nor is there today, any *theology of the secular* that justifies separating any function of life from obedience and duty to God.

God's covenant was made with all of the people of Israel, the elders and officers, the priests and laity, women and children, the sojourner in the camp, from the hewer of wood to the drawer of water. (Deuteronomy 29:10). Judaism is not enshrined nor entrusted to any ecclesiastical structure. It is the heritage of faith of an entire people, some of whom are believers and others rebellious, some ceremoniously pious and others uninvolved, some devoted to works of righteousness and others engaged in pursuit of pleasure. The work of religion is not confined to clerics or to the reciters of prayers. God's *shekinah* is as present in the so-called secular world as it may also be present in the synagogue.

Jews were spared some of the disastrous consequences of such an all-embracing theocracy, however, by virtue of several delimiting concepts:

1. A clear distinction was made between the function of the King and Priest. Whereas Samuel opposed a monarchy and viewed its establishment as an act of disloyalty to God (1 Samuel 8), the Jewish people insisted that the function of

maintaining the civic order required a state authority that would bind the people together and provide them with trappings of nationhood. They recognized, nevertheless, that the king himself had to be subject to God's Law as revealed in the Torah (Deuteronomy 17:18), and that an independent priesthood and a prophetic class provided a restraint on the state, a vehicle for Divine judgment, and the occasion for redress of wrong and collective atonement for corporate guilt. Whenever the offices of king and priest were intermingled, Jewish society suffered, religion was perverted and freedom was diminished.

Thus, Zechariah in his vision of the new kingdom, prophesied that the community of Israel would be replenished through the proper and separate functioning of both a king and a priest, both of whom were considered vessels of God's grace (Zechariah 4).

2. The function of that people who called themselves Israel, was to serve as a witness to God (Isaiah 43:12) and thereby to become a blessing unto men (Genesis 12:3). By the example of their lives they were to be a light unto the nations (Isaiah 42:6; 49:6). Jews never felt it necessary, therefore, to exercise a coercive power over the lives of others, other than that achieved through influencing the heart and the mind by example and suasion.

3. Gentiles did not need to become Jews in order to achieve redemption (Micah 4:5). It was sufficient that the gentile live righteously.[1] All non-Jews who observed the Noachide laws, were entitled to participate in the rewards of the world to come.[2] Faith was not to be coerced on the non-Israelite and the Jews were instructed by the rabbis to be respectful of the dignity of the person of the other, even of the idolater; in fact, the religious wholeheartedness of the pagan in service of his god was offered as a rebuke to Jewish backsliders and seen ultimately as an acceptable offering to God himself—so impressed was God by the sanctity and purity of the pagans' sacrifice (Malachi 1:11).

Ibn Gabirol, 11th Century Jewish poet, sang of this broad-minded view toward the faith of others in the following poetic words:

"Thou art the Lord and all beings are thy servants and thy Domain.
Nor is thine honor lessened, even by those who serve idols vain.
For it is to be one with thee, that is their aim."

Finally, while community sanction could be used to enforce religious practice among Jews, freedom of opinion and dissent were zealously cherished. Gradually rabbinic law modified the penalties imposed upon the nonconformists, until finally no coercive penalty was left except those that are spiritual in nature.

But most significantly, Jewish sovereignty did not long endure and the Jews for the last two thousand years have been without power to coerce anybody, Jews or gentile. It is this historic phenomenon that is most important to an understanding of Jewish commitments in relation to church and state; that is, Jews for so long have been defending themselves against violation from the Christian church and Christianized states, they have so long been positioned in minority status, that the obligation and the opportunity for the responsible use of power have been lacking. Jews have had no need to work out a systematic conception of church-state relationship. Our position has been defensive rather than constructive. We have had cause for suspicion rather than trust and our commitments frequently partake of a rigidity that mask anxiety and fear and powerlessness.

Christians are now gradually becoming aware of the anguish of the Jews. As responsible churchmen assert with relief that the Constantinian age of church-statism is dead, so they realize now that Jews suffered most under the tyranny of that dreadful alliance. Christians fail to realize, however, that religious freedom for the Jew has only very recently been achieved, and it is still not realized everywhere in Christendom.

There is a tendency among Christians to think that the

religious oppression and coercion of Jews was a feature of the distant past—the Middle Ages, the years of the Crusades and the Spanish Inquisition, etc.—and that since the French Revolution and the adoption of the American Bill of Rights religious liberty has been a normative experience. Not so.

The Jew presumes that the civil disabilities and the institutionalized patterns of social discrimination that he has endured, rarely challenged by church or state, are not merely problems of inter-group relations or accidental faults in the democratic structure or a "secularized" form of Jew-hatred. Rather the Jew has always understood anti-Semitism to be a concomitant of Christianity. Thus discrimination was seen as a painfully alive vestige of past church-statism. Not only did American Jews feel imposed upon when the state allowed school teachers to engage their children in Christological affirmations at morning public school devotional exercises, but they also interpreted restrictive housing covenants, disabilities in advancement in industry, discrimination in admission to professional school, all as the inevitable harvest of centuries of Christian teachings of contempt, reinforced by civic legislation.

So expansive have been the frontiers of American society, however, that in this land the Jew has been able to make his way despite such disabilities. Yet constantly we were reminded that the past lived on in the present. For example, the erection of the Nativity Creche on the public commons, for which Jewish businessmen are expected to give donations, the invocation of the Trinity in prayers on public occasions to which the Jews are expected to say "Amen," the scheduling of public school dances on Friday night and football games on Saturday, the high school rally of "Christian Athletes" with their threat of damnation to those who turn their back on Jesus, Sunday closing laws, and the choice of Deborah Goldberg to play the Virgin Mary in the public school Christmas pageant "since Mary was Jewish"—all these rub the old sores and open them again.

Yes, freedom is ours in America, unlike our situation anywhere else in the world in all of history; but if your heart aches and you do not feel quite secure and fully accepted, or if you have a chip on your shoulder, then every little slight and disadvantage takes on a symbolic meaning out of all proportion.

For example, Jewish religious law centuries ago provided the Jew permission to say Amen when a pagan offered thanksgiving,[3] but today, when the Trinity is invoked by a clergyman at the high school graduation or at the Rotary Club, Jews are angered at his insensitivity. So history overrides religious law and sociology explains more about our commitments than theology.

The paradox, of course, is that the more secure we become in America, the bolder our attack on the remaining symbols of state-supported religion will be, even if these symbols are trifles with no important functional significance. The explanation for such behavior is that it takes confidence in the democratic process to exercise it and the closer you come to full equality, the more impatient you are with whatever still blocks its full realization.

One of the first commissions established by the Central Conference of American Rabbis—the first of the four rabbinical associations in the United States—was that on church-state relations. Vigorously this commission campaigned against sectarianism in public school textbooks and religious ceremonials as public school exercises; but significantly, in 1905, the commission cautioned the Jew against instituting litigation. Anxiety over adverse public reaction and the baneful possibility of defeat in State courts that had frequently declared in *obiter dicta* that America was a Christian country inhibited the rabbis.[4]

The B'nai B'rith Youth Organization shortly after World War II disclosed that more than half of Jewish teenagers remained silent or added nonsense words when Christological affiirmations occurred in public school Christmas songs. In such manner these youngsters demonstrated their rebelliousness at being placed in a situation where they had to violate their own religious integrity.

The situation, of course, is now changed. The processes of democracy have been made more secure by the victory over Nazism. Jews achieved a self-respect that motivated courageous questioning of accepted status quo arrangements despite veiled threats of anti-Semitic outbreaks from Christian friends. Most significantly, the Supreme Court extended the guarantees of the First Amendment to state actions and indicated that it would be activist in defending individual liberties. Thus Jews were encouraged to bring their case to the court and they have been further emboldened by their successes.

This very fact that the courts have been the battleground rather than the legislature, however, is indication enough that the position favored by Jews cannot muster a majority vote. Jews cannot yet count on legislators to understand their concern nor on Christian leaders to be sympathetic, although even this situation is now rapidly changing. The Supreme Court, by its courageous decisions, has educated more Americans as to the meaning of religious freedom than the Jews were ever able to achieve, despite enormous expenditure of funds and energy for pamphlets, conferences and negotiations.

I do not intend to discount the fact that hundreds of private meetings between Jewish community relations officials and public school superintendents led voluntarily to the imposition of restraint on missionary-oriented school teachers. Nor do I discount the fact that afternoon teas for teachers achieved some degree of understanding and sympathy and that conferences with denominational church leaders paved the way for a serious reconsideration of church positions on religion in public education. Such activity undoubtedly contributed to a readiness for the acceptance in many quarters of the Supreme Court's decisions. The truth is, however, that it was not until the Court acted that

America fully realized that the nature of our religious pluralism had been radically altered, requiring a change in long-standing practices of state-sanctioned religious affirmation.

For many years, Jews were able to count on Catholic support in their protest against religion—usually of Protestant form and substance—in the public schools; and Jews joined Protestants in opposing Catholic efforts to obtain financial aid for parochial schools. These alliances, however, are now shifting and this accounts for some of the new flexibility we have recently seen in the development of public policy. Most crucial has been the reconsideration of their position by the main line Protestant denominations within the National Council of Churches. Their support for the Supreme Court decisions with regard to prayer in the schools and a child-benefit approach to the distribution of federal poverty and education funds represents not only a reconsideration of philosophy, but an effort on the part of Protestants to be sensitive to human need in an ecumenical age. These Protestants have been most responsive to the dynamic opportunities of pluralism, the obligations of ecumenism, the changing pattern of federal governmental involvement in public life, and most importantly, they have demonstrated a most profound concern for the crisis confronting religion in an increasingly secularized society. Protestants, as the majority of the population, are the custodians of American public policy and with mature self-consciousness they have been grappling realistically with their responsibility and their power. For this they are to be commended. Protestant leaders have been much more flexible than Jewish and Catholic communities where self-interest and minority considerations still predominate. It would be unfair, however, not to acknowledge the significant contribution to ecumenically oriented cooperative studies and actions that have been made by many liberal and sensitive Jewish and Catholic leaders as well.

The most significant rupture in the Jewish community on

church-state issues has been occasioned by the conflict over the expenditure of public funds for church-related schools. Regretfully it appears that internal Jewish politics and self-interest better explain this situation than philosophic judgment about church-state relations, although there is a new philosophic position emerging among some Orthodox and non-Orthodox Jewish leaders which is of significance and which, in fairness, I shall discuss in due course.

Orthodox Judaism maintains the largest system of Jewish all-day schools. In the general revival of religion that has brought thousands of Jews back to the synagogues of each of the Jewish denominations, the number of Orthodox Yeshivot (all-day schools) swelled considerably. Their number has quadrupled in the last fifteen years. In 1964 there were 303 Hebrew day schools in the United States located in 28 states and the District of Columbia and in 95 communities, with a total enrollment of approximately 61,000 children.

To their chagrin, however, Orthodox Jews found that Jewish community, federation and welfare funds were not very generous in support of the all-day schools. 31 Jewish communal federation and welfare funds appropriated $595,631 for the support of Jewish day schools in 1964, with contributions ranging from $1,500 in Syracuse, New York, to $116,000 in Chicago, Illinois. It is estimated, however, that the cost of maintaining a child in a Hebrew day school approximates $500 per child. The total financial need of the day school movement, therefore, approaches the figure of $30,500,000. Federation support is only fractional of this need.[5]

Resistance to support of the Orthodox school has been based in great measure on principled opposition to a separatist ghettoized Jewish educational effort; it is a reflection of the Jewish enthusiastic endorsement of public education. In 1961, at the General Assembly of the nationwide organization of Jewish Federation and Welfare Funds held in Dallas, Texas, this issue of

Jewish communal financing for the all-day school was debated. Amon Deinard, explaining the denial of a grant to the Jewish day school by the Minneapolis Federation, reported that some Minneapolis Jewish leaders held "that an all-day Jewish school was a parochial school and Jews of all people should oppose community financing of parochialism because it is destructive of the American concept of general public education. They believe that Jews should be in the forefront of the community in opposition to anything that would injure the spirit of free education."[6]

The exact opposite attitude toward the centrality of the public school in American education is held, of course, by the supporters of the Orthodox Jewish day schools. Thus, when Rabbi Maurice Sherer, Executive Vice-President of the Agudath Israel of America, testified before the House Education and Labor Committee on the Federal Aid to Education Bill, he warned: "Our founding fathers never intended that our children be raised in a monolithic educational strait jacket . . . Our educational plant is a mosaic with the free play of the many faceted cultures of our people blooming into the moulding of an informed, dedicated and loyal citizenry." Then, in an appeal similar in tone to that made by many Catholic spokesmen, Rabbi Sherer added: "To compel our children because of the staggering financial hardship suffered by their schools, to study in overcrowded classrooms and in make-shift annexes, as is the norm in so many communities, is more than an unjust obstruction to their educational progress—it actually weakens the very structure of the entire American educational effort."[7]

In addition, much of the opposition to Jewish communal support of the Hebrew all-day school movement came from non-observant Jewish leaders of so-called secular Jewish organizations as well as the wealthy constituents of Reform Judaism. Even when funds were allotted to the Orthodox school, the Federation Board members—many of whom were Reform and

Conservative in their religious affiliation and were not quite sympathetic to the Orthodox schools—sought to impose conditions of control over the schools' program and curricula. One must also realize that Orthodox Jews, by virtue of their position in the economic structure of the American Jewish community, are the least capable of maintaining their own educational plant.

Thus Orthodox Jews devised a political strategy that threatened a split in the unified Jewish front on church-state issues unless the Jewish community assumed a larger share of responsibility for the financing of their schools. When the Jewish community failed to respond adequately to this need, the Orthodox acted upon their threat.

Not only did the Orthodox break ranks politically, but they also used the occasion to attack Jewish "secular" agencies as unrepresentative of religious Jewry and to advance themselves as the proper custodians of Judaism's religious heritage.

When Rabbi Amos Bunim, Chairman of the Executive Committee of the National Society for Hebrew Day Schools (Torah u Mesorah), appeared at the Senate hearings on the education bill, Senator Randolph of West Virginia asked him how he could account for the fact that the American Jewish Congress opposed the bill. Rabbi Bunim replied: "The American Jewish Congress does not represent the religious community. It ill behooves this organization to try to protect the religious freedom of the Jewish community or, for that matter, of other faith groups when that religious leadership endorses the bill and sees in it no threat whatsoever to religious freedom and, on the contrary, expects the strengthening of religious freedom to emerge from the enactment of the bill." It is to be noted here that Rabbi Bunim ignored the fact that Reform and Conservative Jewish religious leaders had also joined the American Jewish Congress in opposition to certain aspects of the educational bill.[8]

It needs to be understood also that some of the Orthodox

Jewish community sought public support for the Jewish all-day school, not out of any concern for the enrichment of American education, but rather in light of their commitment to the survival of the Jew as a separatist community. Thus Rabbi Menachem Shneerson, Head of the Lubovitcher Movement, argued in favor of federal aid to the parochial schools in the following language:

> One of the greatest frailties in contemporary Jewish life is the complacency toward the Torah-true education of our youth. In our generation we have become the unfortunate witnesses of the tragic fruits of this complacency—intermarriage and assimilation. Parents who neglected the Torah education of their children, thinking that matters would somehow take their proper course without it, or that it just wasn't that important—without realizing the consequences—have become victims of devastated homes and disgraced families because of their children's behavior.
>
> Elements foreign to Torah way of life beckon the Jew to come and share their society, but the Jew can never acquiesce to this society, for a Jew cannot survive in a life devoid of Torah, just as fish cannot live without water.
>
> Jewish education and the training of youth are the most cardinal precepts of the Jewish faith. Therefore, the entire matter of federal aid to parochial schools as far as Jews are concerned, should rest in the hands of the Hallachikly competent Jewish clergy and certainly not in the hands of Jewish laymen or organizations.[9]

The schism on church-state issues between the Orthodox religious community and the rest of the Jewish community must be seen also within the perspective of Orthodox Jewry's running battle with secular Jewish agencies over their involvement with the Vatican and with Reform and Conservative Jews over their challenge to Orthodox control of Israel's religious life.

In an editorial in the May 21, 1965 *Viewpoint,* publication of the National Council of Young Israel, Rabbi David Hill, describing the involvement of Jewish leaders in the Ecumenical Council, asserted:

> Yet who were these people so anxious to discuss theological problems with the Pontiff? By and large they were representatives of secular organizations, people who have neither the background nor the right to speak on these issues . . . Much of what has developed is a result of amateurish meddling of people . . . who were not qualified to represent the view of Judaism . . . the time has come for Orthodoxy to begin to assert itself. Only Torah-true Jews have the right to speak on these issues.

In an address before the annual meeting of the Rabbinical Council of America, Dr. Zerah Warhaftig, Israel Minister of Religion, attacked the development of Conservative and Reform Judaism in Israel as a "divisive factor." Claiming that two-thirds of the Jews in Israel attend Orthodox services, Dr. Warhaftig exclaimed that Israel was "inextricably bound up and based on the precepts and laws of Orthodox Judaism." Nevertheless, he asserted, "complete, uninhibited and unrestrained religious liberty exists in Israel."

In reply the presidents of Reform and Conservative rabbinical and congregational bodies labeled Warhaftig's claim of religious freedom in Israel to be "a complete uninhibited and unrestrained figment of his imagination." Reform and Conservative leaders added: "The simple truth is that religion in Israel is totally controlled by the Orthodox rabbinate. Non-Orthodox rabbis are denied the right to conduct weddings, officiate at funerals or grant divorces, and have been harrassed by the Orthodox rabbinate in Israel at every step in their efforts to establish non-Orthodox synagogues anywhere in Israel."

The Reform and Conservative leaders also charged that the American Orthodox rabbis who had supported Warhaftig, demonstrated "a pretentiousness that seems to be based on the arrogant claim that the Orthodox alone represent the Jewish religious community, both here and in Israel, and presumes to assume that no other way of Judaism has any reason to exist."

"In America," insisted these liberal spokesmen, "there are

several recognized and acknowledged Jewish religious communities . . . and in Israel there are hundreds of thousands of Jews who are religious, but not Orthodox. The overwhelming majority of Jews in Israel and the United States, whatever their religious commitment, support the basic position of separation of church and state, freedom of religious belief, practice and instruction for all."[10]

Orthodox Jews at last have begun to develop theoretical formulations of church-state relations which not only justify Israel's cooperative relation with religion, but which also provide a support for the Orthodox Jewish position on church-state issues in America. In his report to the Knesset in March, 1962, when the budget of his department was being considered, Dr. Zerah Warhaftig, Israel Minister of Religion, said: "In the last two hundred years it has been accepted by the world that separation between church and state was the most welcome solution; but this solution has failed." The Jewish State, he added, "is uniquely a creation of religious tradition and a realization of prophetic vision. It ought not be considered a goal in itself, but rather must serve as a guardian vessel for the enduring traditional values of the Jewish people—the core of which is a religious tradition."[11]

Similarly, in an interview published by the *Jewish World,* April–May, 1964, Rabbi Joseph Soloveitchik, Dean of Orthodox Rabbis in the United States, explained: "The whole idea of separation is against our philosophy and our faith in the fulfillment of the prophetic promise leading to complete redemption . . . A state based on agnosticism and secularism cannot fit into the outlook of redemption. If this singularity is obliterated in Israel, then what right is there to apply the adjective 'Jewish' to that state?"

Even the former Prime Minister of Israel, David Ben Gurion, not known for his championing of Orthodox Judaism—has suggested that religio-nationalistic elements are all joined together in Judaism, thus making it difficult for the Israeli legislator to know how to separate church and state without doing violence to the spirit of Judaism and thus accounting for Israel's unique pattern of church-state relationship. In an article that appeared in the *Jewish World,* April–May, 1964, Ben Gurion acknowledged that the use of religion as a political weapon and the attempt to impose religious practice distort the spirit of Judaism and harm the nation morally. Nevertheless, added Ben Gurion:

> The controversy about religion in Israel is so involved because of the special nature of the Jewish religion. The issue here is not the same as that of church and state in Christian countries. Judaism differs fundamentally from Christianity in that it finds abstract tenets of faith insufficient and is based on a collection of obligations and prohibitions that embrace man's whole life from the moment of his birth to his death and burial. There is a national religion which has absorbed all the historical characteristics of the people throughout the ages and it is not easy to distinguish between the national and religious strains . . . The United States arrived at the convenient solution of separating church and state not in an anti-religious spirit, but on the contrary, out of a desire to ensure complete religious freedom to all citizens. This solution would be no answer to our problem, even if it were accepted in Israel.

In my own view, Ben Gurion has completely missed the significance of the christianization of culture that occurs in western countries and which explains so very much the pressing need Jews have felt in America to push for separation as well as accounting for the outrage of Christians when the court banned the long-standing practices of religious affirmation in public life. Israel itself will confront this same problem when its religious pluralism becomes more significant. The Muslim and Christian minorities are now weak, insignificant and demoralized. They are incapable of any attack on this "national religion" that pervades Israel, although Protestants in Israel have led a battle against restrictions on mixed marriage. Significantly, therefore, the major tension erupts at that point where church-state intermingling has restricted the freedom of Jewish Sabbath non-observers and liberal Jews who are interested in developing Reform and Conservative synagogues.

Finally, it may be instructive to hear how Rabbi Bernard Casper, Dean of Students at the Hebrew University, Jerusalem, in a pamphlet issued by *Israel Digest* published January, 1963, and entitled "Religious Life," explains why the State agreed to support religious schools. Writes Rabbi Casper:

> Had the State offered only secular schooling free of cost, those parents who wished religious education, would have been under the burden and necessity of paying for the religious tuition of the children themselves; and such instruction would then have remained available only to those capable of meeting the additional financial cost and strong enough in their convictions to make the material sacrifice. There was in point of fact no one who did not see in education a supreme matter of principle which would ultimately determine the faith and the spiritual character of coming generations. Religion has, therefore, been recognized as a fundamental issue and the state has accordingly provided constitutionally for both the religious and the secular parts of the community.

It is not surprising to discover that where Jews have had to work out the relationship of religion to the state in a situation where they are in the majority, their approach to the issue has not been very different from that which characterized the pre-Johannine church-statism of Catholics or the practices of American Protestants of pre-Catholic immigration vintage—with one exception: in Israel all religions are supported liberally. The Israel Government, in fact, goes out of its way to make sure that the state provides for the religious needs of Muslim, Druze and Christians, so concerned is the State not to offend anyone.

Orthodox Jews in Israel expect the State to support religious education, to foster a climate in which religious observances can be encouraged and to legislate the basic moral commitments of Judaism.

Thus, Israel's Orthodox constituency has supported the maintenance of the Millet system that prevailed in Israel during the days of Palestine's Turkish and British rule. By that system each recognized religious community, Jewish, Muslim, Druze and Christian, maintains a system of religious courts that have supervision over personal matters, such as marriage, divorce and burial rites. As well, each community has the right to maintain its own religious school system and observe the Sabbath on the day of its choice. This whole system of church-state community is supported financially by the State. Israel subsidizes up to 70%of the cost of maintenance and replacement for Muslim and Christian schools where Arabic and the Koran or New Testament may be taught, just as it maintains both a Jewish public and religious school system. In the school year 1961–1962, out of almost 370,000 pupils of Hebrew elementary schools, 66.01% attended state schools and 33.99% attended state religious schools. Since 1957 every Jewish state school must also teach a course entitled "Jewish Consciousness," which is designed "to deepen the knowledge of Jewish values and strengthen pupil interest in the affairs of the Diaspora." The curriculum includes Jewish thought, religious law, values and experiences associated with the Sabbath and the holy days. Legislation reflecting the influence of Orthodox Jewry in Israel, also restricts travel and communication on the Sabbath, the breeding of pigs, the right to mixed marriage. It includes censorship of movies, restrictions on autopsies, etc.

The front line in the battle between Orthodox Jewry and the Liberals extends, therefore, from Israel to this country.

I would be totally unfair to the Jewish community, however, were I to suggest, on the one hand, that Jewish positions are shaped only by sociological factors or as a consequence of Jewish defensiveness and minority position, or, on the other hand, as a result of political controversy within the Jewish community. The truth is that there are many Orthodox Jews as well as Reform, Conservative and secular Jews who support an absolute separation of church and state for principled reasons, just as there are some Reform and Conservative rabbis who have joined the Orthodox in an attack on the rigidity with which the Jewish community holds to the principle of absolute separation of church and state. I will conclude this paper by outlining what appears to be the major philosophic positions that remain after this survey of historic and political factors.

For almost all of the years in which the organized Jewish community has issued resolutions on this issue of church-state relations, the case for separation has been based on an interpretation of the meaning of the First Amendment. As Rabbi Eugene Lipman points out in a 75-year review of the actions of the Central Conference of American Rabbis, even the rabbis "for many decades" based "their affirmations and negations on legal constitutional grounds primarily." This "emphasis on legalism" adds Rabbi Lipman, "eventually became a point of conflict."[12]

To their credit, of course, it must be pointed out that the rabbis correctly anticipated the eventual course to be taken by the Supreme Court of the United States. Sensitive to the situation of religious minorities as well as to that of the non-religious in this country, the rabbis properly recognized that even token establishments of religion can interfere with the free exercise of religion and, particularly, when that establishment occurs within the setting of the public school. A review of the issues that concern American Jews clearly indicates that religious practices in the public school were paramount. Protectively, Jews were concerned most of all to free their children from Christian imposition; later in history, Sunday closing laws and the appropriation of public funds for church-related schools came to share the attention of the rabbis.

While some legal experts point out that the Supreme Court's recent decisions evoke a new dynamic concept of "neutrality" as against the more absolutistic and rigid concept of "separation," there is no doubting the fact that the Court by its decision has acknowledged that the emergent religious pluralism of this country requires the cessation of formerly accepted practices of state-sanctioned religiosity. It was exactly this that the rabbis had asserted over and over again in their annual resolutions from 1904 until 1958.

At the 1958 C.C.A.R. Convention, a formal debate on separation of religion and state occurred, in which it was my privilege to challenge the old-established position of the rabbinate. I proposed that the rabbis both "rethink our position" and "use different language to express our convictions, whatever they may be." I urged the rabbis "to stop talking like lawyers on this church-state issue. It is time for our policy statements to reflect our interpretation of the Jewish tradition and our concern for God's will."

I had hoped that Reform rabbis would lead Jews to accept an affirmative obligation "to answer the question of how religion can be related to the state and the institutions of the state." I explained:

> The American people want to shore up our democracy by calling society to judgment before God and by rooting American ideals in His being. The general public accepts the fact that the state may not establish a church. They are in general agreement that it may be going too far to provide outright financial assistance to religious institutions, even non-preferentially. At the same time, however, they are convinced that the social order is not and must not be absolutely separated from the influence of religion. The concept known as Americanism is no longer devoid of religious content despite the howls of cynics, secularists and legalists . . . While the First Amendment was intended to separate church and state, it was not intended to separate religion from the state.

It was known among my colleagues that I supported creative experimental efforts to develop curricular course offerings to teach about religion in the public school curriculum, expanded programs of released or shared time, auxiliary benefits to parochial school children, such as textbooks, bus transportation, medical and health services, and expanded public assistance to the non-religious programs of church-related colleges—all of which policies were looked at askance by the majority of Jewish community leadership.

I particularly attacked the hostility and suspicion toward Christians that had been evident in many of the statements of the C.C.A.R. Pointing to one of these in unbelief, I requoted for them a resolution that the C.C.A.R. had adopted in 1956, dealing with the effort to have the public school take a hard look at its role in character education. The resolution read as follows:

> Continued efforts are being made to introduce the teaching of moral and spiritual values, which impress us as a ruse for introducing religion into the school. While we heartily favor character training in the public schools, we believe this is already being done. We regard the many programs under a host of labels as subterfuge for the introduction of sectarian teaching, whether consciously intended or whether or not we are aware of it. Warning is here issued that Rabbis have been inveigled into untenable positions by accepting the initial invitation to explore the possibilities.

I deplored this resolution by my colleagues and declared: "This summary dismissal of a legitimate concern of the American people, this lack of trust, this lack of faith in the intelligence of rabbis to explore the issue, this cavalier cutting-off of the dialogue, is reprehensible and deserving of our loudest objection."

But then, in order to indicate that I did not favor any and every intrusion of established religion into public institutions, and in order to demonstrate how the language of religious faith could clarify Jewish church-state commitments, I concluded:

> We need to tell the world that we are opposed to the affirmation of God by the public school, not just because this is an alleged violation of the First Amendment, but rather because we abhor the idea that an undefined, colorless, vague, public school god should be foisted upon our children. We want them to know God as the God of the Abrahamic covenant, as the cloud of fire that led us from slavery into freedom, as

the still small voice that answered Elijah's cries, as the whirlwind that spoke to Job's torments. It is out of a concern for the vitality of our faith that we oppose the naive suggestion that God be taught to children without definition and without being clothed in the sancta of any particular historic tradition. This must be the kind of argument that rabbis will write in protest to the sweeping effort across the land to have the public school profess belief in God. We must dramatize the lesson of Judaism that one does not question a man's faith, but rather judges him by his deeds. This is why we squirm at these guides on moral and spiritual values and not just because they are the violation of legal principle. We are not lawyers, we are not secularists, we are rabbis. It is time for our policy statements to speak the language of faith and to use the vocabulary of Judaism.

In response to this presentation, the C.C.A.R. authorized a new church-state commission, to which I was appointed a member, to review our positions and to rewrite them. Regretfully I failed to win any change in the substantive positions that the Reform Movement had taken, but I did succeed in having the rabbis radically rewrite the language with which they supported their position. In the new language adopted in 1960, the rabbis clearly defined those religious and historic commitments that supported their political posture and provided justification for their prior stance. The rabbis asserted: "History furnishes ample evidence to support the conclusion that when religion becomes identified with the state, it often compromises its allegiance to Divine mandate. Alliance of religion and the state has often been followed by diminution of moral sensitivity and a distortion of ethical values . . . When religion becomes a tool of the state, it is rendered powerless to oppose unjust acts of government and is even tempted to use the power of the state to advance sectarian interests."[13]

The rabbis pointed to the fact that "religion has flourished" in the United States where no church can be established and all are dependent upon their own resources and zeal of their faithful for support. "Moreover, in a society characterized by religious pluralism, religious groups in America have learned to regard one another with mutual respect and to discover common ground for working together in behalf of shared goals."

Acknowledging that "the desire to counter the forces of secularism and materialism and to raise the moral standard of our national life was commendable," the rabbis nevertheless rejected "the introduction of religious forms and usages, particularly in public schools. Crime and juvenile delinquency will certainly not be abated by posting the Ten Commandments in the public school classrooms, by erecting a creche outside the city hall or by rote recitation of biblical verses in the public school." Such practices not only constitute a violation of personal conscience, said the rabbis, but then evoking Judaism's formula for the repair of the world, we declared: "Only the unremitting labor of men dedicated to the prophetic ideal in the name of a universal God will ameliorate the problems of our time and bring salvation to the world."

Finally, the rabbis asserted their confidence in the public school as the most significant "instrument of democracy" for our pluralistic society. "We deny that a school that does not engage in religious instruction is godless. Indeed, for the school to assume this function, is to usurp the function of the home and the church or synagogue." Admitting that the home "has gradually yielded many of its functions to other institutions, particularly those pertaining to moral discipline and religious indoctrination," the rabbis urged "the forces of religion" to strive to halt this process. "It should be the prime task of church and synagogue in our day to inspire and guide the family in the great tasks of spiritual regeneration . . ."

While I do not waver from my conviction that such insights and commitments are very applicable to contemporary church-state issues, I still do confess my unhappiness at the fact that fear and defensiveness seem more significant than religious insight in shaping Jewish political position. There is nothing in these words, for example, that ought inhibit the full cooperation of religious institutions in serving the educational needs of the Poverty Program, as long as proper safeguards against evangelism are maintained in the program—as they are. Yet, most of America's Jewish agencies, fearful of the consequences of any church involvement in state functions, have warned that only as a last resort "if it is impossible to utilize publicly owned premises" should a religious institution be used.

There is nothing in the 1960 C.C.A.R. resolution that ought preclude the institution of a program of shared time, particularly one that would bring a larger number of parochial school children under the discipline of the public school. Yet, most of America's Jewish agencies have warned against this whole aspect of the new education bill, so concerned are they that any financial assistance at all will be provided through this program to the church school—so concerned are they lest the private school be strengthened and the public school, therefore, be weakened, or that the administrative need for cooperative planning with church-related school administrators ultimately lead to their control over public school administration.

Thus, I find myself in a minority position inside the Jewish community, even at that moment when the Jewish community finds itself increasingly outside of the new public consensus. Needless to say, I am not happy on either account.

What then do I see for the future, particularly with regard to the implications of this issue for Jewish-Christian relations? While I cannot know for sure, I can point to some significant trends and pressures that I think are important.

The Supreme Court has made it clear that the public school may not engage in liturgical exercises. I consider this decision proper and wise, but as all of us know, and as Protestants have already confessed, such religious exercises for many years had provided Americans with the security that the religious aspect of truth that is part of the heritage of western civilization was somehow more or less adequately being communicated in public education. We now know that this is not the case. All of us have to confront the question of how and in what ways the public school in a pluralistic society is to respond to this problem. What information, if any, and how should the public school inform children concerning the events and ideas of religion? How and in what ways should the public school challenge children to make value choices and to consider the significance of those values cherished in religion for which sanction is provided in each of our faiths by our conception of God?

There is no easy answer to these questions, but I believe that we must ask them and attempt together to work at the answers. If such discussion were held under proper educational auspices, if all points of view were given a fair hearing and no coercion exercised, then I am hopeful that Jews may join creatively in the inquiry. I believe that ways can be found for the public school to exercise its educational function better and to produce a greater literacy among Americans regarding the role of religion and religions in civilization. I also believe that the public school can be made more self-conscious about its limited role in influencing character; and to the degree that value choices do become a matter of deliberate and conscious examination, the public school can play a more significant role in encouraging children to an examination of the options offered them by religion, among the other philosophical positions available in our society.

As we work at these questions, I believe that we will discover that there will be even less hesitation about enriching and expanding the course offerings in religion at the university level. I predict that departments of religion will spring up everywhere and that religious groups will be invited back on to the campus of state universities. We shall realize that the burgeoning state university has become a community in its own right and that religion has a right to be inside that community instead of shunted off to the fringes.

I also think that the constitutionality of the child benefit theory as a technical means for unfreezing public funds for church-related education will ultimately have to be determined again by the courts. There is no denying that in response to emerging public welfare needs—such as the race against communism, the demands of defense, the war against poverty—the majority of the American people have been willing, even eager, to involve the church in cooperative relationship with the state. But there is a considerable minority—Baptists who have refused loans even for their hospitals, and Jews who have opposed the church-state provisions of the National Defense Education Act or the poverty and education and higher education bills—whose warnings and antagonisms must receive fair hearing. Denied victory at the legislative level of policy making, this minority has a right to engage in litigation. All of us must defend that right and protect them from abuse because they will choose to exercise it.

It is my personal hope, however, that the courts will acknowledge that where proper provision has been instituted to safeguard public control over the expenditure of funds and the making of policy, where ownership of property remains under public control and no funds are made available for the direct support of the church, then it is proper and right for church institutions and government to cooperate for the common weal. At this moment, when we have agreed to expand to enormous proportions the role of Government in social welfare, it might be well for us to consider how beneficial, corrective and constructive can be the participation of the church as it involves itself according to its own genius and ability in the reconstruction of our society, even though operating with funds made available through the government.

We are now in a new era in the relations among religious groups. This is the era of the Ecumenical Council, the emergence of dialogue groups, the direct active involvement of religion in racial demonstration and issues of peace, the emergence of a governmental commitment to eradicate poverty and illiteracy once and for all. I am satisfied that God is working in all of this, and if I am to sense his Presence, then I must be open to new experiences and opportunities. I must be ready to hear the other, eager to understand the truth he has nurtured, willing to experiment with new forms and relationships that may better make God's word relevant to the structures of society.

Since I believe that all of society, church and state, stand within His judgment, I cannot easily compartmentalize my religious involvement. Certainly, the structures of the institutional church and the established state need to remain separate and distinct, but by His word God brings men to recognize his unity and the unity of all nature. What I seek, then, are those ways by which we can respect the integrity and the uniqueness of each other's faith and of all institutions in society and yet together cooperatively as one humanity serve Him. This is my Jewish commitment.

NOTES

[1] Tosephta Abodah Zarah 8:4–8; Sanhedrin 56A–60A.

[2] Sanhedrin 105A.

[3] Berakoth 5:22; see also discussion on this point by Rabbi Jakob Petuchowski in *Christian Century,* October 12, 1960, "To the Unknown God."

[4] "Christianity—general Christianity is and always has been a part of the common law of Pennsylvania. . . . It is not proclaimed by the commanding voice of any human superior, but expressed in the common mild account of customary law." *Updegraph vs. Commonwealth,* 11 Serg. and R. Pennsylvania. See also *Vidal vs. Girard Executors,* 2 How. 127, 1844, and *Church of the Holy Trinity vs. United States,* 143, US 457.

[5] See data sheet on Hebrew day school movement prepared by Torah Mesorah, 156 Fifth Avenue, New York City, July, 1965.

[6] See report in Organization and Institutions by Rabbi Arthur Gilbert, *CCAR Journal,* June, 1962.

[7] *Religious News Service,* March 8, 1963.

[8] Torah u Mesorah Report, May, 1965.

[9] *Inter-Mountain Jewish News,* Denver, Colorado, January 29, 1965.

[10] *Religious News Service,* May 28, 1965.

[11] Quoted by Rabbi Wolfe Kelman in *Conservative Judaism:* "Judaism in Israel," Winter 1965.

[12] *Retrospect and Prospect,* edited by Rabbi Bertram Korn, C.C.A.R., New York, 1965, p. 117.

[13] *Ibid.,* pp. 124–126.

BIBLICAL CONCEPTS OF COMMUNITY AND STATE

by

John L. McKenzie, S.J.

THE usual designation for Israel in the Old Testament is *people;* but the English word does not quite render the full meaning of the Hebrew *'am.* A people in Hebrew is primarily a kinship group; and the same meaning appears in related words in the cognate languages.[1] The kinship group is a large family, and the family in ancient Israel was conceived in the clan and tribe structure. The family could not exist outside of this structure; and all who pertained to the same tribe and clan group called each other *brothers.* Where it was necessary to specify that the brother was a sibling, a phrase like "the son of my father" was added—and in polygamous families "the son of my mother," since uterine brothers were considered to be more closely related. But the basic bond which united members of a people was kinship; where real kinship did not exist, an artificial kinship was created.

The effects of kinship can be seen in three ancient Israelite customs which have no counterpart in modern civilized society. The first of these was the most serious kinship obligation, and it comprised a number of duties owed to other members of the kinship group.[2] These duties are summed up in the word which is usually translated *vengeance,* but here again the translation is inadequate. Nor is *defense* an accurate translation, since the duties are not exactly preventive, although the institution as a whole was designed to protect the members of the group. The next of kin was obliged to act if his kinsman was killed or suffered bodily harm or was threatened with the loss of his property. For murder or bodily harm the duty imposed was retaliation upon the offender; and there was no excuse from the fulfilment of this obligation. Our concern now is not with the absence of due legal process, the possibility of error and excess, or the failure to distinguish between murder and homicide. This last distinction appears in Deuteronomy 19:4–13, apparently for the first time in Hebrew law. In a culture which had neither police nor courts the only protection of the individual from violence was the assurance that his kinship group would avenge any assault upon him. The solidarity of the group can be seen clearly in this duty.

The same obligation demanded that the next of kin purchase landed property if the needy kinsman was forced to sell; and this illustrates the second custom, which has to do with the Israelite attitude towards the ownership of land.[3] Land was owned in the first instance by the group, and the individual person was a shareholder. In the book of Joshua there is an unhistorical description of the assignment of land to the tribes by lot; but this unhistorical narrative does reflect the way in which Israelite families shared in the land. The law which requires that the land stay within the clan or tribe comes from a time when the kinship group had been loosened by various social forces; and it reflects the accumulation of large holdings in the hands of landlords. But it again illustrates the solidarity of the group, seen in its possessions as well as in its attitude toward persons. The group protected the individual member, and the individual member had the sacred duty of contributing his part to the protection extended by the group.

The third custom is not only foreign to our ways, but

repulsive; this is the understanding of collective guilt.[4] If a member of the group offends the deity or a member of another group, the entire group is responsible in the sense that any member of the group may be punished. Unless we understand that this punishment was not regarded as unjust, we have not grasped the idea of group solidarity. It was a part of the protection rendered to the individual by the group that the group accepted collective responsibility for his acts. In the story of the intertribal war of Jgs. 19–21 the elders of Benjamin will not deliver the offending members to punishment; such a delivery would have been a betrayal of group responsibility. We are not concerned here with the fact that protection of this kind could render punishment impossible; the offenders were subject to the law of revenge, but in this case the offended person could scarcely hope to deal with an entire town. His own group took means to aid him in his pursuit of vengeance.

Collective guilt is seen in the story of Achan (Jos. 7); here the offender is discovered by lot, but his family perishes with him. While a share in the guilt may be presumed, the extermination of a family for the fault of one is repulsive to our moral standards. Modern scholars suspect that the story of the lot has a background no longer recognized when the story took its present form. If the offender was unknown, the group expiated the collective guilt incurred by drawing lots to select the member who should suffer the punishment. This was a community service like war, work or the duty of revenge; it made no difference which member of the community was punished, so the lot was employed. Here once more we see the idea of group solidarity illustrated.

The kinship group could not endure in the urban-agricultural civilization of the ancient Near East and in Israel it was submerged in other forms, but the idea of blood kinship is echoed in the Old Testament long after it had lost most of its social force. The earliest modification was the idea of covenant people. It has become clear that early Israel rejected the Canaanite city-state community with its king and its feudal aristocracy.[5] Israel was a league of tribes in which the ideal of the equality of each clan, tribe family, and individual was preserved. Israel was a kinship group, although there was a large element of artificiality in the kinship; but the basic bond of Israel was covenant rather than blood. The covenant society which appeared in Israel before the monarchy is without parallel in the ancient Near East, and many of its elements were of enduring effect in the faith of Israel; hence it deserves more than passing attention.

Most biblical scholars have accepted the parallel which Martin Noth has drawn between the tribal league of Israel and the amphictyonic leagues of ancient Greece.[6] The amphictyonic league was composed of city-states which were joined in the maintenance and defense of a common shrine at which all the members worshipped. It was a purely religious association, although such leagues could not fail to have political effects as well. This is substantially the character of the Israelite league. The tribes were united in the worship of one God, Yahweh. The cult of the league was carried on at a central shrine. Noth suggests that the number of twelve, which is paralleled in Greek amphictyonies, represents the months of the year; each member was committed to support the shrine for one month. The league was not political; no central political authority appears in the Old Testament for the tribal league, and this accords with the suggestions of George Mendenhall that the tribal league was an explicit rejection of the city-state system of Canaan. The league had, however, other effects which can be designated as political; but these effects were all dominated by the religious nature of the association.

The covenant was a pact between Yahweh and the tribes and between the tribes themselves. Mendenhall and others have pointed out that the form of the covenant reflects a type of ancient Near Eastern treaty called the suzerainty treaty imposed by an overlord upon a vassal.[7] The overlord promises protection to the vassal. The vassal promises loyalty to the overlord, and the terms of this loyalty are set down in certain stipulations. The gods are invoked as witnesses, imprecations are uttered against the vassal should he be unfaithful, and copies of the treaty are preserved in temples. In some form all of these elements appear in the Old Testament, even including the historical prologue in which the benefits conferred by the overlord upon the vassal are recited. The parallel between the covenant and the treaty form does suggest that Yahweh is "lord," and this title is given to him hundreds of times in the Old Testament; but the force of this title should not be misunderstood. It signifies that Yahweh alone is lord, that there is no king of the absolute type such as existed in the Canaanite city-states. Thus the non-political character of the league is expressed. The tribes were united in a single faith and religious allegiance.

Israelite law corresponded to the stipulations laid upon the vassal in the treaty. These are the terms in which Israelite fidelity is defined. A number of recent studies have shown the importance of the idea of covenant law in early Israel. Numerous parallels can be shown between particular Israelite laws and particular laws found in other ancient Near Eastern legal collections. It is clear that a body of common consuetudinary law prevailed over most of the ancient Near East. But the framework in which law was set in Israel has no parallel. Law elsewhere was not without religious sanction; gods like the Mesopotamian Shamash were the vindicators of law. But only in Israel was law conceived as the revealed will of the deity imposed as a condition of the maintenance of good relations between the people and the deity. There emerges obscurely the idea of Israelite law as defining a peculiarly Israelite way of life in community. The community shared in the sanction imposed by Yahweh. As the law was the will of Yahweh, so it was also the will of the community and not merely of the king. When punishment was inflicted, it was a community process; for unless the whole community supported the law, it was not sustaining its fidelity to the covenant terms.

The allusions to amphictyonic assemblies establish the fact that such assemblies existed, but they do not tell us much about the proceedings. That there were regular cultic assemblies for amphictyonic festivals is clear. The tribes were represented by delegates; it is not clear that every Israelite attended these festivals, and it seems unlikely. The assembly also dealt with questions which concerned all the tribes. One type of such question was certainly the interpretation of law, and it seems that this was left to professional experts. The amphictyonic festivals no doubt included a covenant renewal in which the terms of the covenant were read and the saving acts of Yahweh for Israel were recited and the tribes professed anew their acceptance of the covenant. Possibly covenant offenses of major dimensions were submitted to such an assembly.

We have observed that the league had certain effects which can be called political. The most important of these was the idea of the holy war.[8] The name suggests that war of this type was a religious activity, and indeed it was; but it does not seem that all military action could be called a holy war. Following Gerhard von Rad, we can suggest that the holy war was a war of all Israel; as such it could be declared only by the representatives of the tribes. All Israel was liable to summons in the holy war; the Song of Deborah suggests that the summons was not always followed. It seems very probable that the warriors had a ritual consecration with certain restrictions laid upon them. It may be conjectured that the Nazirite vow indicates the nature of these restrictions; letting the hair grow and abstinence from spirituous beverages and sexual intercourse seem likely. No prisoners or booty were taken; the holy war was not a plundering expedition, and prisoners and booty were destroyed in honor of Yahweh.

This indicates the essence of the holy war; it was a war in defense of Yahweh's land. For the donation of the land in fulfilment of the promises to the fathers was an essential part of the covenant idea. Yahweh was the lord, and the Israelites were his tenants. When they took arms in defense of his land, he was their real leader. He exercised his leadership through the spirit which he imparted to those charismatic heroes whom we call judges. He sends terror and panic upon the enemy, and the Israelites need do no more than pursue them. The holy war obviously seems to be an ideal rather than a real activity; but the theory of the holy war discloses the idea of the covenant.

In the ancient near East every state was a religious community in some sense; but Israel achieved a type of religious community of its own. It was first and foremost a community of faith and of obedience to the revealed law. This unity of faith and obedience was professed by cultic ritual. Failure to live by the law was secession from the community, whether it was the failure of an individual or of a group. The league knew no purely political activity. By its formation of the covenant league Israel professed its belief that law and order could not be achieved by purely political means; they could be guaranteed only by the submission of the group to Yahweh. Apart from him neither the individual nor the group could find genuine security.

These elements of the covenant faith endured long after the league itself had yielded to other social forms; for the league was replaced by a monarchy in the eleventh century. It is evident that the league broke down; to trace the causes of its failure is difficult, and it would take us beyond the scope of this paper. We should notice, however, that the Israelite monarchy took a peculiar form deeply influenced by the traditions of the covenant league.[9] There was, in fact, a constant tension between monarchical institutions and covenant traditions which was never resolved. There seem to have been two types of kingship, the Davidic kingship of Judah and the kingship of Israel, about which we are less well informed. It is possible that the Israelite king was conceived as a purely secular officer, at least during the dynasty of Omri. This dynasty, like several other Israelite dynasties, was established by a military revolt; and it is clear that the dynasty of Omri was deeply hated by those Israelites who were attached to covenant traditions. Whatever be the reasons, Israel never achieved the dynastic stability which was so remarkable in Judah; if the Israelite king had a sacral character —which seems likely, even if we cannot define it—it was not the sacral character of the Davidic ruler.

The brief survey of the kinship and covenant communities we have given shows why many in Israel, represented by the anti-monarchic portions of the Old Testament, did not believe that Israel could have a king. The monarchy is described in the anti-monarchic narrative of 1 Sam. 8:5 as "a king to govern us like all the nations." This designation over-simplifies ancient Near Eastern monarchies, and it over-simplifies them even more to say that in the ancient Near Eastern kingdoms the king was either a god or an image of the god; yet this is the point where ancient kingship clashed with Israelite ideology.[10] Yahweh could be represented by no image; a human king as the earthly representative of the divine king appeared to be a form of idolatry. The king was a visible incorporation of the state; and this also established the state as a kind of anti-god in the person of the king. Furthermore, the absolute rule of the ancient king was in contradiction to the freedom of the individual person under tribal law. In spite of these difficulties, an Israelite kingship was established.

To put it perhaps too simply, the solution in the Davidic monarchy was found in idea of covenant, as pointed out by Walther Eichrodt.[11] The Davidic king enjoyed a covenant relationship with Yahweh not so much parallel to the covenant of Israel as superimposed upon it. He was the vassal of Yahweh, promised eternal rule on the conditions that he was faithful to the covenant. But the covenant to which he was bound included the traditional Israelite law; and thus a restraint was placed upon the rule of the monarch. Within these restraints, the king was the elect of Yahweh, as Israel was his elect people. He became a messianic figure, a salvation hero. The gift of the spirit, which was given as a passing charisma to the heroes of the holy war, rested permanently upon the king. This theoretical basis, it seems, was among the factors which maintained the dynasty of David in Judah for over four hundred years in spite of failures and reversals.

The theoretical basis did not prevent the secularization of the Davidic monarchy and a return to the conditions of the Canaanite city-state which had been rejected by the Israelite amphictyony. These conditions are seen both in the historical books and in the prophets. The monarchy in effect became absolute; the restraints upon it were found only in the words of the spokesmen of the covenant traditions. An aristocracy arose based upon the official class of royal administration, and it may be assumed that it was this aristocracy who owned the large estates of which the prophets speak. The individual Israelite was no longer sure of his land; in fact, indebtedness was habitual. The royal taxes were exorbitant. Equal justice for all Israelites before the law did not exist; the prophets speak often of the corruption of judges by bribery. When Israel and Judah were threatened by Assyria, the first world power, they had neither the national resources nor the moral strength to meet the crisis. The monarchy endured longer than the tribal league, but it was no more successful in assuring peace, law, and order for its subjects. It left an enduring ideal in the messianic king, as the amphictyony left the ideal of covenant law; but neither of these institutions survived as such in postexilic Judaism.

From a historical point of view it is most remarkable that any kind of Israelite community survived the disasters of the eighth and seventh centuries. Other states with larger resources and populations disappeared in the conquests of Assyria, Babylonia and Persia. Yet the petty community of postexilic Palestine recognized its continuity with preexilic Israel. The continuity endured because postexilic Judaism was a community of faith. The content of the faith had undergone modification, but it was the same faith in the same Yahweh. The postexilic community, however, was politically powerless. It was a part of a province of the Persian empire, enjoying local autonomy in local affairs but deprived of sovereignty. Hence it asserted its religious identity even more firmly than early Israel had asserted it, for it had no other identity. There was some degree of archaism in Judaism's assertion of continuity with Israel, but the assertion was genuine. The institutions of the community showed how history had affected Israel.

There was a strange revival of the kinship group. Genealogies become important in postexilic Judaism. Israel and Judah had never been a homogeneous ethnic group, but postexilic Judaism insisted on homogeneity. Under the threat of assimilation the community of blood took on new significance. The Jerusalem group refused to admit the Samaritans, although it is very doubtful that the blood of the one group was purer than the blood of the other. Marriages with foreigners were prohibited, although the prohibition was not really effective. Religious loyalty to Yahweh and kinship loyalty were amalgamated into a single sentiment, with consequences which endured long after the period of postexilic Judaism.

The poles of unity were the cult and the law, each modified from earlier forms. Those who insisted that the temple of Jerusalem be rebuilt knew what they were doing. There the whole community could assemble in cultic worship because the community was extremely small. When synagogues arose in Diaspora Judaism, the unity of Judaism had been forged so stoutly that there was no danger of disintegration. The sacrificial cult could be offered in only one place, the place where Yahweh had willed that his name should dwell. This one place could be kept free of ritual deviations and foreign superstitions. That it was not preserved from other and more serious deviations is a fact of history, but it served its purpose as a bond of community. It was the spiritual home of every Jew. It is doubtful that the temple had as much significance under the monarchy. Then the temple had been identified with the monarchy itself, and it was a part of the symbolism of the monarchy. In the postexilic community it signified the abiding presence of Yahweh, who had judged his people for its sins and had saved it.

More important ultimately was the idea of law. The law was no longer the revealed will of God within a sovereign people; the Jews were subject to the empire of Persia. But the law remained the guide of a way of life, and its directions were sharpened by the study and the interpretation of the law which began in the Persian period and issued in the monumental work of the Talmud. This close study of the law left very few situations in life where there were not explicit directions for a proper Jewish way of acting. We have seen that covenant law was sacred in premonarchic Israel; but in postexilic Judaism the veneration of the law seems at times to go beyond due limits. Perhaps this arose from some psychological necessity which we do not perceive. But we can perceive the results; the results were that a community of law came into existence in which every man knew what every other man expected of him, where the individual could be counted on to respond in a definite way, and where the Jew could be recognized as such both by his fellow Jews and by Gentiles. A result also was that the community which observed the law was assured of its fidelity to God and of his continued good will.

The law was not administered by officers of a tribal league or a monarchy; it was administered by scholars. The most important modification of the law was that it became literature, a part of the Israelite traditions which are collected as the Old Testament.

The people of the law were also the people of the book. I have noticed that there is a degree of archaism in postexilic Judaism. This community was a community of conservatism, of an exaggerated respect for the traditional, which desired to find a root in its traditions for every development, sometimes only by artificial interpretation. But we are looking at the type of community which appears in this period, and under the heading of law as a bond we must include attachment to tradition as expressed in the sacred literature. This was the common wisdom of Judaism in virtue of which Jews remained disdainful of Greek learning and literature.

This survey has led us to the point where Christianity emerges from Judaism, and this is the last form of biblical community which meets us. At this point it may be interjected that this survey helps to explain why some biblical students are political pessimists. A study of the Old Testament shows no political form which serves the purpose of political forms. Even the nonpolitical form of the amphictyony did not survive; perhaps it could not have survived in any case, but it represented an ideal higher than the merely political. Against this background it is scarcely surprising that the New Testament has almost nothing to say about the political community. No doubt this reserve reflects the realities of the first century. The sole political reality of the New Testament world was the Roman Empire, and the subject of Rome questioned the Empire no more than he questioned the weather. The empire was a cosmic rather than a political force, and the New Testament response to the empire is summed up in the direction to give Caesar what is his—without defining what is his.

The community of the New Testament is the Church, and this is the only community which the New Testament knows. That this is a revolutionary community needs no explanation. That it is a community of love based on faith is also so well known that I feel no need for going into this at length; the time and space at our disposal do not permit this. But we can notice that the Church fulfills all the Old Testament themes of community while it transforms them. Fraternal love is a bond stronger than kinship, but it knows no limits within the human community. The Church is not a community of law, but it is a community with a way of life defined by the gospel. It is a community in which all the members are equal in the sense that all are equally Christian. It is a community in which the messianic idea is fulfilled in Jesus Christ, who is the corporate personality of the Church. Indeed he is the unity of the Church. The real nature of the Church is more fully perceived when its background in Israelite history and faith are recognized. There is but one more question which I propose in connection with the community of the Church.

The Church, we noticed, is the only community which the New Testament knows, not in the sense that there are no other societies of men, but in the sense that these other societies fail to achieve true community. The obvious eschatological thrust of the New Testament means that the Church is seen as moving towards the total human community; it will not have reached its fullness until this move is completed. The question is whether the missionary movement of the Church has been carried on with complete acceptance of this eschatological thrust. Have Christians resigned themselves to thinking of the Church as one of many competing communities, as one of several allegiances which men must owe? Have they permitted the Church to become a parapolitical society as effective as the personalities of its leaders, but otherwise no more significant than other mutual benevolent associations? The figure that looms is the figure of the state. How much do Christians allow the state to substitute for the Christian community, knowing as they do that Christian community is postponed by political division? That the modern national state is divisive and not unitive certainly needs no demonstration. The degree to which Christianity has compromised with this factor is difficult to assess.

The question, then, is whether Christians in this area are conscious of their mission, or whether they are fulfilling it if they are conscious of it. It is to be expected that non-Christians will not move towards the fulfilment of Christian community. While it is scarcely to be expected that Christians will stand in the way of fulfilment, can their immobility be described as a form of Christian action? That we do not know how to move toward this fulfilment is obvious; that we do not know does not mean we can never know, and it certainly does not mean that we are excused from effort to find a way. Community is not one of the peripheral features of the Church. As long as it is lacking, the whole gospel has not been proclaimed within the Church. Who is responsible for this?

NOTES

[1] See Johs. Pedersen, *Israel: Its Life and Culture* (London: Geoffrey Cumberlege, 1926) I–II, 29–96.

[2] Roland de Vaux, *Ancient Israel* (Eng. tr., New York: McGraw-Hill, 1961) 10–12.

[3] *Ibid.*, 22.

[4] Johs. Pedersen, *Israel* I–II 263–279.

[5] G. E. Mendenhall, *Biblical Archaeologist* 25 (1962), 66–87.

[6] Martin Noth, *The History of Israel* (Eng. tr., New York: Harper and Brothers, 1958), 85–97.

[7] George E. Mendenhall, *Biblical Archaeologist* 17 (1955), 26–46; 49–76.

[8] Gerhard von Rad, *Studies in Deuteronomy* (Eng. tr., London: SCM press, 1953), 45–59.

[9] Roland de Vaux, *Ancient Israel,* 91–114.

[10] Sigmund Mowinckel, *He That Cometh* (Eng. tr., New York: Abingdon Press, 1954), 21–95.

[11] Walther Eichrodt, *Theology of the Old Testament* (Eng. tr., Philadelphia: Westminster 1961), 436–456.

MORAL SOCIETY AND IMMORAL MAN

by

Michael Novak

IN 1932, Reinhold Niebuhr published a book, *Moral Man and Immoral Society,*[1] which shocked the American Protestant world. The central thesis of that book was "that the Liberal Movement both religious and secular seemed to be unconscious of the basic difference between the morality of individuals and the morality of collectives, whether races, classes or nations."[2] The morality of individuals vs. the morality of collectives: it is plain from Niebuhr's title that he favored the morality of individuals, and judged societies by the standards of individuals.[3] For Niebuhr, what is really real in Christian life is the "vertical relationship" between the individual and God; the ethic of Jesus, in his view, has almost nothing to say about the "horizontal relationships" between individuals in society.[4] For Niebuhr, the individual is the primary reality of Christianity; the community is secondary, instrumental, and inferior; it can never meet the purer standards of the individual.[5]

It will be the argument of this paper, however, that the community, not the individual, furnishes the most accurate model for the discussion of social ethics. What is really real in Christian life is not the individual but the community. We are first baptized into a people, and only secondarily called upon to exercise our own unique individual witness among that people.

Christian *agape* is primarily the love of God poured forth among men, calling into being and vivifying a chosen community, and only secondarily is it a personal, "vertical" relationship between an individual and God. What is really real in Christian ethics is a communal bond among men.[6] The community is the locus in which the individual learns *agape;* the community is the bearer of love, the teacher of love, the household of love. "How can you love God, whom you do not see, if you do not love your neighbor, whom you do see?" (I John 4:20). We do not even know whether we have an authentic "vertical" relationship with God, except insofar as we know that we love our neighbor. Mutual love is the criterion by which we judge the authenticity of our love of God.[7]

In attempting to reverse the priorities between the ethic of individuals and the ethic of communities, we shall, moreover, be gaining a fresh vantage point for assessing the relationships between the church, the individual Christian, secular society, and the state. The conceptual apparatus for assessing these relationships may be governed (1) by the model of an individual's vertical relationship with God, or (2) by the model of an entire community's relationship with God. The choice of the first model has one set of consequences; the choice of the second model has another. Thus the issue of what is primary in Christianity, the individual or the community, plays the role of an important presupposition in considering many problems of church-state relations.

1. *The Meaning of Love*

A complete and fully grounded study of the question we have raised would require a study of the meaning of *Agape* in the New Testament; such a study exceeds our competence.[8] Thus our present argument will not be based upon considerations drawn from a close study of Scripture. On the contrary, it will be drawn mainly from reflection upon certain human experiences. Nearly every man has sometimes loved others; nearly everyone has present in his experience the data out of which our problem arises. The difficulty lies in arranging this data properly, so as to come to terms with all the data and to overlook or to distort none of it. The problem is not to generate new experiences, but to understand correctly and fully experiences which are already at hand.

There are many theories of love, which attempt, some more and some less adequately, to tell us what is happening when we love. It may be useful to resume some of them here. One of the most famous and starkly drawn of the Protestant theories of love is that of the Swedish Bishop, Anders Nygren.[9] Nygren defines love in terms of the individual self: *Agape* or Christian love is selfless, unselfish, disinterested, heedless, self-sacrificing. *Agape* is contrasted with *Eros,* which is self-aggrandizing, self-fulfilling, self-realizing, acquisitive. Obviously, Nygren hopes to portray *Agape* as unselfish, and *Eros* as selfish. But in a subtle way, Nygren's view of *Agape* is also self-centered. The self's attention is drawn to its own purity and selflessness. *Agape* is defined, not by the loveableness of the one loved, but by the purity of the lover; this situation is not changed because *Agape* is a gift from God rather than a personal achievement.[10]

Reinhold Niebuhr disagrees with Nygren, because he thinks that Nygren creates too deep a gap between *agape* and human love; for Christ often used human love as a symbol of divine love.[11] George T. Thomas criticizes Nygren on several similar counts.[12] Still, both Niebuhr and Thomas think that the primary note in Christian *Agape* is heedlessness of self, unselfishness, and self-sacrifice. Even Paul Ramsey, in criticizing Niebuhr's conception of love, decides that *agape* is primarily self-sacrificial rather than mutual.[13]

A quite different approach to *Agape* is possible, however; we might define *Agape,* not in terms of the purity of the self, but in terms of the attention, respect, affection, and effort which the self centers upon the *other.* In this case, the focus of *Agape* shifts from what happens to the self to what happens to the other. Love is defined as willing and acting for the good of the other, as responding to the reality, dignity, and worthiness of the other. *Agape* is, then, not defined negatively as a matter of unselfishness, but positively as a response to the loveableness of the other. This difference is not merely a matter of emphasis; it is a matter of orientation and attitude.[14] The man who tries to be unselfish acts quite differently from the man who attempts to respond generously and realistically to others. The difference is one between an "inner-directed" and an "outer-directed" love though not in the sense which David Riesman delineates.[15] But it does suggest that one man might, quite lovelessly, be concerned with whether his love is sufficiently unselfish, while another may not worry at all about how selfish or unselfish he is but concentrate on responding to others with respect, affection, and service. *Agape,* in short, is not so much unselfishness as it is other-centeredness. To love is to be concerned about the beauty, the dignity, the feelings, and the needs of others; and it is to respond not to what one would like others to be, but to others as they are.

2. *Where Is Love Learned?*

Thus two characteristics of *agape* can be pointed out: (1) *agape* is other-centered, and (2) *agape* is realistic: it responds to others as they are. In order to love, a man must be capable of attention to others, and he must be capable of coping with reality. However, it cannot be assumed that men are born able to love. On the contrary, it appears that infants are at first almost wholly ego-centered. Years may pass before a child is able to respond to others otherwise than as sources of its own security, warmth, clothing, cleanliness, nurture. Only gradually does the child learn to distinguish between himself and others, learning that what pleases him does not necessarily please others, and that what he desires now may or may not be given him. Only gradually does the child learn to distinguish between appearance and reality, between a hot stove and a cold, between his images, desires, illusions, and the hard, stubborn, immovable world of reality. A child in a tantrum may attempt to lift a dresser and throw it at the object of his wrath; but the furniture will not yield just because he wants it to.

In short, children must learn to love. Nor is learning to love merely a matter of purring with contentment like a kitten, returning affection for affection, good behavior for a mother's loving praise. For the time comes in life[16] when playmates do not offer affection to the newcomer, when harsh and cynical outsiders replace the praising mother. What will the growing child do then: close his eyes and cry? To begin to take the steps out into the real world which lead to adulthood, the child must learn to meet others upon their own ground, to respond to the secret word which is the unique reality and identity of each of them. The child must become capable of attending to others; he must cease projecting a world which pivots wholly upon his own ego and its needs; he must place the center of his world not in his ego but in the search for what is real and other; he must become oriented toward reality, and above all to the reality of other men.

Again, man is a social animal. In discovering his own identity, each man discovers that the reality of his life is created by interaction with other lives.[17] There is no such thing as a human atom, no such thing as the pure individual. The human reality is not an "I" but a "we." The man who is psychologically isolated lives in a world of phantasy and unreality. The human consciousness turned inward upon itself does not find reality, not even the reality of the self; it begins totally to lose its bearings and to slip away. On the other hand, to become fully developed as a man, to gain one's own unique identity, one must become capable of reaching out to others, to others as they are in reality and not in phantasy.[18] The only road to personhood lies through community. In this sense, love is the law of human life. Who does not love, does not develop as a human being. Who does not love, is neither healthy, nor able to find himself. To find himself, a man must first find others. To discover who he is, a man must learn who others are.

Thus it is not by accident that in nearly all languages the verb "to know" has the same root as the verb for that fundamental symbol of human love and human realism, marital intercourse. To come to self-knowledge is to come to know oneself through knowing others. Love is creative, because by bestowing it upon one another realistically and truthfully we create persons of one another: we give each other new centers of life and meaning beyond ourselves, without losing our own identity and self-responsibility. There are, of course, some who regard love as ecstasy; some men are eager to escape from themselves. But before love is ecstatic, it is realistic; the lover is not eager to lose himself, he is eager to find the other. When he has found the other realistically and honestly, thus maintaining his own integrity and responsibility,[19] then the lover experiences joy and ecstasy. Such ecstasy is not that of flight from the self, but that of fulfillment of the self. The self is made for others; to find others is to taste reality, and such reality is sweet.[20]

Love, therefore, is learned not in isolation but in community. Love is not learned by pursuing unselfishness, but by pursuing reality and above all the reality of others. Progress in love is progress from phantasy and romance to fact and reality. Other people are real; they are not mere projections of ourselves. Their needs are real. Their wishes, aims, hopes, goodness, weaknesses are real. To learn to love is to learn to respect the real, not to escape from it.[21]

Moreover, it is chiefly living together in community that teaches us to be realistic. Alone, we dream and indulge in phantasy. We are lazy and do not push our inquiries hard enough. We accept as fact what may not be fact. Our criteria of relevance and evidence are slack. Our desires, wishes, and biasses grow luxuriantly where critical intelligence seldom penetrates.[22] But forced to jostle against the standards, criteria, cynical inquiry, and contrary biasses of other men, our laziness is challenged. The reality of other people rubs against us, pushes us, raises new and difficult questions for us. Community awakens us.

It is true, of course, that no community is infinite in its perspectives or totally alive. The horizon[23] of the individual community, like the horizon of the individual, has finite limits. Moreover, each community also has its biasses, presuppositions, special spirit, laziness, particular enthusiasms, areas of apathy. Thus a dialectic[24] is established. At some points, the community prods all the individuals in its midst. At other points, some individuals are the gad-flies of the community, exposing its biasses and failings. No individual man and no human community exhausts everything that men can envisage, understand, or do; progress depends upon the dialectic by which the community raises up in its own midst prophets who, in one respect or another, criticize the community and press it on toward further horizons.

The extent to which individual dissent is essential to this dialectic has been commonly recognized in Protestantism and in the Enlightenment. But the extent to which community nourishes even individual dissent has been commonly forgotten. Thus the theories of individualism common in our society are only partially adequate. For the individual does not develop outside of a community. Prophets are raised up in the midst of the people. The dissenter learns to speak, to distinguish reality from appearance, to prefer integrity to pharisaism, to love persons rather than codes, to differentiate living values from dead traditions, only in the midst of his community. A healthy community needs its own critics just as love needs realism:

phantasy is the disease of communities just as it is the disease of love.

3. *The Role of Society in Morals*

It is not true, then, that man is moral but society immoral. On the contrary, society is the matrix of ethical education; apart from society moral growth is inconceivable. Still, education is not communicated primarily through codes of law, conventions, textbooks, and sermons. Society educates primarily through those relationships between man and man which it allows or encourages men to establish. In order to grow in honesty, perception, reconciliation, courage, hope, and responsiveness to one another, men must learn to prize such qualities; and they will learn even what such qualities are only with one another's help. Who am I? I will learn who I am only through interaction with others. Am I intelligent, honest, realistic, courageous, capable of love? How will I know unless I live with others? Others will tell me, through words or behavior, much that I could never learn through introspection. Moreover, the community with which I identify has formed my notion of what the words "intelligent," "honest," "realistic," "courageous," and "capable of love" mean. A dissenter may insist that the community no longer understands correctly its use of such key words; but to make himself understood at all (even by himself), the dissenter must use such words as derive from, or can now be incorporated into, the common inheritance of his community. A completely personal language is a contradiction in terms.

Several objections to the present line of thought leap to mind. Is not a human community often oppressive, mediocre, or even evil? Must not the individual be ready to stand against the herd? Isn't the differentiation of the individual from the society one of the great achievements of Western culture? Is not the thirst for community a disease which leads to goose stepping, romantic

Fascism or to a drab Communism? These questions seem to show that the source of moral progress is not primarily in the community but in the individual. But the fallacy in the questions is that they seem to think of the community as a single total unit. There is no such "thing" as a society; there are, in fact, only millions of individual men, who live in certain relationships. "Society" is an abstraction, a way of speaking about the different ways in which men are related. We must exorcise from our minds the image of society as a great, grey "thing," standing menacingly behind the countless individuals we see, talk to, shake the hands of.

These individuals, however, are not isolated atoms. They speak, and speech is a communal phenomenon. All are children of other humans. Some of them love one another. Some teach, and others study with them. Some are in the employ of others. They have various ways of arranging for political decisions which concern the behavior of large numbers of them. It is these complex relationships that affect human consciousness that we speak of as *society.* And our thesis is that men become moral only through growing into these relationships; there is no possibility of growing moral in total isolation. One could not even love God if one had not learned how to love by discovering the reality of others; otherwise, there would be no way of defending oneself against illusions in a relationship with one who is unseen and who does not speak.[25]

Thus, while it is true that the organs of a particular church, nation, or social group in which one lives may suppress individual liberty, enforce complacent and apathetic conformity, or command racial injustices of the most flagrant sort, still, the remedy for these diseases does not lie in the attempt to escape from all social relationships. On the contrary, the love of liberty, the pursuit of excellence, and protestation against injustice are learned through social relationships. For such values spring from the acquired ability to distinguish reality from appearances, to discern alternatives, to make judgments based upon evidence, and to decide according to one's judgments. The individual learns these skills through living in a community. The requisite experiences, skills, and dispositions are more accessible in some societies than in others, of course; they are part of the tradition of a free society. But wherever men teach each other to speak, the basic tools of discrimination are accessible for further moral development. The culture in which one lives is the matrix in which the task of moral development is established, and the first steps in personal liberation begun.

Again, the individual could not stand against the herd unless he had learned the distinction between the self and the community, and learned enough from the community to judge when and how the community is betraying its own values or neglecting other values. When the prophet chastises the community, he stands upon the shoulders of the community.

Again, if the differentiation of the self from the society is one of the great achievements of Western culture, still, the view that the individual is independent of society and prior to society is one of the radical exaggerations which endanger the health of Western culture. Individual talent is nourished by the tradition, and tradition is revitalized by individual appropriation.[26] A man is not completely conditioned by his society, for he may critize it; but neither is he independent of his society. A man is born into a community and, appropriating its values and acquired skills, criticizes it. He is not disloyal to his community for using on it the moral skills it has helped him develop.

Finally, there are two senses of community which it is important to distinguish. In a romantic sense, nostalgia for community may haunt the isolated individual; a man who experiences himself as an isolated atom hungers for identification with a group. In this sense, community totally absorbs the individual; the values, goals, and exigencies of the commune are uncritically devoured in exchange for comradeship. This is the sense of community which draws the insecure, the alienated, the threatened, and those incapable of realistic love. Millenial groups in Western history have long arisen out of this nostalgia.[27]

But the second sense of community is not romantic but realistic. The community is not perceived as an escape or refuge. Rather, community is already present because the individual experiences himself as related to others; he is not an "I" merely, but also a "we." He is not isolated, alienated, or unable to love. He has been nourished by a community of which he feels himself a part, and he is free to extend community to others. He is not uncritical; he does not accept all the values, goals, and exigencies of his community as equally valid. He feels a responsibility towards his community, a claim upon him to be intelligent, reflective, honest, and courageous. He does not feel that dissent is disloyalty, for the community of which he is a part does not demand his total submission but the total development of his humanity. Such a community has taught him to seek reality through intelligent and critical judgment, and to respond to others as they are, not as phantasy or pretense suggest. Such a community has maintained a tradition of at least some small measure of liberty, justice, truth, and love. In it a man is free to be himself: both an authentic person and a social animal. Such a community communicates the desire for a free, responsible, and critical life to as many of its members as are receptive to it.

4. *The Open Society and the Open Church*

Love is mutual before it is selfless. It is other-centered rather than non-self-centered; its goal is community of life, rather than the purity of individuals. Man is a member of a community before he is an individual, and he develops as a genuine person through developing more creative, realistic, and profound relationships with others. The basic model for the understanding of human life and action, therefore, is not the atomic individual but the community of persons. Is this community the state? The church? Or neither one?

In the language of political science, the community is prior to the state; the state is an administrative, legal, and technical apparatus for securing certain purposes of the community. In the language of theology, God made his covenant with a people, an *ecclesia,* not with atomic individuals. A Christian is first a member of a people, secondarily an individual believer. The call is not first addressed to separate individuals, who then join together for their mutual protection; on the contrary, a church was first called into being, within which individuals might be nourished in a community of life, faith, and love. Likewise, the national community is not first a group of atomic individuals, who for self-protection create a government by contract; on the contrary, human communities are primordial, and various rules and institutions are from the first implicit in their ways of life.

Consequently, the problem of church and state is not the radical problem in the question of how to relate Christian life to secular life. The radical problem concerns the relationships which obtain between the many human communities which are prior to the two polities, church and state. Insofar as the community of believers has an historically articulated polity, a variety of offices, techniques of communal decision-making, and an unavoidable degree of bureaucratization, the meaning of the word "church" has a secondary, juridical sense. Primarily, the church is the people of God;[28] secondarily, it is an external, more or less bureaucratic polity. The two senses of the word are linked organically; no community can endure through the necessities of history without establishing an effective polity.[29] But the two senses must also be distinguished and their priorities observed, lest the church attempt to be purely "spiritual" and nonhistorical or, on the other hand, become a sepulchre of bureaucracy and legalism.

Similarly, insofar as a large community requires an articulated polity, it gives rise to a state. No national community can survive without government; but the ends of government do not encompass all the ends of the community.[30] In many areas of community concern, in the arts, the sciences, religion, and the like, the state has no competence, or only that marginal competence which restricts abuses against public order: forbidding religious practices, for example, which involve human sacrifice, the use of poisonous snakes, or polygamy. It is extremely difficult to mark off the limits which the state must observe in interfering with the broader life of the community. Criteria for deciding what constitutes an abuse against "public order" and what constitutes an illegitimate intervention of government in the liberty of the community are scarcely to be derived from abstract considerations; abstractions themselves cover too much ground and infringe upon liberty. Thus the history of the community and the concrete circumstances of each instance furnish more limited and less ideologically menacing criteria from case to case.

Nevertheless, a disproportionate amount of attention is usually given to the problems of church and state; for church and state are secondary realities. The church as polity is only an instrument of the church as community, and the state is but one instrument of the culture. When attention is focussed upon the state rather than upon the culture, or upon the church as polity rather than upon the church as people, there is an overpowering temptation to construct a conceptual model with the atomic individual as their opposite pole. The state is taken to be a threat to the individual; individual conscience is brandished as a battlecry against the church. Moreover, the church is understood to be one separate collective, the state another; the dimensions of life in which the individual shares beliefs and attitudes which derive *at the same time* from both his church as community and his civic community are overlooked. Robert N. Bellah, from the Social Relations Department at Harvard, has described in a fascinating paper[31] the role and importance of "civic religion"—a shared body of ultimate assumptions and ways of action—in the life even of a religiously pluralistic society such as our own.

It may be fruitful, then, to concentrate our efforts for a while upon establishing a clearer notion of those communities which are prior to the polities of state or church. If, for example, we now list several ways in which beliefs, attitudes, and techniques of intellectual and moral growth are communicated among men, we may come to see (1) that a community is not merely a collective, and (2) that the morality of the community may not be directly opposed to the morality of the individual. For each man, it seems, benefits by the insights, loves, aims, hopes, and failures he shares with other men. It is in company with others that men acquire and develop what intellectual and moral abilities they have; even the solitude and intellectual or moral loneliness required for certain stages of personal growth have communal significance. For while the community provides the matrix of moral or intellectual growth, the individual must appropriate the basic values and orientations he learns from the community thoroughly and at his own pace.

Some examples from different types of communities may illustrate the role of community life in moral education. In marriage, husband and wife must learn a mode of life more thoroughly other-centered than they have known before. An ideal of unselfishness or of self-sacrifice is inadequate. For the primary reality of married life is not the personal purity or personal generosity of either party, but the degree to which the two persons can communicate in one life. The woman entering upon marriage with the goal of proving her spirit of self-sacrifice had best heed the poet's advice: "Get thee to a nunnery!" Even the act of intercourse between husband and wife teaches them that they are to be each concerned for the other; it is not a symbol of separate ecstasy but of mutual involvement.

Likewise, it is in the matrix of the family that children acquire their earliest moral experiences, begin to associate pleasures and pains with certain activities, develop tastes and skills, and otherwise acquire what Aristotle calls the indispensable starting-points of ethical judgment.[32] Again, it is in the scientific community that young men and women acquire the information, the series of insights, and the criteria of relevance and evidence that enable them to attain critical discrimination. Further, it is in the political community that those attitudes toward fairness,[33] liberty, law, and due process are nourished which make certain kinds of political techniques either practicable or unrealistic; for the same techniques do not work equally well in different communities. Finally, it is in the religious community that the word of God is heard, a context of interpretation acquired, and a tradition of reflection, prophecy, and reformation nourished or neglected.[34]

In each of these instances, the experience, understanding, reflective judgment and even personal decisions of the individual are nurtured and tutored by the community.[35] Rare is the large, historical community so limited that it is easy for the individual to outgrow it; ordinarily, only a few individuals bring to fruition a genuine strand of originality and thus contribute something new to their historical tradition. Thus, few individuals rise to the levels possible in their tradition; most seem to feed upon the community, like harmless parasites, deriving all their intellectual and moral nourishment from it and contributing to it perhaps not even an authenticity of their own. In many ways, therefore, the community may bear in itself moral resources superior to those realized by individuals within it.

The distinction between the state and the culture, and between the church as polity and the church as community, however, makes it possible for us in our time to heighten the dialectic between the community and its individual members. For these distinctions have become operational in recent times through that political wisdom which led to the conception of the open society and the open church. A closed or a total society is one in which all decisions are, in principle at least, subject to review by one authority. Leaders are separated from followers, officers from soldiers, superiors from subjects, staff from inmates. In such a society, the relationships among individuals are established by the attitudes and aims of the leaders; these leaders may be paternal or tyrannical, wise or restrictive. The total society is not, therefore, *ipso facto* an evil society. Nevertheless, our increasing differentiation of belief systems, professions, specialized sciences, economic opportunities, and political options has now rendered the total society obsolete and regressive as a model for the human community.

For the fact is that today there is not one human community; there are many human communities. It seems apparent that a human being may best reach his full potential if he belongs totally to no one community, but partially to many communities. An open society or an open church is designed precisely to accommodate a rich diversity, many voluntary associations, and freedom of choice.[36] But it would be a conceptual mistake to think that the model of an open society or an open church supposes that men are merely atomic individuals, and that individuals as such are the locus of moral power and fruitfulness. On the contrary, the open society and the open church are forms of polity which favor the multiplication of varied forms of community for various purposes. The community remains the locus of human exchange, conversation, stimulation, and development. The open society and the open church support the principle of diversity precisely to nourish as many different kinds of community as necessary or fruitful for human development. The atomic individual, the alienated man, is the man who has not learned how to live in the open society and the open church; since there is no closed society to take care of him, he withdraws into his own guts.

The authentic life of the human community, the lifeblood of moral and intellectual development, is civic conversation;[37] the criterion of a healthy culture is that men speak to one another, and listen to one another. Without speech and listening, there is no moral and intellectual development.[38] This is why segregation is so great a sin, why living in a ghetto is so stultifying, why denominational schools sometimes have an air of unreality about them, why the Iron Curtain is so politically dangerous, and the trivial "hot line" is yet so powerful a symbol.

Men are rapidly filling up this planet and yet they have created no one human community, but a congeries of partly isolated communities. Speaking and listening are not operational in many situations; thus labor unions resort to strikes, minority groups employ coercive pressures, governments engage in wars. If we are realists, we recognize that we do not have, neither at present nor in immediate prospect, a worldwide human community of discourse.[39] For community is organic. It grows by shared experiences, shared insights, shared criteria of relevance and evidence, and shared lives; it is not achieved by treaties, pacts, ordinances, or laws, though these sometimes spring from early steps in its acquisition and make further steps possible.

5. *Conclusion*

The pressures of world population and technical progress make imperative an ethical vision which all men can share. The argument of this paper is that an ethical ideal which conceives of *Agape* in individualistic terms cannot supply that vision. For the primary reality of ethical life is not the atomic individual but the community of life in which the individual shares. *Agape,* whose source is in God, is precisely the highest and fullest form of community life. *Agape* is both other-centered and realistic. Thus those individuals who learn from their communities the experience and the meaning of the communal love which *Agape* makes divine are in a position to reach out to others, and to do so not with illusions but realistically. They are in a position, not only to criticize themselves, but also to criticize their communities, and thus to extend, however gradually and modestly, the *Agape* which they learned in their communities beyond the limits of their communities. In this way, men reach out toward one another across the gaps of silence that separate them. The conceptual model of the open society and the open church enables them to understand that to open civil conversation with one another they do not have to submerge their historical communities in one closed, total society. On the contrary, the whole point of the model of the open society and the open church is that the human community can be a community of conscience and reasonable discourse and mutual respect. In such a community, diversity prospers. Diversity contributes to the fundamental enterprise: that countless finite men in their variety may mirror back the infinite loveliness of God.

NOTES

[1] Charles Scribner's Sons, 1932; paperback edition with new preface, 1960.

[2] Preface, 1960 edition, p. ix.

[3] In his introduction to *Man's Nature and His Communities,* Scribner's, 1965, Niebuhr cites the remark of a young friend who chided him that he should have called the book *The Not so Moral Man in His Less Moral Communities.*

[4] See "The Ethic of Jesus" in *An Interpretation of Christian Ethics,* Meridian Books, N.Y., 1963, p. 45.

[5] In his introduction to *Essays in Applied Christianity,* D. B. Robertson writes: "It has been said by numerous people, speaking from a number of positions, that Reinhold Niebuhr has given little attention to the question of the church." Meridian Books, N.Y., 1959, p. 11. Prof. Robertson tries to redress this judgment; but Niebuhr's basic conceptual model is, until *Man's Nature and His Communities,* at any rate, the individual. But even in 1956, Niebuhr wrote that he "has increasingly recognized the value of the church as a community of grace;" he spoke of this as "only a growing recognition."

(*Reinhold Niebuhr,* The Library of Living Theology, vol. 2, Charles W. Kegley and Robert W. Bretall, eds., Macmillan, p. 437). Thus Niebuhr's own underlying development appears to have been in the direction of a new conceptual model based upon community.

[6] I am indebted to a stimulating discussion on this theme by Professors Robert N. Bellah and Krister Stendahl at a planning session for *Daedalus* Magazine, held at the home of the American Academy of Arts and Sciences in Brookline, Mass., on October 15–16, 1965. A transcript of the meeting is in preparation. An article by Professor Bellah on "Civic Religion" will appear in a forthcoming issue of *Daedalus.*

[7] Caught in a lifelong darkness of faith, St. Therese of Lisieux in 1895 described in a line of one of her poems her criterion for finding God:

Car je te vois dans les âmes, mes soeurs,
La charitè, voilà ma seule étoile . . .

(*Histoire d'une ame,* Office Central de Lisieux, 51, rue du Carmel, 1946, p. 330). See also I John 4:12–13: "No man has ever seen God; but if we love one another, then we have God dwelling in us, and the love of God has reached its full growth in our lives. This is our proof that we are dwelling in him, and he in us; he has given us a share of his own Spirit."

[8] See Ceslaus Spicq, O.P., *Agape in the New Testament* Herder: St. Louis, 1963.

[9] For a brief statement, see "Eros and Agape" in *A Handbook of Christian Theology,* M. Halverson and A. A. Cohen (eds.), Meridian Books: N.Y., 1958, pp. 96–101; the masterwork is *Agape and Eros.* Westminster Press: Philadelphia, 1953, esp. the "tabulation of contrasts," pp. 208–210.

[10] In interpreting the "transvaluation" of pagan by Christian love, specifically as it was worked out by Aquinas, Nygren falls into a conceptual error made prominent among Thomists by a brilliant writer who died in his youth, Pierre Rousselot. Both Nygren and Rousselot interpret human love as a "higher" version of sensitive desire. But for Aquinas, the model of sensitive desire—acquisitive, self-aggrandizing—is not adequate for describing the love of human beings. The human spirit is capable of realistic judgment, and thus of relating itself to others, not as it would wish them to be, but as they are. Love is willing the real good of the other—it is not *amor,* nor even *benevolentia,* but *dilectio,* and not only *dilectio* but *amicitia.* Moreover, as *caritas* this love is wholly a gift from God and is not in man's power to attain, or to increase; and only God's wisdom, not human reason, is its rule. See *Summa Theologica,* 2.2., q.24.1.ad 4 and 24.10;q.23.6.ad 1; q.27.2 and 27.5, etc. See also P. Rousselot, *L'Intellectualisme de St. Thomas* Beauchesne, France: 2nd edition, 1924, and *Pour L'histoire du problème de L'amour au moyen age* Paris, 1933, and the critique by L. B. Geiger, *Le Problem de L'amour chez S. Thomas d'Aquin* Montreal, 1952. Also, G. Gilleman, *The Primacy of Charity in Moral Theology,* Newman: Westminster, Md., 1961.

[11] Contrast *An Interpretation of Christian Ethics,* p. 218 n., where Nygren is cited with approval, with *The Nature and Destiny of Man,* II, p. 84 n., where Niebuhr writes that Nygren "makes the contrast [between *eros* and *agape*] too absolute." In both cases, Niebuhr uses Mt. 7:11 as the basic text. See Niebuhr's fuller discussions of Nygren in *Christian Realism and Political*

Problems Scribner's, 1953, pp. 162–68, and *Faith and History* Scribner's, 1949, pp. 178–79.

[12] *Christian Ethics and Moral Philosophy,* Scribner's: N.Y., 1955, pp. 42–58, esp. 54.

[13] Library of Living Theology, vol. 2, pp. 104–106.

[14] Ramsey, *ibid.,* writes as though the point of mutual love were to secure the good of the self as well as the good of the other. More exactly, it is to make the aim of the self to become attentive to the good of the other. The concentration is upon the good of the other. Self-sacrifice may be required in the process, as a means or condition, not as a goal. Moreover, *Agape* is a gift of God, a share in God's own life, and thus to say with Scripture "Let *Agape* be among you" (Ramsey, *ibid.,* p. 106) is to say: "Let the mutual love you share among you be transformed by grace into God's own love." In this way, ordinary mutual love is kept under the judgment of a different standard (*Agape*) than that of human intelligent love (*dilectio*), but the discriminate judgments of such ordinary healthy love are not simply abandoned.

[15] Cf. *The Lonely Crowd,* Doubleday Anchor Books: New York, 1953, pp. 19–48.

[16] See the discussion of *"variations in moral and ethical sensitivity* in accordance with stages in the development of human conscience," in Erik H. Erikson, *Insight and Responsibility:* W. W. Norton, New York, 1964, p. 221.

[17] "Yet to grow in the individual, ethics must be generated and regenerated in and by the sequence of generations . . . The chosen unit of study must be the generation, not the individual." *Ibid.,* pp. 228–29.

[18] "The failure of basic trust and mutuality has been recognized in psychiatry as the most far-reaching failure, undercutting all development." *Ibid.,* p. 231.

[19] "I would call mutuality a relationship in which partners depend on each other for the development of their respective strengths." *Ibid.* Erickson's recognition of possible inequalities *to be taken account of* in a healthy relationship is a helpful modification of the Aristotelian notion that a genuine, uncorrupting friendship must be based upon a fundamental equality. But see *Nicomachean Ethics,* VIII, vi, on "The Friendships of Unequals."

[20] Nygren's strategy is to by-pass human judgment in his attempt to glorify God. Like Peter Lombard, against whose theory Aquinas directed the first question of his Disputed Question on Charity, Nygren (cf. George T. Thomas, *op. cit.,* p. 54) tries to identify God himself with *Agape,* so that the human self is displaced. The strategy of Aquinas is to allow the human self and its discriminating judgment full exercise in its attempt to reverence, respect, and respond to the reality of others; but then to say that the gift of *Agape* gives man a created participation in God's own love, which exceeds the measure of even perfect human mutual love, by drawing it into the life of God's wisdom and God's love. Perfect human mutual love (which in actual history is impossible for man without grace to sustain; cf. *De Veritate* q.24, a.12) is not rejected nor demeaned, but placed under the judgment and necessity of a divine measure of love.

[21] On the realism of love, see Eric Fromm, *The Art of Loving,* Harper's:

N.Y., 1956; C. S. Lewis, *The Four Loves,* Harcourt, Brace, 1960; and Jacques Maritain, "Some American Illusions" and "Marriage and Happiness," in *Reflections on America,* Scribner's: N.Y., 1958, pp. 131–45.

[22] For a systematic account of various patterns and levels of such bias, see Bernard Lonergan, *Insight,* Longman's, Green & Co.: London, 1958, pp. 191–206; 217–44.

[23] See Bernard Lonergan "Metaphysics as Horizon," *Gregorianum* 44 (1963), pp. 307–18.

[24] For an analysis of philosophy as dialectic, and a theoretical construct of a fully developed community—"Cosmopolis"—see Bernard Lonergan, *Insight,* pp. 217; 225–41.

[25] Cf. I Jn. 4:12–13.

[26] See T. S. Eliot, "Tradition and the Individual Talent," *The Selected Essays of T. S. Eliot,* Harcourt & Brace: N.Y., 1950.

[27] See Norman Cohn, *The Pursuit of the Millennium,* Harper Torchbooks: N.Y., 1961. Among Roman Catholics, Father Riccardo Lombardi's Better World Movement seems to be a contemporary version of dangerous and romantic millennialism.

[28] Cf. Vatican II, *The Constitution on the Church,* ch. 2.

[29] See, e.g., Yvres Simon, *Nature and Functions of Authority* Marquette University Press: Milwaukee, 1940.

[30] See, e.g., Jacques Maritain, *Man and the State,* University of Chicago Press: Chicago, 1956, ch. 1.

[31] Working paper, for private circulation, for *Daedalus* Planning Session, Brookline, Mass., 1965.

[32] *NE,* I, iii, 5–7; I, vi, 5–7; II, i, 8; etc.

[33] See John Rawls, "The Sense of Justice," *Philosophical Review* 72 (1963), pp. 281–305.

[34] See, e.g., Lehmann, *Ethics in a Christian Context,* Harper's: N.Y., 1965; G. Tavard, *Holy Writ or Holy Church,* Harper's: N.Y., 1959.

[35] For an excellent account of the many ways in which the church is a human community, see James M. Gustafson, *Treasure in Earthen Vessels,* Harper: N.Y., 1961.

[36] See my "Diversity of Structures: Freedom within Structures," *Concilium.* 1 (1965), pp. 103–13, and "The Free Churches and the Roman Church," *Journal of Ecumenical Studies* 2 (1965), pp. 426–47.

[37] Aquinas notes three fundamental inclinations or tendencies in man, of which the third is most specifically human: "that he might live in society." In following this inclination, he says, man learns "not to harm those with whom he dwells in conversation." *S.T.* 1–2.94.2.

[38] On the need of civil discourse, see John Courtney Murray, "Natural Law and Public Consensus," in *Natural Law and Modern Society,* John Cogley (ed.), World Publishing Co.: N.Y., 1963, pp. 48–81; also Walter Lippmann, *The Public Philosophy,* Mentor Books: N.Y., 1956.

[39] See R. Niebuhr, "The Illusion of World Government," *The World Crisis and American Responsibility,* Ernest W. Lefever (ed.), Association Press: N.Y., 1958, pp. 85–104. Contrast with Cardinal Ottaviani's impassioned plea for a "world republic" in the closing debates of the Second Vatican Council.

NATURAL LAW IN THE TEACHINGS OF ST. PAUL

by

Markus Barth

1. *The Many Meanings and Places of the Natural Law and Its Unique Function*

AMONG recent writers it is the Freiburg philosopher of law, Erik Wolf, who in a most comprehensive and penetrating way has compassed the meaning of Natural Law in the history of philosophy, law, theology. He has presented the issue in systematic form. The sum of his extensive historical and systematic studies is presented with admirable brevity and clarity in his booklet *Das Problem der Naturrechtslehre*[1] and, even more concisely, in his amazingly different, though logically consistent articles on *"Naturrecht"* in the second and third editions of the Encyclopedia *Religion in Geschichte und Gegenwart.*[2] Erik Wolf distinguishes ten meanings of nature and nine meanings of law which have played a major role in the history of reflection on Natural Law. The possible combinations of these meanings yield no less than ninety definitions of Natural Law! We present only a simplified selection:

We may call "natural" what is proper to man, in distinction from what is proper to animals or things. We may consider natural what was originally true of man, e.g. during a golden age. The natural may be sought in the causality and determination found in evolution. Others would locate it in the demands of reason and consequently insist that the natural is independent of history and subject only to the freedom and the responsibility of reasoning. The loftiest notion of the nature of a thing identifies nature with a Platonic idea, or with the ideal of something. But who will deny to others the right to consider natural the domain of impulses, instinct, senses, including the urge to survive or the will to power? Again, others hold, not without reason, that it belongs to man's nature to be a social being and to recognize certain value in the fate or the contractual forms of social existence.

By "law" we should certainly not solely understand something specific either written or codified, a given constitution such, for example, as marriage and divorce laws. The English concept of law covers not only the Latin *jus* and *lex* and the German *Recht* and *Gesetz* but, among other things, all forms of oral and written expressions, respective intentions, rules and principles of juridical thought, the whole process leading to legislation, the whole apparatus for administration and enforcement of a given order (from the police force, to courts, to prisons), and all the people involved in one or another of these activities, institutions, or formations.

When reference is made to Natural Law, then law may mean either an objective order believed to be in, above, or under the mass of legal principles, constitutions, laws, statutes, customs, or practices, whether conceived esthetically, to be in evolution or entire disorder. Or law may be identified with the claims of the conscience, i.e. of the individual or of specific groups (as the family, or a minority) over against the organized society or majority. Also law may be regarded as the right which the opinion, consent, or drift of society, or of a given time, or of its heroic spokesman, has over both the individuals and masses. *Zeitgeist, das gesunde Rechtsempfinden des Volkes;* perhaps a

Führer-principle can then be the embodiment of law. What is right may also be identified with an idea of righteousness, or with all that contributes to human happiness, or with those things which are opportune, feasible, and successful under given conditions. Finally we mention the yearning for the good old times: that which is hidden in tradition and changes but underlies them all may be "the" law by which all laws are to be measured.

It is impossible first to select one or two concepts of Nature and Law and then to decree that their combination alone yields viable definitions of Natural Law which can be compared to Paul's teaching. But it makes sense to reduce the great number of natural Law concepts to workable size by asking for the origin, seat, epistemology, and validity ascribed to this Law.

Some seek law in a deity like Dike. For Stoics like Kleanthes, Zeus, nature, reason, moral conduct are ultimately identical. To submit to the Father Zeus, to use one's reason, to live according to nature—this is the law incorporated in the free man. Living according to the harmony of the divine with the natural and the reasonable, he is a law to himself.

Other Natural Law schools, however, represented e.g. by Hugo Grotius, proclaimed that the Natural Law exists and is true, even if there be no God. They found the seat, recognizability and guarantee of Natural Law outside any deity, in the law itself or in man. It was argued (on Platonic and other grounds) that all that is finite, changing and relative can exist is such only because there is an infinite and abiding absolute. Thus the unique idea of law was distinguished from the many existing laws; and the idea was treated as the metaphysical presupposition of the many laws in the world of phenomena. The function of this idea, which was called Natural Law, was not only to explain why the varied and varying phenomena existed and why a quest or yearning for essential right, or a remembrance of it, could not be quenched. Much more, the idea of the right (*to dikaion*) served as an ontological imperative and methodological instrument to criticize, limit, and direct or inspire the existing laws. Recognition of Natural Law has therefore made men free and able to engage responsibly in the establishment of better laws and a better order; but also in the critique and overthrow of systems of tyranny. Men like Grotius, Pufendorf, Thomasius expressed in different ways one great thought: man's humanity is determined by law; but law is not determined by man.

Others traced the seat of Natural Law to man. In one or another form, anthropology rather than religion or metaphysics was declared to be its epistemological tool and the guarantee of its validity. It has been argued that Natural Law cannot be proven mathematically, physically, or logically because it is nothing but the sum of a human experience. This experience, in turn, was ascribed to individual yearning, to the indelible operation of conscience in all great or real men, or to a *consensus Gentilium.*

Whether the law itself or man was made the starting point, to deny Natural Law was equivalent to denying man's humanity and to establish it was to call man to true humanity. The endeavor of the seventeenth and eighteenth century philosophers of law was, in this regard, identical with the intention of the Nuremberg Trials after World War II and the faith of Pope John XXIII proclaimed in *Pacem in Terris.*

In view of the many meanings and possible foundations of Natural Law, it is impossible to leave the discussion of this topic only to theologians or only to philosophers or exclusively to lawyers, logicians, psychologists or moralists. For Natural Law has proven to be a vision so inspiring or a problem so immense that the combined resources of theology and metaphysics, jurisprudence and logic, history and anthropology are indispensable to a morally responsible and ethically applicable treatment of the issue. I cannot judge whether the apostle Paul was aware of these requirements and able to fulfill them. But an interpreter of Paul, who is charged to discuss Paul's relation to the Natural Law, is faced with the assignment of bringing together a man who is hard to understand (2. Pet. 3:16) with an entity that defies a clear definition.

It might be argued that Natural Law need not necessarily be treated as an unsolved religious, metaphysical, ontological, etc., problem. Should it not be possible to start out from the contents of Natural Law (rather than from its definition, foundation, recognizability, validity) and simply compare its contents with the subject matter of Paul's message? If this approach is chosen, a new problem immediately raises its Gargantuan head. For what is the content of Natural Law? With Sophocles many might argue that this law is unwritten (*agraphos*) and therefore, cannot be spelled out. But another stance is also possible. The principle that contracts must be kept (*pacta sunt servanda*); the demand of mutual equity (*suum cuique*); the Golden Rule in its positive or negative formulations; the right of the fittest to survive; the *jus talionis* ("an eye for an eye"); something like the categorical imperative; authority as embodied in father, prince, or state; or the right to live primitively from tradition or in revolutionary manner on the basis of advanced reasoning; or axioms saying (e.g.) that the purpose of marriage and sexual intercourse is to produce children—these and many more have been suggested. Like Augustine, Scholastic divines and the Reformers found the Natural Law expressed in the Decalogue and/or in the commandment of love. Others saw in the *Haustafeln*[3] convenient summaries of generally accepted or acceptable equity. On the whole, the great thinkers of the West have given preference to the foundations laid by the Stoic teachers over the suggestions made by Epicureans or admirers of man's potential for tyranny.

No doubt, specific historical, cultural, ethnic, if not personal conditions, have always contributed heavily to the respective definitions of Natural Law. It is easy and cheap, upon the ground of the apparent changeability and relativity of Natural Law interpretations, to punish the whole concept with contempt or neglect. However, there is no need to throw out the baby with the bath. For though no unambiguous, universally valid answer has as yet been provided, the human yearning and search for Natural Law may have a legitimate place among other necessary or desirable human endeavors. However, it should be admitted that as yet a clear concept of Natural Law is not within sight.

But one thing is clear in the matter of Natural Law: independent of the questions of whether its existence can be proven, whether its perception can be ascribed to reason alone, or whether its contents can be defined is the fact that Natural Law has often exercised a specific function. More precisely, those speaking of Natural Law have attributed to that Law a necessary and vital service. The function of Natural Law is "unequivocally and always one and the same: it serves for a foundation, limitation and direction of positive-historical, human law and it is its critical gauge."[4] Natural Law is an attempt to answer such questions as the following: Is it possible to have a better law established than the laws currently valid? Why is it necessary to rely upon that which is right and to criticize distorted concepts and practices of law? What is the rightness of right and how can it be justified? The answers given in the name of Natural Law have been manifold, if not contradictory. But notwithstanding their shortcomings these answers made a difference. We mention as historical examples the French Revolution, the American Declaration of Independence, the Encyclical *Pacem in Terris,* and we might add (though explicit reference to Natural Law may be missing from some oral and written statements) the stance of conscientious objectors and freedom fighters who engage in civil disobedience precisely because they feel entitled and compelled to do so by a law that is higher than Federal, State and Communal laws.

Though appeals to a higher, even the Natural Law, have

often been made in opposition to the demands of current religion, political powers, society and custom, they need not necessarily or always be revolutionary. Even the rights of the ruling prince, the established religion, or the conservative element in society have frequently been sanctioned, defended or increased by appeals to Natural Law. If some believed that Nature and Law, as if by definition, were opposites to the grace and the Gospel of God, others found it necessary to state precisely that the Natural Law is a gift of the gracious God, recognized by the gift of reason, to be used for the protection of the freedom of religion, including the freedom of preaching the Gospel of Jesus Christ. Not only philosophers of the State and Christian theologians, but also Jews have become defenders of Natural Law. S. S. Schwarzschild[5] shows how Maimonides, Spinoza and other Jews handled the problem of Natural Law in its relation to the Sinaitic Law: The legendary Noahite or Adamite Commandments were given a dignity equivalent to the pagan concept of Natural Law.

The fact that Natural Law has found promoters and defenders among theologians leads directly to the core of our task.

2. The Problem of a Christian Natural Law

The very concept "Christian Natural Law" is a contradiction in terms. If there be Natural Law, it can be neither Roman Catholic nor Protestant, neither Christian nor Jewish, neither religious nor atheistic. For all these attributes refer to specific historic conditions that have been set by necessity or by chance; they are not simply "natural." When posited factors qualify and determine a given jurisprudential reflection the result will certainly be different from the supposedly simple, natural, legal, or generally human essence of Natural Law. Natural Law is meant to be universal and timeless, despite its changing concretizations and applications. A "Christian Natural Law" would necessarily be so qualified by the coming of Christ and faith in him that non-Christian thinkers would have to classify it with positive law!

Still, it is possible to speak of the teaching and the evaluation of Natural Law by Christian thinkers. For again and again two things have been affirmed at the same time: faith in Jesus Christ and belief in Natural Law. A summary report on the development of this combination from the times of the second century Apologetes and of Emperor Constantine through Augustine and the Scholastic variations to the Reformation, the age of Enlightenment, and the 19th and 20th century reflections, is given *int. al.* by Ernst Wolf.[6] While the Apologists endorsed main elements of Stoic teaching, Augustine developed a subtle ontological interrelation of God's eternal law, the natural law, and the human laws. He subdivided the realm of God-given positive laws by distinguishing the law of Christ from the law in every man's heart and the Mosaic Law. Thomas combined the Augustinian heritage with Aristotelian, Roman, Canonistic and Biblical materials and gave the Natural Law a predominantly teleological function: Man is to participate in and to conform to the Eternal Law; the gift of reason enables him to derive from Eternal Law or Eternal Reason whatever is necessary to make Human Law participate in the true nature of Law.[7] Natural Law discerned by the light of natural reason thus stands somewhere between the Eternal Law and Human Law.[8] Just as in Augustine's teaching the special revelation contained in the Bible is said to confirm and to complement Natural Law, so also in Thomas' teaching. Up to the present many Roman Catholic discussions about Natural Law seek to restore or reaffirm what Thomas said or to probe the validity of his criteria. But the special interest of canon lawyers and moral theologians is not shared by those who concentrate their attention more upon the Bible that Aristotle, and more on revelation than nature and tradition.

The position of the Reformers to Natural Law has not yet been clarified in a satisfactory manner. While it would appear that their teaching of *Solus Christus, Sola Gratia, Sola Fide, Sola Scriptura,* should have led them to a radical questioning, if not elimination, of concepts of right, law, and reason which might compete with revelation and justification by grace and faith alone, they retained a considerable amount of Stoic and Medieval thoughts. Erasmus, Melanchthon, and Zwingli are outstanding among those whose thinking was deeply influenced by the humanistic heritage.[9]

One special trait of latter-day Lutheran theologizing on Natural Law must not be by-passed: each in his own way, P. Althaus, W. Elert and F. Gogarten attempt to subsume Natural Law under the tutelage of the triune God. Natural Law is now identified with an *Ur-Offenbarung* and is said to be contained in the *Schöpfungsordnungen.* Thus it comes under the protection of God the Father whose work is redeemed and completed but by no means antiquated or repudiated by the work of Jesus Christ, the Son. Scandinavian scholars, but also Emil Brunner, reflect similar thinking. Outside the continent, the concept of middle axioms promoted by J. H. Oldham and J. Bennett may be considered an attempt to keep Natural Law alive among Protestants.

How relevant is Natural Law in present day discussion? Attention may be drawn to the fact that the same Erik Wolf who in 1930 predicted a "glorious resurrection" of Natural Law thought observed, somewhat sadly, in 1960 that we are now in a new period of "the eternal return of jurisprudential positivism." Personally I have observed that in the United States it is rather difficult to find among lawyers, philosophers or theologians many who attribute importance to this topic. The proverbial pragmatic orientation of the American mind may explain the coolness to Natural Law. But it is certainly no proof of the irrelevance of the theme. Not only have strong revolutionary movements been motivated by intelligent reflections upon Natural Law but also great pleas for peace have been based on it. If nothing else, the last Pope's famous encyclical should certainly recall this potential of the Natural Law concept.

In *Pacem in Terris,* John XXIII does not conceal his devotion to God's special revelation in Jesus Christ and the Scriptures.[10] But what he says in the body of this document on the rights and duties of man, of political authorities and nations among themselves and in relation to the world community is untiringly, even repetitiously based upon "the nature of man" (#6), "the rights of man" (#11), "Natural Law" (#12, 13, 18, 20; cp. 46) or the "natural rights" (#28). Jesus Christ the "prince of peace" is described in moving terms as the reason for the Pope's raising his voice. The raised voice pronounces above all not Jesus Christ but Natural Law; the rights of man and their consequences for politics, armaments, and social life are exalted. Certainly it would have been feasible to place the references to Isaiah 9:5; Eph. 2:14–17; John 14:27 and to the resurrection stories at the beginning of the encyclical and thus to enter the realm of social ethics from a Christological and Biblical foundation (as e.g., the proposed *Confession of 1967* of the United Presbyterian Churches does). As things stand, the main body of the encyclical speaks so well for itself that except for a few orthodox theologians or pious spirituals nobody would find the Pontifical declaration less appealing, stringent, and relevant, if the brief concluding Christological postscript had been omitted.

No reason is explicitly given for the prevailing argumentation on the Natural Law basis. It can be surmised that in this address to both the Roman Catholic community *and* to "all men of good will" Pope John wished to avoid an explicit argumentation from Jesus Christ or the Bible. The Bible is read only by a part of mankind; Jesus Christ is confessed by an even smaller part. The majority of interested persons might have considered a reference to God's special revelation an indication of a particularist trend.

A suspected intention to make converts to Christianity might have caused resentment among non-Christians. Thus references to Christ and the Bible might have had a restrictive and divisive effect and limited the appeal. Natural Law recommended itself as being potentially more unifying. In favor of this law, Thomas Aquinas is explicitly quoted twice. That element in Thomism which reflects Aristotelian and Stoic teaching appeared to establish a common denominator which in cultural matters could meet the interest and consent of the ecumene more successfully than Christ or the Bible. The tremendous success of *Pacem in Terris* not only among Christians of many denominations but among religious and non-religious people all over the world appears to prove, on a pragmatic basis, how right the calculation was and how much can be achieved by reference to Natural Law.

Still, the success alone of a given belief and procedure cannot sufficiently prove the truth and validity of an axiom or argument. Not only humility but also a false condescension; not only care for efficient communication but also an attempt at pontification; not only a defense of timeless truth but also the attempt to negate one's specific situation and limitation may play a part wherever particular revelation is subdued. God's particular revelation in Christ included rather than excluded the promise and gift of peace to those near and those far.[11] Traditionally, the mission of the church to those outside the church in matters both doctrinal and moral has been understood rather in terms of preaching Jesus Christ and in calling to faithful obedience to him than of an appeal to Natural Law. Certainly whenever Christians turned their attention to social ethics they were more readily and frequently inclined to refer to Natural Law than when they dealt with other special fields of doctrine and morals. But if social ethics is to become an integral part of the church's theology and mission, it can hardly claim for itself principles, rights and methods that may flatly contradict or secretly invalidate the norms to which other theological disciples are subjected. How can Christians speak of social ethics without learning from Christ and referring to him? The question must be asked: Is it Biblical to suggest, to enhance or make use of Natural Law? Is Jesus Christ attested to and glorified, both in the church and for all men, or is confession to the triune God made, when Natural Law is employed and exalted?

If there be a *Natural Theology* beside the Theology of Revelation, then these questions will have to be answered in the positive. Indeed, if Natural Theology is a solid basis upon which theology and mission may build, the existence and salutary function of *Natural Law* will not be questioned. The belief in Natural Law is a child of the axiom of Natural Theology. Christian theologians who say *A* will gladly and naturally proceed to saying *B.* Theists and Deists of a non-Christian origin have done the same. Those religious defenders of Natural Law who go so far as to proclaim that it is valid "even if there be no God," may feel wonderfully supported even by pronouncedly atheistic and agnostic philosophers, jurisprudential thinkers and moralists. The search and enthusiasm for Natural Law may then well be the acme and epitome of Natural Theology. But we must ask again: Is this Natural Theology and its brain child, Natural Law, Biblical?

It is amazing that Christian (and Jewish) champions of Natural Law have time and again sought justification in Biblical passages. Thomas, the Trent and the Vatican Councils, F. Gogarten and E. Brunner, John XXIII—to mention only a few instances—are fully convinced that the special revelation vindicates the general, natural, or creational revelation. We call this fact amazing because if there really were a valid Natural Theology and Natural Law, and if its defenders by use of reason or conscience alone were fully convinced of their stance and method they need not ask and would not seek Biblical support or confirmation. We said already that the Bible and its testimony to

Jesus Christ fall under the category of the "positive." Therefore, they cannot possibly validate, in any substantial sense, what is supposedly true apart from the revelation of God in Jesus Christ. The Bible does not speak of things that are or may be true "even if there be no God." And it can certainly not prove their validity.

But reference to the Bible *has* been made in order to support Natural Theology and Natural Law. It is specifically Paul who has been called to the witness stand. If Paul's testimony endorses them, then both have to be called Biblical doctrines. In that case, both have a legitimate place in the church's theological, missionary, and ethical thought and work.

3. The Epistle to the Romans and Natural Law

Among the Pauline texts the following utterances are quoted as evidence of the apostle's positive attitude to Natural Theology and Law: the Areopagus Speech (Acts 17:22–31); the passage dealing with God's wrath and man's inexcusability (Rom. 1:18–32); the text describing Gentiles who fulfill the law because it is written in their hearts (Rom. 2:14–16); and finally the exhortation to be subject to the powers that be (Rom. 13:1–7). Since the first two texts are alleged "proof texts" for Natural Theology rather than specifically for Natural Law we limit ourselves to some exegetical remarks on Rom. 2 and 13. In these two chapters Paul comes nearest to the result anticipated by the supporters of Natural Law.

Rom. 2:14–16: "*When Gentiles who have not the law do by nature what the law requires, they are a law to themselves, even though they do not have the law. (15) They show that what the law requires is written on their hearts, while their conscience also bears witness and their conflicting thoughts accuse or perhaps excuse them (16) on that day when, according to my Gospel, God judges the secrets of men by Jesus Christ.*" Among the innumerable scholarly attempts to uncover the meaning of this passage we mention specifically F. Flückiger's essay "Die Werke des Gesetzes bei den Heiden"[12] and his discussion of Rom. 2 in *Geschichte des Naturrechtes.*[13]

The wider context of the quoted words treats of the revelation of God's wrath which reveals that Gentiles and Jews are equally exposed to God's righteous condemnation.[14] The more immediate context (2:16–29) shows that precisely the man who might seek to exempt himself from God's verdict by condemning his fellowman, cannot dodge the judgment. He can escape least of all when he seeks security in the status of a law-possessing, circumcised Jew. Gentiles who fulfill the law will put the self-styled judges to shame; only "doers of the law will be justified," even when they are Gentiles. Paul's task is to announce that precisely in this way God will hold judgment through Jesus Christ (2:13–16); obedient Gentiles will make the disobedient Jews blush!

In describing the Gentiles' justification Paul uses several terms that were current coinage in Stoic diction of the Hellenistic and early *post*-Christian period. The contrast of "having a law" to "doing the (requirement of the) law" may reflect the distinction between positive and natural (*thesei-physei*) law. The reference to nature (*physis*) recalls either the "law of nature" and the slogan "live according to nature" which were popular among Stoics. The phrase "they are a law to themselves" may take up the dogma that the wise man in using his reason is a king, who is subject to no law because he is a law to himself. Also the mentioning of the "conscience" may be due to Stoic influence—though C. A. Pierce[15] has convincingly shown that other non-Stoical influences such as folk-wisdom and second-hand philosophical jargon may have played a much stronger role than is commonly assumed. At any rate the reader of Rom. 2:14–15 cannot deny that there exist parallels to Paul's diction and thought. The conclusion derived from the parallel elements was most frequently that Paul, just as the Stoics, affirms the Natural Law.

However, similarities in diction do not always prove identity of intention. Even historical posterity and resemblance are not sufficient proof of causal dependence and identical conviction. Indeed, there are elements in the text which call for more intensive study and thought than accumulation and citation of "parallels."

a) Paul says twice in vs. 14 that the Gentiles of whom he speaks "have not the law." The context[16] makes it abundantly clear that Paul has in mind the law of Moses. According to Paul Gentiles are "lawless"[17] because they don't have this, the Sinaitic law. God's law is a privilege granted to Israel alone (Rom. 3:2; 9:4). But do the Gentiles have another law? Paul never affirms such a thing. The non-gods whom they served according to Gal. 4:8 are in no wise identified with the Mosaic Law that served as Israel's pedagogue and kept them enslaved (Gal. 3:19–4:5). Least of all does Romans 2:14 inform us that the Gentiles "have another law," e.g. the Natural Law. For "they have *not*" what is called law.

Of course, Paul knows that Gentiles have their constitutions and codes, statutes and regulations, customs and mores; in Old Testament diction such rules were called *hukim,* as distinct from the *Tora* given to Israel. *Hukim* and *mishpatim* were also incorporated in the *Tora.* In Rom. 7:1 Paul refers to the Roman's knowledge of "law"; he may mean in that passage both the Biblical and the Roman order of marriage and divorce. But when the apostle speaks explicitly of "another law" beside the holy law of God or beside the law of faith, of the Spirit of righteousness or of Christ[18] he means most distinctly *not* Natural Law or the Noahite Commandments. The life according to that "other law" is according to Paul most devastating. It makes war against God and his holy law and it is directly opposed to justification by God in Christ. We conclude that Rom. 2:14 does *not* affirm that Gentiles have a law distinct from Moses' law or that this law is Natural Law or that because of their submission to Natural Law they will be justified.

b) The term "by nature" (*physei*) qualifies, in Paul's statement, the fulfillment of the law and not the law itself. Paul does not speak of a law *of* nature (*nomos physeos*) like the Stoics did. The meaning of the noun "nature" is as ambiguous in Greek as in English. Already Aristotle distinguished first four, then seven different meanings.[19] Paul himself uses the term in different senses. It is possible that *physei* ("by nature") in Rom. 2:14 means either "in reality" as in Gal. 4:8; or that it means[20] "by instinct, voluntarily, freely," if not (as in Eph. 2:3) "completely, thoroughly." Augustine, in turn, suggested again a different understanding: on the basis of II Pet. 1:4 he assumed that Paul referred to the "divine nature" of which Gentiles had become partakers by their rebirth and baptism.[21] While the meaning of *physis* in II Peter is not necessarily decisive for the interpretation of a Pauline passage such as Rom. 2:14, the tendency of Augustine's interpretation is noteworthy. Gentile Christians rather than unregenerate Gentiles are apostrophized in this passage, according to him.

c) It appears that Paul was conscious of the ambiguity of the words "do by nature the requirements of law." In order to prevent as much as possible a misunderstanding of his first sentence, he repeats much of vs. 14 in vs. 15. If we translate literally, the term "work of law" replaces the "things of the law"; the idiom "written on the hearts" is substituted for "by nature"; the "showing the work" is analogous to "doing the things." There is no Hebrew equivalent to the Greek term "nature"; all the more is the "writing on their hearts" a specifically Hebrew idiomatic expression. The idiom Paul chose for explaining the "doing by nature" appears to have been coined by Paul's favorite among the Old Testament Prophets, Jeremiah. "I will put my law within them and I will write it upon their hearts; I will be their God, and they shall be my people."[22] According to the prophetic context, the distinct features of that people of God are that God has made a new covenant with them; they no longer need to instruct one another in the knowledge of God, for their sins are forgiven. This people is the eschatological people of God. If Jeremiah equated the New Covenant with the recreation of Israel and Judah only, it was Paul's assignment to announce that by Christ's death and resurrection the New Covenant embraced Jews *and* Gentiles. It is clear that in Rom. 2:28–29 Paul alludes to that "circumcision of the heart" which according to Deut. 10:16; 30:6; Jer. 4:4; 9:26; and Ezek. 44:7, 9 was to be the mark of God's true people. Most likely, in Rom. 2:15 he makes a similar allusion to a prophetic idiom and prediction. In this case the Gentiles mentioned in Rom. 2:14–15 are Gentiles joined to Israel by Jesus Christ in the New Covenant. Paul would then say: The Gentiles who believe in Jesus Christ and fulfill the law by love[23] will put the fleshly Israel to shame in God's judgment.

d) While Rabbinical teaching frequently expressed the thought that in the Last Judgment Israel would sit in judgment over the Gentiles, there exist also rare statements indicating that Gentiles who did *de facto* the things of the law would inherit eternal life. "There are righteous ones among the nations who have a share in the world to come."[24] The book of Jonah narrates that God uses penitent Gentiles as examples to make his Jewish servant blush. And according to Matt. 12:41–42 and Luke 11:31–32 Jesus himself reversed conceited Jewish expectations by announcing that the Queen of Sheba and the men of Nineveh would stand up against the wicked generation (of Jews) and condemn them in God's judgment. This was a strong statement and it is little wonder that it did not endear Jesus to the obstinate among his audience. We consider it probable that Paul in chapter two of his epistle to the Romans refers to Gentiles for the very same reason and with the same intention as did Jesus according to Matthew and Luke. This interpretation would, of course, support Augustine's understanding of Rom. 2:14–15.

e) The witness of the "conscience" mentioned in Rom. 2:15 is probably not a testimony found in every man's heart. Whenever in other passages[25] Paul refers to the conscience, he appeals to something that is operative in Christians. "There is a conscience only in connection with the word of God, a terrified conscience only under the world of wrath, a comforted conscience only under the Gospel."[26] Conscience in the New Testament is, as I Pet. 2:19 puts it, "consciousness of God" as he is revealed in Jesus Christ and his work. Unless we wish to fill Paul's reference to the "conflicting thoughts" with random psychological observations or guesses, we have to interpret that conflict under the auspices of Rom. 7:15–8:1. In this passage Paul describes the believer in Christ as a battlefield on which a merciless war is going on between the misery of his failure to fulfill God's will and his knowledge of acquittal by Christ. The Gentiles apostrophized in Rom. 2:14–15 obviously do not possess "peace of the soul" on the ground of security or evangelical preparation under a Natural Law. But they live at the same time under the accusation of their own heart and the defense of God's verdict.[27] When Paul in Rom. 9:30 states: "Gentiles who did not pursue righteousness have attained it, that is, righteousness by faith," he means definitely Gentile-Christians. Equally in Rom. 2:14, the term "Gentiles" means most likely Gentile-Christians.

f) The final verse of the passage treats of God's judgment, the hidden things of men to be revealed, the Gospel preached by Paul, and Jesus Christ. All that Paul said previously about the obedience of the Gentiles is hung upon one peg: the judgment of God which is placed in Jesus Christ's hand and proclaimed by Paul. If the place and the means of the justification of Gentiles by Christ is the presupposition then they obviously do not possess a righteousness of their own: e.g. a natural sense of equity or an innate power and will to obey which would exempt them from a surprising revelation before the bar of Christ. Scholars like J. Moffatt and R. Bultmann have been aware of the fact that Rom. 2:16 withdraws and destroys all statements supposedly made in favor of Natural Law in the ver. 14–15. Moffatt solved the problem by a little operation which seemed to promise the salvation of Natural Law. In his translation of Romans, he transfers the verse Rom. 2:16 behind 2:13 where indeed it makes good sense. "Doers of the law will be justified on the day when God will judge. . . ." Bultmann[28] reckons 2:16 among the glosses that were added by a later hand to Paul's letters. Thus the verse is *de facto* eliminated. But since there is not one manuscript by which this transfer is vouchsafed and since the transposition or elimination are obviously arbitrary measures of tendential criticism, we had better abstain from these operations. The place in which Rom. 2:16 stands in all Greek texts, reveals that the gracious judgment of Jesus Christ rather than Natural Law saves the Gentiles from condemnation and makes specific Gentiles, even Gentile Christians, witnesses against the claims of disobedient Jews.

Rom. 2:14–16 is *in toto* a reference to the gracious judgment of God as it is proclaimed by Paul throughout Romans. With Jesus in his allusion to the converted Ninevites, Paul points out that the justification and faith of Gentiles shall move Israel to repentance. In summation: This passage neither discusses, nor endorses, nor promotes Natural Law.

We turn now to a second text: Rom. 13:1–7. "*Let each person be subject to the governing authorities. For there is no authority except from God, and those that exist have been instituted by God.* (2) *Therefore, he who resists the authorities resists what God has appointed, and those who resist will incur judgment.* (3) *For rulers are not a terror to good conduct, but to bad. Would you have no fear of him who is in authority? Then do what is good and you will secure his approval,* (4) *for he is God's servant for your good. But if you do wrong, be afraid, for he does not bear the sword in vain; he is the servant of God to execute his wrath on the wrongdoer.* (5) *Therefore, one must be subject, not to avoid God's wrath but also for the sake of conscience.* (6) *For the same reason you also pay taxes, for the authorities are ministers of God, attending to this very thing.* (7) *Pay all of them their dues, taxes . . . revenue . . . respect . . . honor to whom honor is due."*

Important surveys on the past and present interpretations of this passage have been written by K. H. Schelkle,[29] A. Strobel,[30] E. Käsemann,[31] and G. Bauer[32] in *Antwort.*[33] While Origen was inclined to see in this text an ethic at a pre-Christian level that could not be binding upon a pneumatic Christian, Chrysostom discovered in it a visionary anticipation of the Christians' relationship to the emperor Constantine. John Knox, elaborating upon a lead given by the last chapter of Calvin's *Institutes,* saw no objection in Rom. 13 to overthrowing a tyrannical regime. Luther understood the civil government as an agency of God's left hand, which required unconditional submission. It was left to German and Scandinavian theologians[34] to repudiate the intervening enlightenment theories of Hobbes, Rousseau and others by the above mentioned theorem of an *Ur-Offenbarung* or *Schöpfungsordnung* which is supposedly embodied in the State and sanctioned by Romans 13. Also the Pauline *Haustafeln* with their prescriptions for the husband-wife, parent-children, master-slave relationship were drawn into the discussion as a support of the revelation of God through the natural orders. Quite apart from God's special revelation, so it was argued, the very existence of authority and superiority in human society demonstrates the presence and validity of a natural order and imperative valid for all men.

A break-away from a Natural Law interpretation of Rom. 13 became first visible when in the wake of J. Weiss' and A. Schweitzer's work the weight of eschatology in Paul's teaching was seriously pondered. Obviously the apostle expected that

Jesus Christ would very soon return in glory to establish fully God's kingdom on earth.[35] Why then did this revolutionary and courageous man develop a social ethics so astonishingly conservative as Rom. 13 appears to reveal? Two answers have been offered for choice: Either Paul was so totally dominated by the conviction of an immediate return of the Lord that he felt it superfluous or detrimental for Christians to become involved in such earthly matters as marriage, revolution, improvement of existing political or social conditions. Or at the time of writing Romans, Paul had despaired of his fervent hope and therefore recommended to the Christians of this later time to make their peace with the present evil age and to strive for the respectability granted to law-abiding citizens. In either case an evaluation of the relative situation of the Christians in the course of *Heilsgeschichte,* rather than the endorsement of a positivistic Natural Law theory, appeared as the key to understanding Paul. Marxist historiography can make use of these interpretations of Rom. 13 for anti-Christian polemics. But also thinkers influenced by the Christian Social Gospel movement made use of it—usually for combatting the relevance of both Paul's eschatology *and* his alleged conservatism.

A still more recent interpretation employed the argument of the eschatological school and came out with an even more revolutionary exegesis. The final turn in the exposition of Rom. 13 was made possible *int. al.* by M. Dibelius[36]; it was spearheaded by G. Dehn[37]; it was then taken up by K. Barth, W. Schweitzer, W. Künneth, and especially by O. Cullmann.[38] Ernst Wolf[39] has summed up the evidence of this new interpretation and has shown what consequences it entails.[40]

The new interpretation bids farewell to the Patristic, Scholastic and partly Reformation hypothesis according to which Paul presupposes a direct ontological connection between the State and God. Wherever this connection was upheld, Paul's exhortation did not look too different from what any law abiding

Jewish, Greek or Roman citizen, with or without an underlying Stoic or Roman Natural Law theory, would maintain. But the more recent interpreters of Paul understood him to argue upon a strictly *heilsgeschichtliche* basis. The authorities of which he speaks were still accepted to be the Roman officials and institutions. But a new dimension was added: these powers and structures were identified with the principalities and powers, the angels and/or demons to which Paul often refers. Not every contemporary of Paul equated the highest political authorities with divine or Satanic powers. At his time deification and worship of emperors had not yet reached Rome. But some Jews of Paul's time spoke e.g. of an Angel of Persia, and of supernatural beings or heavenly messengers who, in obedience to God or in defiance of his will (cp. Gen. 6:1–2), took care of every position filled with authority including, e.g. the supervision of wells. An ancient divine kingship pattern of Canaan, which considered the kings to be representatives of deities, or deities incarnate, also Persian angelology or demonology may have contributed to this belief. Paul does not simply deny this belief concerning the existence of "heavenly powers" that are partly under Satanic control. But he affirms that all these principalities and powers, lordships and rules, names and persons, whether they are good or evil, had been or were about to be subjugated at the feet of Jesus Christ.[41] The "rulers of this world" ignored Christ, but they could not do away with him by crucifying him (I Cor. 2:8). Christ's death, resurrection and enthronement on high are mentioned by Paul as the cause and means of their submission. Christians are equipped with the power of the Spirit and the whole armor of God to resist vicious attacks from their side (Eph. 6:10 ff). From these texts the conclusion may be drawn that only because of Jesus Christ's victory over the invisible and visible "authorities" were Christians expected to pay taxes and grant honor to whom revenue and reverence are due. It is obvious that if this interpretation can be upheld through a careful study of Rom. 13:1–7, Paul's statements on the Christians' relationship to the political authorities can no longer be used as a buttress of Natural Law.

Three observations should indeed urge us to prefer the newer to many older interpretations.[42]

1. In Rom. 13 Paul uses the singular and plural forms of the Greek noun *exousia* for describing political authority. While the singular of *exousia* means in Pauline diction and in common New Testament and secular usage "freedom, right, capability, realm, authority" and has usually nothing to do with angels or demons—the plural form *exousiai,* often together with other similar nouns, means in Paul's epistles invisible, heavenly, angelic or satanic powers that make themselves felt on earth. Paul does not refer to these powers for their own sake, as if they formed an ingredient of his world-view, quite independently of his faith in God and witness to Christ. But when outside Rom. 13 especially in Rom. 8; Colossians and Ephesians, he mentions them, he does so in order to assert that they are all submitted or will be subjected to Jesus Christ's feet.[43] Equally the Gospels speak of "demons" only when they are about to be exorcized by Jesus Christ. While Jewish practitioners of the kind of the seven sons of Skeuas mentioned in Acts 19:13 ff. probably announced their knowledge of demonology in order to interest people in their own tricks of expelling demons, Paul refers in his epistles to the principalities and powers only in the context of their subordination to Jesus Christ.

In Rom. 13:1 the apostle uses the plural *exousiai* which in all his other epistles has angelologic or demonologic connotations. In verses 1 and 2 he refers to the submission of every principality to God. In literal translation: "they are put in order by [or under?] God." Like Pilate's authority over Jesus Christ (John 19:10–11), so theirs over the Christians is the result of a specific gift or act of God. In the context (ver. 4 and 6) Paul shows (as he also does in Rom. 8) that these principalities are not necessarily Satanic and evil. By calling the political rulers servants or liturgical ministers of God, he designates them colleagues of his. He conceives of his own ministry as a liturgical service (Rom. 15:16 etc.). The same Jesus Christ who brought him into that service, has, according to Col. 1–2, Eph. 1, and I Cor. 15, also proven victorious over superhuman powers. Whatever potential or actual, religious or mythical honor and rank were attributed to them, they are yet "under God" or "from God" (Rom. 13:1). Not naked fear,[44] but an attitude befitting fellow servants of God is recommended to the Romans. Paul proceeds in his choice of vocabulary in consecutive steps from principalities to power, from rulers to servant, from ministers to the tax-collector and any person deserving of honor. Each time he shows that the dignity of magistrates is dependent upon God who has ordained them, who wills the good and fights the evil, who is known to the conscience and is honored when his servants are honored.

In starting out from the supposedly mythological or superstition-laden term "principalities" and ending with the sober duties of paying honestly the taxes due and greeting respectfully the bearers of office, Paul gives an example of demythologization. He demythologizes the political sphere. Nero and Caligula, the powerful Senate and the last tax collector are neither gods, nor fate, nor the devil incorporated. They are just powers overcome by Christ's victory, men placed in God's service and used for a good purpose. Many, if not all of them, may not be believers; but they, like all inhabitants of the Roman Empire and its capital, live yet from God's grace. Jesus Christ is Lord over all (Phil. 2:10–11)!

2. Rom. 13:1–7, as is the case with all *paracleses* contained in Rom. 12–15, stands under the heading of Rom. 12:1–2. "For God's mercies' sake" (as they are described in Rom. 1–11) Paul exhorts the Christians in Rome fearlessly to discern the will of God, to recognize and to do what is good. It is most surprising,

but also most important that Paul does not presume that he alone, or maybe other Christians with him, can give sufficient guidance and help for conduct obedient to God. Rather God also has servants outside the church; they also are to be listened to and obeyed. The husbands, parents, and masters to whom, according to the *Haustafeln,* the Christian women, children, and slaves render honor and service may (as is shown by I Cor. 7:12–16) often have been as unconverted as were the Roman officials. But "in the Lord" the subjection and obedience of those freed by Christ is the right thing. Christ recognized the authority given by God to Pilate (John 19:11). Christians walk in his footsteps when not only in domestic matters the authority of husband or master is recognized, but when they acknowledge God's sovereignty also in political matters (I Pet. 2:13–25). Since the admonitions contained in Paul's (and I Peter's) *Haustafeln* are all based upon references to the Lord Jesus Christ and since in Rom. 12:1 the mercies of God are explicitly mentioned, it is most arbitrary to consider Rom. 13 a piece of political ethics which stands independently beside or over the special ethics valid for Christians.

3. Beside Christ's victory and God's mercies there stands a third argument: Paul appeals to the conscience of the Romans and asks for obedience freely rendered. It is unlikely that the author of Rom. 13 had forgotten what he wrote in Rom. 8:2, 21 and in Gal. 5:1, 13. In those passages the freedom of the men liberated by Jesus Christ's death and resurrection, rather than fear of wrath or calculation of merit, is the ground of obedience. Freedom according to Paul is not a possession or quality man has by nature. But it is the fruit of redemption by Christ as Israel's freedom was the purpose and result of the Exodus. When in Rom. 13:5 Paul asks for obedience to the state "not only because of the wrath [meeting the evildoer] but also because of the conscience" he appeals to a specific awareness of the Christians which is distinct from other reasons for obedience. The wrath of

Leviathan or the stringency of a Social Contract might be respected without faith in God. The obedience "from the heart . . . with good will" which Paul expects of servants (Eph. 6:6–7) and which has its analogy in conscientious submission to the political servants of God (1. Pet. 2:13 ff), cannot be argued, legislated or voted. Also this obedience cannot be based upon a legal basis from which the living God is excluded. In the Bible only the covenant of God with man provides a trustworthy foundation for a fitting conduct of life. It is probable that in Rom. 13:5, just as in Rom. 2:15, the conscience created, nourished, and judged by the word of God is meant. Not a natural revelation or law perceived and skillfully handled by everybody's reason, but special acts of redemption and revelation which create a freedom that means responsibility, and a responsibility that is enthusiastically borne are then the objective and subjective presupposition of the exhortation given in Rom. 13:1–7.

In short, as free men, rather than because of their captivity under a law, Christians will pay taxes and fees and render honor. It appears that precisely the hidden emphasis on freedom of the conscience and on responsibility for the political government made it possible that Rom. 13 was not only understood as a conservative muzzle, damper, or quencher of more liberal thought but led from one emancipation to another and finally toward the development of democracy and the welfare state. Rom. 13 declares every citizen and every subject responsible for the control of the evil and the strengthening of the good. The use of Rom. 13 from Chrysostom's to Luther's and Hitler's time to glorify absolute State power is therefore suspect of being a frightful distortion.

Many conclusions may be drawn from the three arguments just listed. One is that Paul does not argue on the basis of Natural Law. Christ's victory over all principalities; God's mercy shown to believers and non-believers; the service rendered to

God by ministers in and outside the Church; and the freedom of the Christians interpreted as their responsibility for the common good—such things are proclaimed in Rom. 13:1–7. Each of these elements is dependent on God's history with man, even the so-called *Heilsgeschichte.* But an appeal to nature, law, or Natural Law is not found in this passage.

Thus the two key-witnesses in Paul's letters, Rom. 2 and Rom. 13 fail to indicate that Paul knew of Natural Law, borrowed from it, relied upon it, or formally endorsed it. Only if other strong and reliable witnesses could be quoted in favor of Natural Law, might the issue be opened anew.

Indeed, other testimonies might be dug up from Paul's epistles. Passages like Phil. 4:8 ("Whatever is true, whatever is honorable . . . just . . . pure . . . lovely . . . gracious . . . worthy of praise, think about these things") and Col. 4:1 ("give what is right and fair") show that Paul was not a narrow minded bigot setting his own judgment and insights above all current standards. He acknowledged that outside Israel, the church and the apostolic preaching good and honorable things might be found and that they are worth pondering. In Rom. 1:26 and I Cor. 11:13–14 he referred to things which are "natural" or "taught by nature." But it is impossible to assume that these occasional positive hints regarding decency are equivalent to the affirmation of Natural Law. Paul certainly does not say that these natural, general, and extra-ecclesiastical elements are solely and precisely the "foundation, limit, and directive" of the specific ethical exhortations valid for Christians. If they fail to be such a foundation, limit and directive, then they do not fulfill the function of the Natural Law as it was described earlier in Part I. We cannot consider such passages as those just cited as endorsements of Natural Law.

Still, the prevailing negative result of the preceding paragraphs cries out for implementation by positive statements. We ask now: If not Natural Law, what else, if anything, is the basis, sets the confines, and furnishes the inspiring power which gives Paul the right and the freedom at the same time (a) to affirm the holiness and righteousness of the Law given through Moses, (b) to criticize the universal validity and applicability of inherited positive (Mosaic or Rabbinical) laws, and (c) to proclaim the "law" of God, of Christ, of the Spirit, of faith, of righteousness to all Jews and Gentiles? It appears that Paul could by-pass any reference to Natural Law and its function on only one condition: if he knew of an alternative and if he was convinced that it was so much better than Natural Law that all supposed or actual glory of the latter would fade away and vanish in its burning light.

4. Paul's Alternative to Natural Law

There is no passage in Paul's letters in which the apostle affirms that nature in general or human nature in particular is bad. But he speaks in such a manner of the fall of the first man and of the grip of sin and death on all men that many of his interpreters understood him to teach total depravity of human nature, or of nature itself. In whatever way his teaching is summed up or reproduced it is certain that he announces: Not by law or the rule of law, but by grace the damage ushered in by Adam is repaired and overcome.

Also there is no text in Paul's writings in which this servant of Christ asserts that law, or the law of Moses specifically, is a bad thing. But he elaborates in such fashion the limits of the law given to Israel and the freedom of Christians from the strictures of that law that many misunderstood him to be an antinomian. It is certain that in Paul's preaching the deficiency of the law as a means of salvation is not proven by references to the quality, right or power of nature but by the proclamation of Christ through the Gospel.

Therefore it is neither law nor nature, and certainly not the combination of both in "Natural Law" which are the Archimedean point upon which Paul sets his lever. Paul's praise of the law given by God; the criterion by which he measures and judges its purpose, validity and application; and the compelling force and directive which causes him to give specific commandments, exhortations and suggestions are all interdependently grounded in one and the same name and event: Jesus Christ is the righteousness of God incorporated on earth. In him God deals with all peoples and creatures on earth. He establishes their right before God and one another. He is also the revelation of what is right. The judgment of God, as announced by Moses and the Prophets, as carried out on Calvary and Easter, as proclaimed by the apostolic witness, as embraced in faith by Jews and Gentiles, as to be manifested on a world-wide scale on the Last Day—this judgment which Paul usually calls "justification" takes in Paul's thought the place which in jurisprudence, philosophy, natural theology or ontology has often been attributed to Natural Law. Therefore, Paul does not need to refer to Natural Law, he has no use for that Law in any of its aspects.

But others had use for it. Who has a right to condemn or even wonder at people who because they lack knowledge of Jesus Christ and justification by grace should take refuge in a great and workable idea? The noble and lofty, the searching and concerned among them had necessarily to seek for something above, in and under the perennial or ever-changing, the necessary or arbitrary positive laws. Not only is it true that "there ought to be a law" to judge all laws; but the actual labor invested and the success harvested in finding that law and submitting to its dictates were and are most respectable. Honor to whom honor is due!

And yet, we have also to call a spade a spade. In our enlightened and tolerant era it may appear rude and uncouth to speak of idolatry. It is certainly Paul's conviction that precisely those who called themselves "wise" exchanged the glory of the immortal God for images and became fools.[45] Natural Law, as promoted among Christians, is either the radiance of the glorious righteousness of God himself or it is an image of that glory, fabricated in man's mind and serving as an idol. Paul utters a distinct opinion concerning name and place of the true image of God. He affirms that Jesus Christ alone is the glory, the image, the wisdom of God by which God is known and worshipped (I Cor. 1:24, 30; 11:7). Is it, therefore, wise to locate the glory of God somewhere beside or outside Jesus Christ, e.g. in creation and its order, or in the conscience or reason of every man? God's work *is* wonderful, and man specifically a most admirable creature. But should he be admired at the expense of Jesus Christ? Many have upheld and defended a God-likeness of man in competition with the way followed by the Son of God, from glory to death and to highest honor. But it is questionable whether the revealed glory and image of God were exalted by this defense of a natural God-likeness of man. Paul does not distinguish a Fatherly righteousness or a righteousness imparted to his creatures from the righteousness manifested in Christ.

Also, a Spirit- or Wisdom-Theology has been developed. It seeks to attribute to the Spirit and Wisdom functions that the New Testament ascribes to Jesus Christ. But Paul's Christology does not permit a splitting of the deity into three separate agencies or gods. What the Old Testament and Apocryphal Writings say on the Spirit or the Wisdom, is by Paul[46] understood as statements about Christ.[47] Finally, Paul's Christology was considered a supplement to his anthropology. But anthropology is for Paul not a theological discipline beside Christology; it is rather one of its ingredients and consequences.[48]

We may call Paul narrow or fanatic but we have to admit that he neither wanted nor pretended to know anything nor to have any wisdom at all "except Jesus Christ" (I Cor. 2:2). This may be the reason why we find no passage in Paul in which issues such as the righteousness of God, justice among men, or the validity of law are discussed upon the basis of Natural Law. Paul considered and treated the righteousness revealed in justification as a sufficient criterion for the treatment of all questions concerning Law. "You are not under law, but under grace . . . You are slaves of obedience to righteousness . . . Yield your members to righteousness . . . I appeal to you by the mercies of God."[49]

It may be important to emphasize that neither a specific doctrine of sin nor a special concept of law but awareness of redemption and revelation by Christ are the causes of Paul's freedom to abstain from Natural Law arguments. If it were different, then at least a negative function of Natural Law might be saved: to reveal and validate man's quest to justify himself, or to vindicate his laws out of his own resources. Augustine's doctrine of grace appears to be largely dependent upon his (originally Manichean) doctrine of evil. A rigid dualism might require some tempering by a negative Natural Law theory which supposedly upholds the monarchy of the Good. But Paul is not Augustine. Some more specific observations are necessary to undergird these propositions:

1. Together with the books of Exodus and Deuteronomy, Paul assumes and teaches that the law exists only upon the basis of God's love, election and covenant. He makes much of the fact that the law was given after and not before God's promise was made and his covenant was established.[50] The dependence of the gift, function and fulfillment of the law upon the election and covenant of grace has been beautifully pointed out in a long essay by M. Noth[51] and in a penetrating study by G. Mendenhall.[52] Paul considers law not as a presupposition, opportunity or possibility upon which righteousness, peace, life and blessing may eventually sprout and blossom. It is for him a consequence or confirmation of life previously promised, righteousness previously recognized, a covenant and inheritance previously established. Thus Paul admits that the positive laws given by God in the course of history have a foundation, limit and orientation. Yet the ground of law is not a ubiquitous, timeless, general law

residing in the stars, in the realm of ideas, or in man's conscience, reason or experience but God's eternal election as it is carried out and revealed in the covenant between God and man. Therefore, election (or covenant) is a Pauline alternative to Natural Law.

2. The law which Paul calls holy and righteous and which is to be upheld and fulfilled by love wherever Jesus Christ is preached and believed[53] is the same law which is also described as working wrath, bringing curse, being inept regarding justification and not necessary for the salvation of Gentiles.[54]

(a) Paul might certainly be claimed as a supporter of the distinctive existence and functions of both Natural Law and Positive Law, if his concept of the "holy" law could be equated with the Natural Law or a timeless "will of God" and if his reference to "works of law" had a specific connection with Positive Law; i.e. the Sinai Law, or the circumcision commandment. But a careful study of Paul's vocabulary, historical allusions, and theological thought reveals that whether he speaks of the holy law or the works of law he treats of the law given to Israel on specific occasions or of certain selections made from its many commandments.

(b) Paul does not teach that the Sinaitic law has a potential or necessary role to play in the conscience of each individual in such a manner that nobody could be saved without submission to it. But he affirms in extended discourses[55] that the law's function is limited to Israel. Even within Israel's history it has only a restricted range; it rules from Sinai to the Messiah's coming (Gal. 3:17–25). All Jews, including Jewish Christian missionaries like Peter and Paul, had to go through the school, the prison, the humiliation formed by the law. The Jews were subject to the curse threatened by it. But Paul fights passionately the notion that Gentiles ought to be exposed or submitted to the same law and the same curse. Paul might be claimed for the support of Natural Law—if he had proclaimed that the Sinaitic Law, or at least the Decalogue, was imposed by God upon every human being and if he had considered the Sermon on the Mount, or similar calls to love, an additional ("new") law which makes sense only upon the basis of the former. But Paul neither identifies the Sinai legislation with an event that subjects every man to Moses' Law, as if it were "by nature," nor does he distinguish Sinai Law and Messianic Law in the way that Natural and Positive Law are distinguished in jurisprudence.

The law of love which is most likely identical with the law of the Messiah, the Spirit, the law of faith[56] which is essential in the sanctification of every Jew and every Gentile lies neither in the nature of the Sinai legislation nor in the nature of an ideal truth nor in an innate human conscience. It is a specific gift, or (in the language of philosophy of law) a positive law; for it is essentially connected with the coming, person, work and glory of Jesus Christ crucified and risen, preached and believed. Jesus Christ (or the love poured out by God) is a Pauline alternative to Natural Law.

3. According to Paul the righteousness of God has come to grips with the unrighteousness of each man and all men. The meeting of Him who is right with the many who are wrong takes place in the judgment of God which is executed upon and by Jesus Christ. Prophets and later Jews expected that one day a judgment would be held in which God would establish theodicy, vindicate his servants, squash his enemies. Paul's specific task was to announce to the whole world that this judgment had come, how it was accomplished, to whom its amazing outcome was due, and what it means for daily life and future hope. Without denying that there will still be a future court day to manifest God's righteousness in world-wide fashion, he affirms that both the full wrath of God and his righteous way of saving by grace have already been revealed.[57] Upon the basis of the condemning and acquitting judgment held at Calvary and

Easter, Paul calls for conversion, faith, decision, obedience. On the same basis he gives at times the most detailed "positive" advice or warning. The judgment of God holds fully and exclusively that place in Paul's theology which in some systems of thought and reflection were ascribed to Natural Law. God's righteousness as revealed by Calvary and Easter supplants the function of Natural Law.

4. From the form and result of this judgment essential insights may be gained regarding the relationship between love and righteousness. Scholars like A. Nygren, E. Brunner, R. Niebuhr have taken up an Augustinian and scholastic axiom when they ascribe (in various ways) to natural man some competence concerning the discovery and administration of righteousness, while they reserve the gift and exercise of *agape* (love, charity) to Christians alone who believe in forgiveness. Pauline statements, e.g. on paying fair wages, on right behavior, on women's hairdos, on the function of courts[58] may be quoted to support this distinction. For they seem to affirm that upon the accepted general background (of virtues, or of some unwritten or written law) the specifically Christian virtues are to shine. Why should not the general background of virtues which culminate in righteousness be understood as a representative of Natural Law and gladly be affirmed as the potential and necessary stage of the special gift of God, even love as "posited" by Jesus Christ and faith in him?

We answer: neither the Deuteronomic, Prophetic, Psalmistic, nor Pauline concepts of either righteousness or love permit this division. Love is robbed of its steel and granite contents when it is set over against righteousness; righteousness loses its passionate, edifying, altruistic core when it is supposed to be independent of forgiveness, care, and protection of fellowman. The one cannot be without the other. In Biblical terminology, both are the true and inseparable modes of faithfully keeping the covenant of God. Because of this covenant man is not man without responsibility to the community of men; the exercise of justice and love of neighbor are the only way to fulfill this responsibility. God himself is the guarantee of the right of the neighbor to be loved. By intervening in man's history in ever new acts, God protects that right. Faithfulness to this God causes man to exist truly, righteously, and authentically. But we cannot stipulate that existence in itself, apart from Jesus Christ is *per se* oriented toward faith. The specific act of God, not a general dialectic of righteousness and love, calls responsible existence into being. Where God's covenant is proclaimed and kept, not only God's right but also the rights and the responsibility of the community, the neighbor, the stranger and every member of God's people are upheld. Therefore, the juxtaposition of moral man and immoral society (or vice versa) and the corresponding distinguishing of the realms of love and righteousness, or of special (revealed) and general (natural) ethics have no room where the Old and the New Covenant of God is proclaimed. The grace of God's judgment and the crisis forced upon sin by the gift of God's love is Paul's answer to arguments based on Natural Law.

5. The same Paul who appears so narrow when he reduces all theological issues to their Christological basis and sums up all his Christology in statements on justification is also educated and open enough to dwell upon solutions of the problems of man's existence that were sought outside God's covenant people. In his epistles he makes allusions to stances taken on the basis of sensory perception and reasonable judgments. He makes use of his knowledge of various cultic forms of religion and of individual relationships with God. He is far from condemning all that was upheld by moralists and philosophers in the fields of sex, economics and politics. Just as the formation of the Old Testament canon included the incorporation of dicta, books and

collections of pagan origin[59] and as the Old Testament history included "holy pagans" (J. Daniélou) of Melchisedek's and Cyrus' kind, so Paul's vocabulary, thought-pattern, and actual teaching makes free and frequent use of rare or popular Hellenistic elements. Not only the Areopagus Speech, but Paul's teachings on God, on the obedience of the Christians and possibly on Baptism and the Lord's Supper reveal such borrowing. *Nil humanum a me alienum puto*—so Paul might have said of himself. Especially his doctrine of justification has a deeply humanist and humanitarian concern: even the salvation of the humanity of man. The scope of Christ's work according to Paul was far more than a small slice of humanity, its problems and endeavors. Jews and Gentiles, the whole of mankind, the "world" was according to II Cor. 5:18 ff reconciled to God. From all this the conclusion might be derived that the natural was not obliterated by the grace Paul preached, but on the contrary saved, sublimated and perfected. At least it might be argued that the general search for truth, righteousness and religion found among some, if not all men was used by Paul as a point of contact, from which he was able to ascend to higher spheres. Does Paul, therefore, if not on an ontological basis, then yet for solving the problem of communication, presuppose, uphold and use Natural Law (or Natural Theology)?—We answer: While the breadth and depth of Paul's humanism and his skill in communication are patent, it is impossible to derive or to distill from Paul's teaching and preaching a system of cooperation between nature and grace, Greek wisdom and the Gospel of Jesus Christ. Paul's intention was to build upon *nothing* else than Jesus Christ and to preach *only* the Gospel. It was Paul's conviction that the Gospel of grace (supported as it was by the evidence of the Spirit) was sufficient to speak for itself, to establish contact with people dead in sin, to convince opponents outside and distorters inside the Church. The Gospel, whether it was preached by himself, the Jerusalem Christians, or gain-seeking individuals was for Paul an alternative to any system of thought that would have preserved an honorary place or essential role for Natural Law.

Conclusion

The absence of positive references to Natural Law in passages like Rom. 2 and 13, and even more the presence and dominant role of alternatives throughout Paul's epistles make it impossible to appeal to this Apostle as a defender or promoter of Natural Law. Where the covenant of election, the love of Jesus Christ, the universal and gracious judgment of God are preached and where the Spiritual power of the Gospel is trusted there is neither need nor room for Natural Law. The apostle Paul argues not only without reference to Natural Law, but against it.

But other parts of the Bible, foremost among them the Wisdom literature, would require special research before it could be stipulated that the whole Bible shares in Paul's stance. Since the Bible does not contain a unified system of doctrine, its interpreters should be open for surprising results of further scrutiny. But as to Paul's relationship to the ambiguous concept of Natural Law, the result is unambiguous.

NOTES

[1] C. F. Müller, Karlsruhe 1955, 2nd ed., 1959.

[2] Vol. IV, 1930, cols. 445 ff; Vol. IV, 1960, cols. 1353 ff.

[3] Colossians 3:18 ff; etc.

[4] Erik Wolf, *RGG,* 3rd ed., Vol. IV, col. 1356, cp. 1358.

[5] "Do Noahites Have to Believe In Revelation," *Jewish Quarterly Review* 52, 1962, pp. 297 ff; 53, 1962, pp. 31 ff.

[6] "Christliches Naturrecht," *RGG,* 3rd ed., Vol. IV, cols. 1359 ff.

[7] *S. Theol.* Prima Secundae quaest. 19, art. 4 and 9; quaest. 93, art. 3 secundum, quoted in *Pacem in Terris* #38 and 51.

[8] L.c. quaest. 91, art. 1–3.

[9] An adequate treatment of the manifold views produced by theologians and philosophers of and after the age of Enlightenment and by Anglican scholars following R. Hooker's combination of trust in reason and faith in

incarnation and the fantastic arguments produced under cover of interpretations of Thomas, Luther and Calvin is beyond the scope of this paper.

[10] ##10, 47, 167 ff; the English Translation, edited by the National Catholic Welfare Conference is used.

[11] Ephesians 2:13–17.

[12] *Theol. Zeitschrift,* Basel, 1952, pp. 17 ff.

[13] Zollikon-Zürich, 1954, pp. 295 ff.

[14] Romans 1:18–3:20.

[15] *Conscience in the New Testament,* London, 1955, pp. 13 ff.

[16] Especially Romans 2:17 ff; 3:19; also Romans 5:13–14, 20; Galatians 3–4.

[17] Romans 2:12; I Corinthians 9:21.

[18] Romans 3:37; 7:22–23; 8:2; 9:31; Galatians 5:2.

[19] *Physics* II, 1, 192b; *Metaphysics* IV, 1014b–1015a 19; see R. M. Grant, *Miracle and Natural Law,* Amsterdam, 1952, pp. 4 ff for a discussion.

[20] See Liddell and Scott, *Greek–English Lexicon,* s.v. II 4b; III.

[21] *De Spir. et Lit.* XXVI, 43 f.

[22] Jeremiah 31:33; cp. 32:40.

[23] Romans 13:9; Galatians 5:14; 6:2; James 2:8.

[24] T. Sanh. 13:2; b. Sanh. 105a; cp. BQ 38a; S Lev. 18:5.

[25] E.g. in I Corinthians 8:7–13; 10:25–29.

[26] Ernst Wolf, "Gewissen zwischen Gesetz und Evangelium," *Peregrinatio* II, 1955, p. 116.

[27] Cf. I John 3:19–20; see also Luther, *Schol. in Rom.* WA 56, pp. 203–204.

[28] *Theol. Lit. Ztg.* 72, 1947, pp. 197–202.

[29] "Staat und Kirche in der patristischen Auslegung von Rom. 13:1–7," *Z.N.W.,* 44, 1952/3, pp. 223 ff.

[30] "Zum Verständnis von Rom. 13," *Z.N.W.,* 47, 1956, pp. 67 ff.

[31] "Rom. 13 in unserer Generation," *Z.Th.K.,* 56, 1959, pp. 316 ff.

[32] "Zur Auslegung und Anwendung von Rom. 13:1–7."

[33] *Festschrift für K. Barth,* Zollikon-Zurich, 1956, pp. 114 ff.

[34] Under the influence of Hegel's philosophy!

[35] As e.g., I–II Thessalonians; I Corinthians 7 and 15 indicate.

[36] *Die Geisterwelt im Glauben bei Paulus,* Göttingen, 1909.

[37] "Engel und Obrigkeit," in *Theol. Aufs.* f., K. Barth, Munchen, 1936, pp. 90 ff.

[38] *The State in the New Testament,* New York, 1956.

[39] "Remarques theologiques sur Rom. 13," *Foi et Vie,* 1961, #3, pp. 25 ff.

[40] Cp. also his several essays on Justification, Law, State, and Social Ethics in *Peregrinatio* I, Munich, 1954, II, 1965.

[41] In Col. 1:20; 2:15; Eph. 1:10, 20–23; 4:8; I Cor. 15:25–27; Rom. 8:38–39; Phil. 2:10–11; cp. I Pet. 3:22; Heb. 1:13; 2:7–8.

[42] Cp. for the following M. Barth and V. Fletcher, *Acquittal by Resurrection,* New York, 1964, pp. 46–48; 99–150.

[43] Especially in Rom. 8; Colossians and Ephesians.

[44] Or angel-worship; cp. Colossians 2:18; Revelation 22:8–9; I Corinthians 11:10.

[45] Romans 1:23; in contrast to a frequently found interpretation of this

passage we believe that Paul here accuses both Gentiles and Jews of idol-fabrication.

[46] As well as by John 1:1–5; Hebr. 1:1–4; Matt. 11:25–29.

[47] I Corinthians 1:18–2:16; Colossians 1:15–20.

[48] Romans 5:12–21; Philippians 2:5 ff.

[49] Romans 6:14, 16, 19; 12:1.

[50] Romans 4:13 ff; 9:4; Galatians 3:17 ff.

[51] "Die Gesetze im Pentateuch," *Gesammelte Studien zum Alten Testament,* Munich, 1957, pp. 9 ff; tr. Philadelphia, 1961.

[52] "Law and Covenant in Israel and the Ancient Near East," *Biblical Colloquium,* Pittsburgh, 1955.

[53] Romans 3:31; 7:12, 14; 10:31; 13:9.

[54] Romans 3:20–21, 28; 4:15; 6:14; Galatians 2:14, 16, 21, etc.

[55] Especially in Romans 4 and 5:12 ff; Galatians 3–4; II Corinthians 3; also in Galatians 1–2; Philippians 3.

[56] Mentioned in Galatians 6:2; Romans 3:27; James 2:8.

[57] Romans 1:16–3:31.

[58] Colossians 3:4; Philippians 4:8; I Corinthians 11:6 and ch. 14; Romans 13:3–4.

[59] Cp. especially Proverbs 22:17 ff; 30:1 ff; Job.

ST. THOMAS AQUINAS ON NATURAL LAW

It is unfortunate for us that St. Thomas has been misinterpreted more often than not. Thus, it used to be the custom to think of him as hardly more than a baptized Aristotelian. At other times he has been interpreted as a Cartesian rationalist. Yet, in fairness it must be admitted that the original difficulty lies in the text of St. Thomas himself. Therefore, it may be appropriate to say a few words about the peculiarities of thirteenth century writing, particularly because they affect the question now before us.[1]

To St. Thomas, who was after all a professional theologian, sacred theology (*sacra doctrina*) includes, besides the revealed word of God, any other sort of information that may assist in making it understood; this includes philosophy, any philosophy —that of the Christian Boethius, that of Isaac Israeli, the work of an Islamic Avicenna, or of a pagan Proclus. Motivating this unabashed borrowing was the conviction that all truth comes from God and thus the confidence that reason and faith could not in principle oppose one another. Perhaps this openness to every sort of learning could be called the humanism of medieval theology. Humanism or not, it sometimes leads the modern student to ask if a conclusion proceeds primarily from Scriptures or more especially from philosophy. This question arises in connection with St. Thomas' teaching on natural law.

The medieval text is not only enriched by profane learning as well as sacred; every sort of information is introduced by means of quotations from predecessors. Unless they come from Scriptures, these quotations (*auctoritates*), in spite of their Latin name, do not have a final authority. On the contrary, they initiate discussion after the manner of Aristotle's dialectical use of other men's opinions. Since he had little knowledge of the historical situation in which his predecessors wrote their opinions, the medieval theologian had to interpret them as well as he could. Conscious of his historical ignorance, he was cautious enough not to disagree with them. However, that did not prevent him from interpreting them in such a way as to make them consistent with the truth as he saw it. As a result, St. Thomas uses the words of Boethius, for example, to say things that Boethius could not possibly have said. Did St. Thomas know exactly what he was doing? In a surprising number of cases historians have discovered that he did. Each case, of course, must be judged on its own merits. Yet, for the modern reader the medieval practice of repeating time-honored statements with a frequently new but always respectful interpretation (*pia expositio*) can be troublesome, to say the least. In connection with the problem at hand, we might ask whether St. Thomas' use of the term "law" as the title under which he discusses eternal law, natural law, human positive law, and divine revelation is not an example of the "respectful interpretation."

Aristotelian terms and procedures constitute another formidable barrier for many modern readers of St. Thomas. The medieval theologian's use of Aristotle is understandable considering that the undergraduate program which prepared students for professional studies was largely devoted to a study of Aristotle's works. One instance of this usage that should be mentioned here is the Aristotelian definition. When Aristotle defined a notion he did not try to describe the entity it represented either in terms of all its individual instances nor precisely by leaving them out. Rather, he attempted to express the thing's intent, that which it was inclined to be. Thus, a definition sets forth a kind of ideal; even if the thing being defined is a vice such as cowardice, its definition presents a disposition that individuals may approach or approximate without ever fully realizing it. Consequently, when St. Thomas defines law as an ordinance of reason promulgated for the sake of the common good by someone who has the care of the community,[2] he does not believe that every rule which is called a "law" realizes this definition. He means that unless a rule includes all these elements to some degree, whatever else it may be, it is not a law. To be unfamiliar with these Aristotelian usages is a sure road to misunderstanding.

A cluster of other peculiarities may be quickly mentioned before turning to our immediate business. These difficulties fall under the heading "Scholastic style." As a professor of the thirteenth century, St. Thomas taught pupils who did not have paper on which to take notes because the supply of papyrus was cut off from Europe. In that oral culture a teacher spoke in short sentences using the smallest possible number of technical terms. This style was carried over into most of the published works since they were written by hand on very expensive parchment. Add to these economical measures the fact that the medieval writer was more often than not addressing students for whose sake he had carefully to organize his material and the result was that his style was both cut and dried. This very conciseness can be most deceiving. Consider, for example, the few lines in the *Summa Theologiae* where St. Thomas summarized for students the proof for God's existence from the evidence of motion. Then turn to the many pages devoted to that single argument which he wrote in the *Summa Contra Gentiles* for the guidance of missionaries to the Aristotelian-minded Moslems of Spain. Brevity of statement and definiteness of language do not mean that nothing else could be said nor that qualifications are excluded. Accordingly, when St. Thomas repeatedly speaks of "reason" as the "rule and measure of human acts"[3] he does not at all mean reason in an unqualified sense.

In light of the above remarks, it is easy to see why a medieval writer might be misunderstood by us today. All the features mentioned above characterize St. Thomas as a man of his age: his 13th century humanism, his conservative terminology, his Aristotelian procedures and his Scholastic style. The fact remains that in synthesizing the views of his numerous predecessors within a context that was intentionally Christian,[4] St. Thomas shows a greater perceptiveness than many other thinkers whether before or after.

1. *The Essence of Law*

Examining the more immediate context of our subject, we find that law is a part of "sacred teaching."[5] This teaching begins with a study of God; it continues with a discussion of the procession of creatures from Him; and it concludes with a long account of the return of all creatures to their source.

St. Thomas' treatment of the "return" constitutes three fourths of the entire *Summa Theologiae.* This part of his work is also divided into three sections, the last of which is the longest. The first section considers man's destiny in God; the second examines the human activities that lead toward or deviate from that end; the third section treats entirely of "our Lord and Savior Jesus Christ who, according to the words of the angel, saves his people from their sins."

In the middle of his account of the creatures' return to God and while dealing with human actions, St. Thomas asks what the sources of human action may be. He maintains that they are both intrinsic and extrinsic.[6] The intrinsic sources (*principia*) are the soul's various powers along with the good and evil habits of those powers, that is to say, the virtues and vices. There are two extrinsic sources of human activity: the devil, inclining us toward evil through temptation; and God, moving us toward the good by instructing us with law and by helping us with the grace we need to follow it.

This brief résumé gives us the setting for our question. St. Thomas approached law primarily as a theologian and only secondarily as a philosopher. Such, at least, is his own view of the matter. For he tells us that the theologian begins with God as the rule of human action while the moral philosopher begins with human reason.[7]

What is law then? Or rather (remembering the requirements of an Aristotelian definition), what does law tend to be? It is a kind of instruction. It is no less than that; but it is no more either. For if law is to guide man back to God, man must at the same time be assisted by grace.

Let us examine this notion of law as instruction more closely. Law, says Aquinas, is a "rule and measure" of actions.[8] It rules by commanding and forbidding. Now, to command and to forbid are functions of reason. Consequently, law is something belonging to reason as the word "instruction" suggested above.

Indeed, one may follow Aristotle's usage by calling reason itself the rule and measure of human actions because it is their source (*principium*) precisely insofar as they are human. For Aristotle, reason is the measure of actions because it is by means of our reason that we direct ourselves toward ends.[9] In this terminology, whatever is the immediate source of a whole class of things is called the "rule and measure" of those things; thus, for example, unity is the source and measure of the entire class of numbers. Yet only because reason takes into account some end or good is it the source of directives.[10] Consequently, although it may sound awkward it is correct to say that an end is the source of reason's being a source of directives.

One more element must be observed in the interplay of factors that are involved in law-making: an end can influence reason only through the mediation of the will.[11] In other words, it is due to the fact that one wills the end that reason issues its precepts regarding things ordained to the end. Evidently, a law is willed by the legislator. Nevertheless, his directive must be in accord with reason if it is not to be lawless.

To say that the reason productive of laws is moved to do so by the will is to say that the reason in question is "practical reason."[12] This is an Aristotelian expression designating reason insofar as it regulates conduct.[13] When reason functions precisely for the sake of knowing as in pure mathematics it is called "theoretical," "contemplative" or "speculative." In short, this is a distinction in terms of function, not in consequence of really distinct powers. It remains a distinction of capital importance. In enunciating laws, practical reason does not seek so much to inform the one who hears them as to guide his action. Its purpose is not precisely understanding but good conduct. Or, if understanding be itself a kind of activity, at least it is not that sort of activity which law aims to induce. Law does not tell us how things *are,* except incidentally; it tells us how our actions *ought to be.* Granting this qualification, law remains a kind of instruction which, like any other sort of teaching, cannot by itself elicit compliance. Still, it is that effect which the instructions of practical reason attempt to produce. The utterances of theoretical reason, on the other hand, aim at nothing more than an expression of the things it contemplates.

Finally, it should be noticed that a rule of action may be a law either essentially or by participation.[14] That rule is essentially a law which is present in the reason of the legislator. As found in its subjects, a law may be present as no more than the inclination to an end which is produced by the rule that is essentially a law. Such an inclination is called a law by participation. As present in reason, a law may exist in practical reason's act of directing conduct or in the universal proposition that reason has produced to embody that directive and which it can recall as needed.[15]

So much for the first element in the definition of law: it is a directive or ordinance of practical reason.

Secondly, law must be enacted not merely for some private purpose but for the common good.[16] Just as reason is the source of human actions, so in reason itself there is something which is the source of both the actions and the fact that reason produces them. Now the primary source in all practical matters is the last end. Given that the last end of man is blessedness,[17] law must mainly concern itself with the order found there. Besides, inasmuch as individual men are merely members within the whole community of mankind, law must be concerned with the blessedness of all. If then, law is ordained chiefly to the common good, no other precept will be lawful except insofar as it regards the common good. Evidently, the "common good" is not some state or quality that all men now enjoy[18] but the goal or end that all aim at because it is already present somehow in the practical reason of each.

While law aims at the good common to all men it does not exclude particular ends. Indeed, particular ends ought to have the law applied to them but always in accordance with the common good.[19] In this sense one can say that "the common good comprises many things."[20]

Thirdly, the essence of law requires that not merely anyone make laws but only the one who has the care of the community.[21] The principle involved in this requirement is as follows: directing things to an end is the concern of the one to whom that end belongs. For example, as we noticed earlier, laws are present not only in the minds of legislators but also by participation in those who are subject to the laws. Thus, insofar as the subject shares the law received from his rulers he "is a law to himself."[22] Similarly, a free people that is competent to make its own laws has even greater authority than the person who rules that community merely as its representative.[23] The principle St. Thomas uses seems quite general: whether it be a private person or a community or the leader of a group is not important; the one whose goal is at stake has the authority to regulate the manner of achieving it. In the case of regulations which are laws and which therefore look first and foremost to the common good, the power to legislate "belongs either to the whole people or to a public personage who has the care of the whole people."[24]

Consequently, although anyone in his merely private capacity can advise others and thus perhaps lead them toward the common good, he cannot do this so efficaciously as to lead all sorts of persons by this means.[25] In the case of those who require coercion he would lack the power to enforce the law. Since a law directs activity toward the good common of all, it ought to have this coercive power. Only the community as a whole or its ruler possesses this quality. Therefore, they alone can make laws.

If coercive power goes hand in hand with the authority to legislate and therefore with laws themselves, it does not follow that law has no other power than that. The intention of the lawmakers should be to make men good.[26] It is true that men are good through virtue. The purely human sort of virtue is acquired by personal effort and the theological kind of virtue man can have only as a gift from God. Still, being accustomed to good action contributes to both; "for it causes the acquired virtue, while it disposes to infused virtue, and preserves and fosters it when it already exists."[27] Law, therefore, does not fulfill its purpose unless it governs human actions insofar as they are conducive to virtue.[28] However, law accomplishes this effect primarily by being obeyed. It seeks to be obeyed in three ways: by its commands, which in various ways prescribe all the acts of virtue;[29] by its prohibitions which forbid evil acts; and by its permissions which allow all acts that are indifferent of themselves, that is to say, not distinctly good or evil.

To insure obedience, law makes use of punishment and the threat of punishment. This action of law does not lead to virtue directly but sometimes, through doing what one ought out of fear of punishment, one is led to act in the same way with pleasure and of one's own accord.[30] Laws, then, seek to achieve compliance in two ways: precisely through being the directives that they are; and, further, by inducing us to assent to them. Because anyone can employ advice or reward to bring about compliance with his wishes, these are not the inducements peculiar to law.[31] To punish, however, pertains exclusively to an administrator of law and that is why coercive power is said to be proper to law.[32] From these remarks it is clear that law has a two-fold power: of its very nature it has a directive force leading to virtuous action; and it has a coercive power for the sake of inducing compliance with its directives.[33]

Now since the coercive power of law is applicable only for the sake of bringing about obedience in recalcitrant subjects, strictly speaking no man can coerce himself. What is more, this power extends only as far as the authority of the ruler in question.[34] In short, for St. Thomas, the power to coerce seems to be one with the power to make laws. The principle he employed above seems to apply in both cases: it is proper to the one to whom the end belongs to regulate the individuals under his authority in such a way as to achieve that end.

The fourth and final component in the definition of law is that it be promulgated.[35] The reason for saying so is the above-mentioned fact that a law is imposed on others as a rule and measure of their actions. However, the imposition or application of a law in such a way as to bind those who are its subjects is accomplished by informing them of it. In other words, unless it is made known, a directive can have no force, and without binding force a directive is not a law. As we saw at the outset of this discussion, law is a kind of instruction.

From the foregoing account, then, we gather St. Thomas' definition of law. "Law is nothing else than an ordinance of reason for the common good, promulgated by him who has the care of the community."[36]

2. *The Eternal Law and the Natural Law*

After discussing the essence of law, St. Thomas asks whether the following are truly instances of law: (1) the eternal law; (2) the natural law; (3) the human law; (4) the divine law; and (5) the law of sin. It will be helpful to our understanding of the natural law if we examine these in turn. The "law of sin" or "law of the members," however, is a law only in so derivative a fashion, perhaps merely by metaphor,[37] that we shall not include it in this survey.

The expression "eternal law" comes from St. Augustine.[38] But even without it St. Thomas would probably have found another term to describe the origin of all government in God. The reason for saying this is the fact that the doctrine of God as Creator requires that every creature have its exemplar in its source.[39] Now, that is what the eternal law is for St. Thomas. If law is a dictate of practical reason emanating from a ruler and if the universe is ruled by divine providence then the very notion, or exemplar, of the government of things in God is law.[40] But, since the divine conception of things is eternal this kind of law must likewise be eternal.[41]

The eternal law is not eternally imposed on creatures because they are not eternal. Still, they are contained in the Creator's preconception of them along with the way in which they will be governed.[42] Just as it is not eternally imposed neither is this law eternally promulgated in the sense of being forever learned by creatures. Yet, because the conception or Word of the Father expresses all things in His knowledge, the Word contains the eternal expression of the law for creatures. Taken in this way, the eternal law is promulgated.[43] Furthermore, as human actions are ruled by laws or, more simply, by human reason, so the subjects of the divine government are said to be ruled either by the eternal law or by divine reason.[44] When we think of the source of all government we speak of the "divine reason." But this is no other than the Word, or Son, of God made known to us through revelation.[45] Insofar as He is naturally born of the Father, the Son is not subject to the eternal law but in some fashion "rather is Himself the eternal law."

In this light, the other three types of law, natural, human and divine, will appear as different ways in which the creature is subject to the eternal law or participates in it.[46]

Perhaps the principal stimulus for St. Thomas' account of natural law is the traditional interpretation of *Romans* ii, 14 (the Gentiles, who have not the law, do by nature those things that are of the law). The accepted commentary on this passage describes the law in question as "the natural law whereby each one knows, and is conscious of, what is good and what is evil."[47] Moreover, this interpretation seems to be corroborated by other Scriptural and traditional texts as well as by the evidence of man himself.

St. Thomas reminds us that a law can be in a person in two ways: essentially, as it is in the reason of the legislator; and participatively, as it is in the subject of law.[48] Since everything subject to divine providence is ruled by the eternal law, it follows that all things partake in that law to some degree by having imprinted on them their respective inclinations to their proper activities and ends.

Now, rational creatures are subject to divine providence in a more excellent way through sharing in providence inasmuch as they care for themselves and others. This is to say that the rational creature has its inclination to its proper activity and end by having a share in the eternal reason itself. "This participation of the eternal law in the rational creature is called the natural law." Thus, in answering the question, "Who showeth us good things?" the Psalmist replies: "The light of Thy countenance, O Lord, is signed upon us" (*Ps.* iv, 6). St Thomas takes this to mean that we are able to discern good from evil by the light of natural reason. This discernment is also the function of the natural law. Besides referring to the natural law as the rational creature's participation in the eternal law we may also speak of it as the imprint of the divine light upon us.

Has St. Thomas meant to say that the natural law and the light of reason are the same thing? Not quite. As we saw in our discussion of law in general, law is a directive or pronouncement of reason. The fact remains that the rational creature participates in the eternal law through sharing in the eternal reason. As a result, only the rational creature's participation in the eternal law is called a law.[49] Strictly speaking, irrational creatures are not governed by the natural law but only by the eternal law and the inborn tendencies which are its imprint.[50] Of man, then, we must say that he is naturally subject to the eternal law or receives by nature an imprint of the divine light in two ways.[51] Like every other creature, man has a natural inclination toward his proper activity and his proper end. In addition to this, man has some knowledge of the eternal law. Since the second sort of subjection will help us to understand the first, let us begin with man's knowledge of the eternal law.

Only God and the blessed who see Him know the eternal law as it is in itself.[52] But every rational creature knows it more or less through knowing some truth. Every truth is a reflection or participation of the unchangeable truth. Now all men know the truth to some extent; at least by knowing the common principles of the natural law. As to other truths, some know more, others less. In any case, everyone knows the eternal law through knowing something of the natural law.

What are these "common principles of the natural law" that everyone knows? In other places St. Thomas refers to them as "seeds of the virtues," as principles that are "indemonstrable," "self-evident," "naturally known," or "primary" and, more simply, as "moral precepts."[53] Why they should be called "seeds of the virtues" or "naturally known principles" we shall consider when we examine the natural law as an inborn tendency. St. Thomas calls them "self-evident" (*per se nota*) or "indemonstrable" because in each case the predicate is contained in the notion of the subject.[54] Of course, to the person who does not know the definition of the subject such a proposition could not be self-evident. Accordingly, some axioms may be self-evident to all, others only to the sophisticated.

Since the principles of the natural law relate to matters of action just as the first principles of theoretical knowledge relate to the conclusions of demonstrations, a comparison may be helpful. First, we should observe that there is an order of apprehension in human knowledge proceeding from the simple to the more complex and this is true whether reason proceeds theoretically or practically. Thus, theoretical reason first grasps being, or the fact that something exists. The word "first" in this statement does not signify priority in time. It simply means that whatever else a man understands, this is included in it. On the notion of being and its opposite, not-being, is based the first indemonstrable principle of theoretical knowledge; namely, that the same thing cannot be affirmed and denied at the same time. In saying these things, St. Thomas is evidently following Aristotle.[55]

Now, insofar as reason is directed to action, the good, or that which is desirable, is the first thing reason apprehends. One says this because anyone who acts always moves toward some end as though it were desirable or good. Consequently, the first indemonstrable principle of practical reason is based on the notion of the good. The principle is as follows: good is to be done and promoted and evil is to be avoided. On this all the other precepts of the natural law are founded. This means that the things which reason naturally apprehends as good for man are included under the precepts of the natural law as things to be done and their opposites to be avoided.

It follows, then, that practical reason naturally apprehends as good every end toward which man is naturally inclined. Man's natural inclinations are of three sorts. First, just as every substance tends to preserve its own being, man is inclined to maintain human life and all the means needed for its preservation. Correspondingly, man is inclined to ward off all the obstacles to this end. Secondly, inasmuch as he has a nature similar to other animals, man has an inclination toward sexual intercourse, the education of offspring and so on. Thirdly, by virtue of his reason man is inclined to the properly human good which is the knowledge of God and life in society. Everything belonging to this inclination also belongs to the natural law; for example, to shun ignorance, to avoid offending those with whom one must live, and so forth.

Evidently, there are several common principles of the natural law in accordance with man's multi-leveled nature and varied inclinations. Indeed, all actions tending toward personal excellence or virtue are included under the natural law inasmuch as it is proper to man to act reasonably.[56]

Something else has also become clear. If propositions like "human life is to be preserved" and "ignorance is to be avoided" are principles of the natural law, then the natural law is a work of man's reason. That is exactly what St. Thomas maintains. Properly and essentially the natural law is not innate because, as we saw at the beginning of our account of the essence of law, a law is something constituted by reason (*per rationem constitutum*).[57] As man makes speeches so he makes the precepts of the natural law.

Let us grant then, that man knows the eternal law in knowing the natural law and he knows the latter in reasoning about the ends toward which he is naturally inclined. Let us also grant that all men know at least the common principles of the natural law. Needless to say, the universality of this knowledge supposes that the humans in question are neither infantile nor unconscious, nor otherwise radically prohibited from exercising their understanding.[58] Still, we are inclined to wonder, is this really possible for all "normal," conscious adults?

St. Thomas has already suggested a partial answer to this question. We have heard him say that all virtuous actions are included under the natural law inasmuch as they are virtuous or according to reason. Yet, insofar as virtuous acts are of specific kinds not all of them are prescribed by the natural law, or, therefore, known to everyone. Thus, we might say that it is proper for man to wear clothes because, while nature did not give them to him, he invented them by art.[59] Similarly, although the distinction of possessions was not established by nature it was devised by human reason for the benefit of man's life. Still, these humanly contrived devices belong to the natural law not in consequence of answering to a specific natural inclination but on the condition that nature does not ordain their contraries. Here, then, is not only a qualification to the comprehensiveness of the natural law but also another indication of what that law includes: it includes everything to which man is naturally inclined as well as all those things that are not contrary to man's nature but are beneficial to human life. In any case, insofar as specific kinds of virtuous action are not required by man's natural inclinations they are not required by the natural law.

Another reason for saying that not all men know the natural law equally well is based on a point we have already seen; namely, that man shares in the eternal law both by natural inclination toward his proper end and by knowledge of the eternal law. Now, in those who are wicked, both forms of participation are corrupted by vicious habits. Contrariwise, in those who are good, both inclination and knowledge are perfected.[60] In spite of the corruption of man's knowledge of the natural law through wickedness, no amount of moral evil can obscure from his view the common principles but only the particular conclusions that might be drawn from them. Thus, although a man cannot fail to know that he ought not offend others, the ancient Germans are said to have seen nothing wrong in theft.[61]

What are the common principles of the natural law that no man can fail to know? St. Thomas does not seem to have attempted an exhaustive catalogue of them. He has merely said that they are indicated by the inclinations corresponding to the various levels of man's nature and that the most important inclination is to act reasonably. He has also said that the common principles are less specific than the commandments of the decalogue, although these last seem to be among the most evident conclusions to be drawn from the common principles.[62]

The question of the immutability of the natural law is evidently linked with that of its universality. As St. Thomas sees it, the first principles of the natural law cannot be changed although its secondary principles or proximate conclusions may be in certain unusual cases.[63] The more particularized or remote from the first principles a conclusion is the more susceptible of change it will be. Thus, it is a first principle to act according to reason. It is a proximate conclusion from this principle that goods entrusted to another should be restored to their owner.[64] In certain instances this might not be reasonable, for example, if the goods were to be reclaimed to fight against one's country. Finally, if it be laid down that the goods held in trust are to be restored with certain detailed guarantees and only under very precise conditions, this stipulated principle would hold in even fewer cases and will be quite susceptible of change.

The above changes are by way of subtraction from the secondary precepts of the natural law. But other changes are possible by way of addition.[65] In this way, many things benefitting human life have been added over and above the natural law. In this connection we recall the things men have devised for the improvement of human life when the natural law did not prescribe to the contrary.

In general, because the first purpose of law is the common good and secondly the order of justice and virtue whereby the common good is attained and preserved, no precept expressive of these purposes can be changed.[66] Consider one case. The intention of a law against murder is to be understood as forbidding an act that is unjust or without due cause. But, since the killing of an enemy of the common good may conceivably be for due cause such an act would not be murder. Insofar as this sort of law contains the notion of justice it is unchangeable; but, insofar as it attempts to determine what murder is by making application to individual cases it is open to variation after the manner of the law described above concerning the restoration of goods entrusted to another.

In brief, there is a certain group of common principles of the natural law known to all men. Through reasoning about the ends toward which he is naturally inclined man comes to know these reflections of the eternal law. Yet, as prominent as human reason is in the foregoing account of man's participation in the eternal law, St. Thomas maintains that human reason is not of itself the rule of human activity. It is the principles impressed upon it by nature that are the general rules of everything relating to human conduct.[67] When he speaks of the principles "impressed upon" reason by nature, St. Thomas recalls to our attention the fact that man is subject to the external law through his natural inclinations even more profoundly than he is through his knowledge. In the same vein, St. Thomas says that the natural law is instilled into man "through being part of his nature."[68] We now know that this is not the natural law considered properly and essentially. What is it then?

The natural law is two things: it is the will's natural inclination toward man's last end; and it is the intellect's innate capacity to know the end as well as the order of human actions indicated by that end. Reason's innate capacity to know the proper order of human activity is sometimes referred to as the inborn "habit" or predisposition to know the common principles of the natural law.[69] Given that it is a natural capacity, this habit may be said to "contain" the common principles; yet it contains them only as a potentiality contains its possible actualizations. St. Basil named the habit "synderesis." Aristotle's "intuitive reason" provided the theoretical background.[70]

By professing this doctrine of natural inclinations, "impressed" principles and innate habits, St. Thomas tries to avoid two extreme positions.[71] On the one hand were the Platonists who thought that man was by nature fully equipped with every form of personal excellence or virtue and needed only to remove the obstacles to their appearance. On the other hand were the followers of Avicenna who maintained that the virtues which embellished man were entirely the product of some external agency. To St. Thomas the middle ground held by Aristotle is "nearer the truth." According to this view, intellectual and moral excellence is in us naturally insofar as we have the ability to acquire it. The completion or perfection of that excellence is not present naturally but depends upon our action.

In the Thomistic theory of the natural law, innate tendencies are prior to knowledge in importance. Among these tendencies priority is given to the inclinations of intellect and will. It is not entirely clear, however, whether the intellectual or the volitional tendency is primary in man's participation of the eternal law. It is clear that insofar as man's participation becomes conscious the immediate source of this awareness is the reason of man as perfected by the inborn tendency called synderesis. However, St. Thomas is not quite as clear when we ask: What is the immediate source of the aspect of goodness that the intellect inclined by synderesis first recognizes? The answer to this question may be the will. In any case, the following interpretation is proposed without any pretension of doing full justice to a delicate question.

The will's natural tendency toward its end is actualized by an end presented to it in the practical reason.[72] But whenever reason moves by commanding, as it does in matters of practice, it moves under the power of the will.[73] The will itself is moved only by its proper end, an apprehended good. Now, an end considered as good is the object of the will before it is the object of reason.[74] This seems to mean that man's natural volitional tendency toward the good is the primary source of the aspect of goodness seen by the practical intellect. If it is correct to say that the will's natural tendency is the primary specifying principle of practical knowledge,[75] then it would seem to follow that man's participation in the eternal law is accomplished first of all by his loving and only secondarily by his knowing.

The fact that reason pronounces the moral law is its own achievement. But what it pronounces it has found already present within itself due to the natural inclination of the will. The natural law was not actually or articulately present; yet, it was to be found in the intellect's awareness of its last end. It follows then, that reason is the discoverer of natural law rather than its inventor. Because the natural law is finally promulgated through man's discovery of it, Lottin has underlined the "intrinsicist" character of the Thomistic theory.[76] This is to say that natural law appears to be less an extrinsic principle of human action than an intrinsic one. It is not so much a law (*lex*) imposed from without as a person's own realization of what is right (*jus*).[77]

3. *Conclusion*

It is impossible, within the scope of this article adequately to examine the Thomistic notions of human and divine law on the basis of which one might approach the problem of church-state relations.

Briefly we might note that in Aquinas' view all laws are derived from the eternal law insofar as they partake of right reason.[78] Properly considered, human law limits itself to questions of justice;[79] apparently it is concerned with the more private virtues only insofar as they affect community life. Human law seeks to lead men to virtue but without prescribing everything that is good or prohibiting everything that is evil. It falls short of the eternal law without doubt. Yet, it should not be blamed for the limited good that it can accomplish.[80]

Both human law and divine, or revealed, law are determinations of the precepts of the natural law.[81] This is to say that they both articulate what was naturally prescribed and they make definite things that were mere possibilities in the natural law. The latter type of specification is an addition to the natural law which attempts to make concrete the steps whereby man may more effectively reach his last end. This progressive development within law from natural to human to divine is apparent even within the divine law itself. Thus, St. Thomas considers the New Law, or the Gospel, to be an explication of what was merely implicit in the Old.[82] What is more, it is a law of faith and love where the Old Law was a law of fear.[83] Indeed, the New Law "consists chiefly in the grace of the Holy Spirit."[84]

Although the divine law may be a determination of the natural law, everything that belongs to the natural law was included in the Old Law and is now contained in the New.[85] The great difference between natural law and divine is the fact that man's fulfillment of natural law is not enough to cause man's justification before God.[86] Not even the Old Law could do that. The explanation is to be found in the fact that neither natural law nor the Old Law conferred grace. At best, the Old Law signified the New and, in some cases, disposed men to it. In fact, without grace man was unable to fulfill the requirements of either the natural law or the Old Law.[87]

Is it possible to suggest in terms of the above account that the natural law again be considered as a minimal basis for state-church conversations? It goes without saying that this is not to exclude the divine law as a maximal point at which all men should converge. But, if St. Thomas is to be believed, the ever-present basis for the mere possibility of discussing good and evil conduct is the universal awareness that there are norms which human beings ought to observe simply because they are human. In St. Thomas' terminology, this obscure and incomplete but universal awareness is man's knowledge of the natural law.

To say that this knowledge is obscure and incomplete is to remind ourselves of the fact that only the most common principles of the natural law are universally acknowledged. The secondary and more particular precepts are by no means known to all. We have seen that the principal reasons for this deficiency are evil habits and ill will. If this is true then the church as the people of God should be more qualified than other groups to say what the secondary precepts, or more necessary conclusions, of the natural law are. Unfortunately, mere membership in the church is no guarantee of grace. Besides, in St. Thomas' judgment, many people who are nominally outside the church are yet the recipients of divine grace. As he puts it, there have always been some people belonging to the New Testament who have never had the Gospel literally preached to them.[88] Therefore, it would seem that a good number of people both within the church and without may be expected to have a better than average knowledge of the natural law—not, of course, under that title.

At the same time it must be admitted that church and state have distinct concerns. The state, in particularizing the precepts of the natural law to fit specific situations, is concerned primarily with the temporal tranquillity of the civil community. The church, engaged in the analogous task of applying the divine law to daily life, seeks to bring man to that end which is everlasting happiness.[89] In principle, at least, there should be no conflict between state and church; their characteristic aims are different.

When all this has been said the fact remains that the natural law and the divine law include each other in different ways. The natural law, unwittingly, awaits its fulfillment in the divine. The divine law includes the natural as the whole includes the part. Similarly, while all citizens are not believers, all believers are citizens. Living in distinct but not quite separable domains, they should not be surprised at the constant tension between them. Both might remember that no human is perfectly clear before the fact as to the most particular and concrete implications of the good for man. All are called, according to the varying degrees of their knowledge, to cooperate in working out the minimal requirements of a life that is human. This, in the eyes of St. Thomas Aquinas, seems to be the unfinished business of the natural law.

NOTES

[1] The bulk of what is said in this discussion on "Problems of Interpretation" may be found more fully explained in M. D. Chenu, *Introduction à l'Étude de S. Thomas d'Aquin,* Montreal, Paris (1950). References that follow are to the following works: Grotius, *De Iure Praedae Commentarius,* trans. G. L. Williams, New York, London (1964), pp. 8, 9; *The Rights of War and Peace,* trans. A. C. Campbell, Universal Classics Library, Washington, London (1901), pp. 22–25. St. Thomas Aquinas, *Summa Theologiae,* Ottawa (1941), I–II, 93, 3 *sed contra* and 93, 4, *ad* 2. Hereafter this work will be referred to as *S.T.* O. Lottin, *Le Droit Naturel chez Saint Thomas d'Aquin et ses prédécesseurs,* Bruges, Paris (1931); *Psychologie et Morale aux XIIe et XIIIe Siecles,* 7 vols., Louvain (1948–1954). J. Maritain, *The Rights of Man and Natural Law,* New York (1943); *Man and the State,* Chicago (1951), chapter IV.

[2] *S.T.* I–II, 90, 4.

[3] *Ibid.,* 1.

[4] *S.T.* I–II, *Prologus.*

[5] *Ibid.*

[6] *S.T.* I–II, 49, *Prologus.*

[7] *Op. cit.,* 7, 6, *ad* 5.

[8] *Op. cit.,* 90, 1.

[9] *Nichomachean Ethics,* VII, 8 (1151a 16).

[10] *S.T.* I–II, 1, 1.

[11] *Op. cit.,* 90, 1, *ad* 3.

[12] *Ibid., ad* 2.

[13] *Nichomachean Ethics,* VI.

[14] *S.T.* I–II, 90, 1, *ad* 1.

[15] *Ibid., ad* 2.

[16] *Nichomachean Ethics,* VI.

[17] *S. T.* I–II, 90, 1, *ad* 1.

[18] *Ibid., ad* 2.
[19] *Op. cit.*, 90, 2.
[20] To avoid confusion with extraneous conceptions of man's last end I have translated *beatitudo* as blessedness rather than, in the more usual way, as happiness. Reasons for doing so may be found in the lengthy discussions of *beatitudo* in the earlier part of the *Summa Theologiae.* More often than not those discussions open with Scriptural texts, the bulk of them being from the Apostle, John; *cf. S.T.* I–II, 2–5.
[21] *S.T.* I–II, 90, 2 *ad* 2.
[22] *Ibid., ad* 1.
[23] *Op. cit.* 96, 1.
[24] *Op. cit.* 90, 3.
[25] *Ibid., ad* 1 where the discussion centers around *Romans* ii, 14.
[26] *Op. cit.*, 97, 3, *ad* 3.
[27] *Op. cit.*, 90, 3.
[28] *Ibid., ad* 2.
[29] Aristotle, *Nichomachean Ethics,* II, 1 (1103b 3).
[30] *S.T.* I–II, 92, 1 *ad* 1; 63, 2 & 3; *cf. Wisdom* viii, 7.
[31] *S.T.* I–II, 92, 1.
[32] *Op. cit.*, 92, 2.
[33] *Ibid., ad* 4.
[34] *Ibid., ad* 2 & 3.
[35] *Op. cit.*, 96, 5.
[36] *Ibid., ad* 3.
[37] *Op. cit.*, 100, 9.
[38] *Op. cit.*, 90, 4.
[39] *Ibid.*
[40] O. Lottin, *Psychologie et Morale,* II, 29.
[41] *De Libero Arbitrio,* I, 6 (*P.L.* 32, 1229).
[42] *S.T.* I–II, 93, 1; *cf.* I, 14, 8.
[43] *S.T.* I–II, 91, 1.
[44] *Ibid.* St. Thomas refers to *Proverbs* viii, 23.
[45] *S.T.* I–II, 91, 1, *ad* 1.
[46] *Ibid., ad* 2.
[47] *Op. cit.*, 19, 4.
[48] *Op. cit.*, 93, 4, *ad* 2.
[49] *Op. cit.*, 93, 2–6.
[50] *Op. cit.*, 91, 2.
[51] *Ibid.*
[52] *Ibid., ad* 3.
[53] *Op. cit.*, 93, 5, *ad* 1 & 2.
[54] *Op. cit.*, 93, 6.
[55] *Ibid.*, 2.
[56] According to the order of the quotations the references are: *S.T.* I–II, 63, 1; 91, 3; 94, 2; 94, 4; 94, 4; 99, 4.
[57] *Op. cit.*, 94, 2.
[58] *Metaphysics* IV, 3 (1005b 29).
[59] *S.T.* I–II, 94, 3.
[60] *Op. cit.*, 94, 4.

[61] *Ibid.*
[62] *Op. cit.,* 94, 5, *ad* 3.
[63] *Op. cit.,* 93, 6.
[64] *Op. cit.,* 94, 4.
[65] *Op. cit.,* 100, 11.
[66] *Op. cit.,* 94, 5.
[67] *Ibid.,* 4.
[68] *Ibid.,* 5.
[69] *Op. cit.,* 100, 8.
[70] *Op. cit.,* 91, 3, *ad* 2.
[71] *Op. cit.,* 106, 1, *ad* 2.
[72] *Op. cit.,* 94, 1.
[73] *S.T.* I, 79, 12; *cf. Nichomachean Ethics* VI, 6 (1141a 7).
[74] *S.T.* I–II, 63, 1.
[75] *Op. cit.,* 9, 1, *ad* 2.
[76] *Op. cit.,* 17, 1.
[77] *Op. cit.,* 19, 3, *ad* 1.
[78] *Cf.* J. Maritain, *Existence and the Existent* (New York, 1948), chapter II, "Action."
[79] O. Lottin, *Psychologie et Morale,* II, 91.
[80] *Ibid.,* p. 97; *cf.* A. P. d'Entreves, *Natural Law, An Historical Survey,* New York (1965) pp. 77–78.
[81] *S.T.* I–II, 93, 3.
[82] *Op. cit.,* 100, 2.
[83] *Op. cit.,* 96, 2; *ibid., ad* 2 & 3.
[84] *Op. cit.,* 99, 3, *ad* 2; 99, 4.
[85] *Op. cit.,* 107, 3, *ad* 3.
[86] *Ibid.,* 1, *ad* 2 & 3.
[87] *Op. cit.,* 108, 1; *cf.* 106, 1.
[88] *Op. cit.,* 94, 4, *ad* 1.
[89] *Op. cit.,* 100, 12; *cf.* 106, 2.
[90] *Op. cit.,* 100, 10, *ad* 3; *cf.* 109, 2 and 4, *ad* 1.
[91] *Op. cit.,* 106, 3, *ad* 2; *cf.* 106, 1, *ad* 3.
[92] *Op. cit.,* 98, 1.

NATURAL LAW IN CALVIN[1]

by

Arthur C. Cochrane

WHEN Josef Bohatec published his exhaustive study, *Calvin und das Recht,* in 1934, he did so in the conviction that scholars who had written on the subject of natural law in Calvin since the beginning of the twentieth century—Ernst Troeltsch, August Lang, von Beyerhaus, and Emile Doumergue—had not done justice to "the factors to which prominence must be given in the problem of natural law." "There is lacking," he wrote, "a description of nature as the source and origin of natural law, as well as the psychological and ethical presuppositions of natural right. There is lacking a clear demarcation of the purely natural elements from those determined and limited by Christian knowledge, and a presentation of the synthesis of both attempted by Calvin. There is lacking an answer to the question concerning the historical origin of the doctrine of natural law. Above all there is lacking a discussion of the relations between the doctrine of natural law and Calvin's other world of ideas."[2] However, at the very time when Bohatec was concerned about the historical, psychological and allegedly synthetic features of Calvin's doctrine of natural law, the urgent *theological* question was being raised, namely, whether Calvin teaches the reality and possibility of a natural knowledge of God's will by means of a natural law. This question was seen within the framework of the larger question: whether there is an actual natural knowledge of God's being and nature. The issue was urgent because it involved the very existence of the Evangelical Church in Germany in its struggle against the "German Christians" who were affirming a natural knowledge of God and His will in German blood, race, soil and history. In the theological debate at that time the issue came to a head with the publication of Emil Brunner's *Nature and Grace* and Karl Barth's *No! Answer to Emil Brunner* in 1934.[3]

Brunner contended that "nature is for Calvin both a concept of being and a concept of a norm, and over and over again we meet with the expression: *natura docet, natura dictat,* which for him means almost the same as: God teaches—i.e., the will of God, which has been implanted in the world from creation, the divine rule of the world teaches. It is therefore quite natural for Calvin to use the concept of the *lex naturae* and also that of the order of creation in the same sense. . . . The will of God, imprinted upon all existence, implanted in it from creation, can therefore be recognized as such."[4] Moreover, although the divine order of nature has been affected not only subjectively but objectively, "it is not affected so much as to render the will of God, the 'rule' of nature invisible."[5] God can be known from God's works in nature and in man himself, and this is not a "confused knowledge" but "something highly important and necessary for the Christian" who knows the Word of God. The knowledge of God from *experientia,* i.e., from the experience of God's preserving and providential grace, is "not made superfluous by faith in the Word of God, but on the contrary remains an important complement of the knowledge of God derived from Scripture."[6] However, it is only a "partial" knowledge. "We can know his wisdom and omnipotence, also his justice and even his goodness, but not his forgiving mercy."[7] According to Calvin, Brunner argued, the relation of revelation in Scripture to that in nature is twofold. First, "through Scripture the revelation in nature is both clarified and complemented"; and secondly, "Scripture shows us the heart of God, which is not revealed in natural revelation."[8] This "applies especially to the knowledge of the divine will from the *law* and the natural ordinances"—which is the aspect of the problem that particularly concerns us in the present paper.

"We know the law of God in our reason or conscience. This *lex naturae* is identical in content with the *lex scripta,* though the *lex scripta* is necessary to make again perfectly clear the writing of the *lex naturae* which has, as it were faded. But Calvin is concerned to point out that the *lex scripta* has no other function but to make the *lex naturae* effective again. For the *lex naturae* is the will of God in creation."[9] "Even fallen man still has—thanks to the 'portion' of the *imago* that he has retained—an immortal soul, a conscience in which the law of God is indelibly and irremovably implanted. But he also has an inclination towards truth and a capacity for recognizing truth" because "the *imago,* which man retains, is the principle of the theologia naturalis in the subjective sense, i.e., of that knowledge of God derived from nature, of which man is capable apart from revelation in Scriptures or in Jesus Christ."[10]

To this Karl Barth replied that although "Calvin spoke of a *Duplex cognitio Domini* from creation and in Christ," whenever he spoke about a natural knowledge of God through creation he only said "what is said about it in Romans 1:19 f., 2:14 f., Acts 14:15 f., 17:24 f. He did not regard it as a capacity which man has retained."[11] Calvin did not "search in reason, history and nature for another source of revelation beside Scripture, for one that would supplement Scripture. . . . His theology was as a matter of principle only interpretation of Scripture and not also anthropology and philosophy of history and nature."[12]

"The possibility of a real knowledge by natural man of the true God, derived from creation, is, according to Calvin, a possibility in principle, but not in fact, not a possibility to be realized by us. One might call it an objective possibility, created by God, but not a subjective possibility, open to man. Between what is possible in principle and what is possible in fact there inexorably lies the fall. Hence this possibility can only be discussed hypothetically: *si integer stetisset Adam* (*Inst.* I, 2, 1; 'if Adam had remained upright') . . . . . The possibility which, according to Calvin, man in fact has, is to know and worship the gods of his own heart."[13] Furthermore, "Calvin always used the idea of the possibility of a 'natural' knowledge of God (objectively based on the fact that God is revealed in all his works) in the sense of Romans 1:20, or rather in the sense of the whole passage, Romans 1:18–3:20. It serves to demonstrate the fact that man is without excuse. The fact that God is revealed in all his works is God's scriptural testimony to us against the ignorance of man. It points out that man's inability to know him is his guilt.[14]

Finally, the knowledge of God in Christ includes a real knowledge of the true God in creation. But this does not mean there is "a second, independent kind of knowledge, so that the circle would become an ellipsis after all—as if our reason, once it had been illumined, had of itself (*per se*) gained the power of sight. . . . Knowledge of God from creation came to Moses, not by free speculation, but strictly in view of the history of salvation." And what the Reformer had to say about God in nature and history was nothing but the proclamation of Christ and exegesis of Scripture.[15]

This, then, was the way in which the problem of natural law in Calvin was articulated by Brunner and Barth within the context of the knowledge of God, and in this form it has persisted down to the present day. The specialists in Calvin research joined in the battle. On the Continent Gunter Gloede sided with his teacher, Emil Brunner,[16] whereas Peter Brunner,[17] Peter Barth,[18] and later Wilhelm Niesel[19] marshalled evidence from Calvin's writings which substantially supported Barth's view. The controversy spread to English-speaking countries. T. F. Torrance in his book, *Calvin's Doctrine of Man* (London 1949), especially in the last two chapters on Natural Theology, definitely upheld Barth's interpretation of Calvin, although he made no reference to the Barth-Brunner debate or indeed to "works on Calvin, ancient or modern, so that this presentation might be free from the imputation of partisanship," as he informs us in the preface. Similarly Torrance's brother-in-law, Ronald S. Wallace in his two volumes, *Calvin's Doctrine of the Word and Sacrament* (Edinburgh 1953) and *Calvin's Doctrine of the Christian Life* (Grand Rapids 1959), appears to agree with Barth, though he too makes no mention of the contributions of Calvin scholars. However the controversy came out in the open with the publication of Edward A. Dowey's book, *The Knowledge of God in Calvin's Theology* (New York 1952), in which he defended Brunner's position against the strictures of Karl Barth, Peter Barth, Peter Brunner and Wilhelm Niesel. In the same year (1952) the first edition of T. H. L. Parker's work, *Calvin's Doctrine of the Knowledge of God,* appeared, in which he showed that Calvin's so-called concessions to natural theology are considerably less than is generally supposed and must be interpreted in the light of his Christology and theology of revelation. To the American revised edition of 1959 Parker appended a penetrating criticism of Dowey's book.[20]

It will not be the task of this paper to review the arguments, much less the evidence adduced from Calvin, of these two scholarly books. However, we would be less than candid if we concealed our conviction that according to Calvin there is no natural knowledge of God for the Church and no natural knowledge of His will through a natural law implanted in all men from creation. When it is borne in mind that for Calvin the Incarnation, life, death and resurrection of Jesus Christ is the one unique revelation of God to which the Scriptures of the Old and New Testaments bear witness, and that his theology was exclusively exegesis of Scripture, and when one considers in particular his exegesis of Psalm 19, Romans 1:19 ff., 2:14 ff., Acts 14:15 f., 17:24 f., in the *Institutes* and in his commentaries, it is impossible, we believe, to attribute to Calvin a second independent source of the knowledge of God and His will in history, nature and man himself. The heart of Calvin's teaching is this: "God is made known to us in no other way than in Christ . . . it hence follows that we are blind as to the light of God, until in Christ it beams upon us."[21] The revelation of God in Christ is so complete, so exclusive and so unique that "all theology, when separated from Christ, is not only vain and confused, but is also mad, deceitful and spurious; for, though the philosophers sometimes utter excellent sayings, yet they have nothing but what is short-lived, and even mixed up with wicked and erroneous sentiments."[22]

If, then, we are warranted in concluding that for Calvin the revelation God has given of himself in Christ is complete and exclusive, does this imply that in his thought the *lex naturae* only has the negative value of rendering man inexcusable?[23] Does this mean that for all intents and purposes the concept of natural law no longer can have any positive significance for Christian Theology? Have we come to an impasse, a sort of dead end, as far as a doctrine of natural law is concerned? Have we finally disposed of it, so that now it can no longer hold any interest for an evangelical theologian? It is notorious how a problem we thought we were rid of keeps cropping up in a new form or in a new context. The problem of natural law, at least in Calvin, will not die down. Calvin's writings, especially his commentaries on the Pentateuch and his sermons on the Book of Deuteronomy and the Book of Job, are so full of references to *ius naturae, lex naturae, ordo naturae, sensus naturae, communis sensus,* to conscience, reason and experience, that the subject cannot be brusquely dismissed. Moreover, however much one may disagree with the main thesis propounded by Edward Dowey, and before him by Josef Bohatec, one cannot ignore the mass of citations they have collected from Calvin that have no connection with the judging function of natural law. "The assumption of some contemporary theologians that natural law has no place in the company of Reformation theology," writes John T. McNeill, "cannot be allowed to govern historical inquiry or to lead us to ignore, minimize, or evacuate of reality, the positive utterances on natural law scattered through the works of the Reformers." He adds: "The bearing of natural law upon theology in these writings still calls for clarification."[24] Just such a clarification will be attempted in the remainder of this paper.

The Doctrine of Man: the Order of Nature

The Christological Basis of the Doctrine of Man: the Imago Dei

The knowledge of man is included in our knowledge of God. "It is evident that man never attains to a true self-knowledge until he has previously contemplated the face of God, and come down after such contemplation to look into himself."[25] "When we have seen God, then we begin to feel and know what we are."[26] "We cannot know God without knowing ourselves."[27] Moreover, man has his creaturely being and the knowledge of his being only in and by the Word of God. "We must maintain what is declared in the first chapter of John, that the life of all things was included in the Word, but especially the life of men. Wherefore by this sign (the tree of life), Adam was admonished, that he could claim nothing for himself as if it were his own, in order that he might depend wholly upon the Son of God and might not seek life anywhere but in him."[28] Consequently it would do violence to Calvin's thought to consider man's existence, or any natural law governing it, outside of Christ or the Word.

The basic concept Calvin employs to define the nature of man is the *imago Dei.* The image of God in which man was created remains even in fallen man. But since it is so corrupted and deformed by sin, it cannot be directly perceived in man. Therefore, "the true nature of the image of God is to be derived from what Scripture says of its renewal through Christ . . . [for] Christ is the most perfect image of God."[29] "Christ was even then the image of God. Hence, whatever excellence was engraved upon Adam, derived from the fact that he approached the glory of his Creator through the only begotten Son."[30] "Christ is not only the image of God, in so far as He is the eternal Word of God, but even on His human nature, which he has in common with us, the likeness of the glory of the Father has been engraven so as to form His members to the resemblance of it."[31] As T. F. Torrance has observed, "whether in man originally or in man renewed in Christ, the image of God is basically that which God sees and fashions in his grace."[32] The image of God consists in a vertical relation of man to God in Christ and a horizontal relation of man to man. "God sends His Word to us in order to be joined to us and that we might be united to Him."[33] But it is with the horizontal relationship of man to man that we are particularly concerned in this paper.

The Order of Nature: Humanity

Calvin employed the concept *ordo naturae* with reference to the order governing the physical universe.[34]

> "Experience clearly shows," Calvin says, "that the voice of God is heard even by dumb creatures and that the order of nature (*naturae ordo*) is nothing else than the obedience which is rendered to Him by every part of the world, so that everywhere His supreme authority shines forth, for at his bidding the elements observe the law laid down to them, and heaven and earth perform their duty. The earth yields her fruits; the sea flows not beyond her settled boundaries; the sun, moon and stars perform their courses; the heavens, too, revolve at stated periods; and all with wonderful accuracy, though they are destitute of reason and understanding.[35]

Calvin, however, does not apppear to have any interest in an independent physical order of the universe. Rather the universe exists for the sake of man, for the sake of the order of human nature. "The Lord himself by the very order of creation has demonstrated that he created all things for the sake of man."[36]

"The whole order of this world is arranged and established for the purpose of conducing to the comfort and happiness of man."[37] Moreover, the obedience which the physical and animal world render to the order of nature is an example of the obedience men should render to God,[38] and the order of nature mirrors and confirms "the spiritual grace of God."[39] Calvin therefore does not develop any particular cosmology or scientific view of the order of the universe. "Therefore we must not commence with the elements of the world, but with the Gospel which sets Christ alone before us with His cross and holds us to this one point."[40] "That means," as T. F. Torrance has rightly observed, "that there can be no naturalistic understanding of man. . . . The world is to be understood only in relation to man, and in relation to man who himself has been made for God! Man cannot be understood by his relation to the world."[41]

Consequently when Calvin uses the term *ordo naturae,* he usually has reference to the order or structure of *human* nature. Sometimes Calvin identifies the *lex naturae* with the objective order of man's being, and sometimes with man's subjective apprehension of the order of nature. As we shall have occasion to observe later, much of the misunderstanding of Calvin's thought about natural law is due to a failure to distinguish between natural law as the order of nature and natural law as man's knowledge of himself. For the sake of clarity we will therefore first deal with the order of human nature and then with natural law.

According to Calvin man is a "social animal." "The commencement (of human society), therefore, involves a general principle that man was formed to be a social animal."[42] "All men are our brethren, because they are related to us by a common nature. Whenever I see a man, I must of necessity, behold myself as in a mirror: for he is *my bone and my flesh.*"[43]Moreover, although this aspect of the image of God in man has been so horribly distorted as to become unrecognizable, yet the Christian has to regard all men as having been created in and as still possessing the image of God.

"Though the greater part of men break off, in most instances, from this holy society, yet their depravity does not violate the order of nature; for we ought to regard God as the author of the union."[44] "We are not to look at what men deserve in themselves, but to attend to the image of God which exists in all, and to which we owe honor and love."[45] "We cannot but behold, as in a mirror, our own face in those who are poor and despised, who have come to an end of their own burden, even though they are utter strangers to us. Even in dealing with a Moor or a Barbarian, from the very fact of his being a man, he carries about with him a looking-glass in which we can see that he is our brother and our neighbor."[46]

Marriage as the Pattern of the Order of Nature

The classic example of this horizontal aspect of the image of God, namely, that man is a "social animal," or what Karl Barth has called the Magna Charta of humanity, is marriage. It is especially conspicuous, Calvin writes, in that sacred bond "by which the husband and the wife are combined in one body and one soul."[47] "Adam was taught to recognize himself in his wife, as in a mirror; and Eve, in her turn to submit herself willingly to her husband."[48] Adam could not perceive such an image in any of the animals, for none was "adapted to Adam" or possessed "such affinity of nature, that Adam could choose for himself a companion for life."[49] Adam and Eve were created one flesh, for Adam "now saw himself who had before been imperfect, rendered complete in his wife,"[50] in order that they might "cultivate mutual society between themselves."[51] The woman is "a kind of counterpart, for she is said to be *opposite to* or *over against* the man, because she responds to him."[52] She is man's "helper," though "the obligation of both sexes is mutual."[53] The fact that the blessing of God in marriage is now "neither perceived nor flourishes" is because "the order of nature which God has appointed, has been inverted by us. . . . Still, marriage was not capable of being so far vitiated by the depravity of men, that the blessing which God has once sanctioned by his word could be utterly abolished and extinguished."[54] Yet it was God's purpose that marriage should illustrate what it means to be truly human to one another and to love one another.[55]

The Order of Nature Consists in Brotherly Love Between Man and Man

The order of human nature is not a mere co-existence of man with man. It is an order in which man exists positively *for* his fellow-man. It expresses itself in brotherly love. In the Parable of The Good Samaritan Jesus teaches, Calvin tells us, that "the word *neighbor* extends indiscriminately to every man, because the whole human race is united by a sacred bond of fellowship."[56]

As R. S. Wallace has pointed out: "The order of nature is that God has united all men together and has set them in this world so that each can help the other; unless we live in peace and concord one with another we prevent the order of nature. But no matter how wicked other men are, and no matter how little they deserve to be reckoned as our brothers and neighbors nevertheless nothing that they can do can alter this order that God has decreed and which we are bound to observe. The wicked man, or the man who hates us and harms us, must still be regarded by us as in the image of God."[57]

"The word, *neighbor,* includes all men living; for we are linked together by a common nature, as Isaiah reminds us, 'that thou hide not thyself from thine own flesh.' (Isaiah 58:7). The image of God ought to be particularly regarded as a bond of union; but, for that very reason, no distinction is here made between friend and foe, nor can the wickedness of men set aside the right of nature."[58] Therefore, self-love is the very opposite of love of the neighbor. It is the denial of the order of nature. "The two affections are opposite and contradictory; for the love of ourselves leads us to neglect and despise others."[59]

Love is served when justice and order are preserved in society. The man who loves will see to it that the rights of all men are maintained. Consequently he will affirm and defend the civil magistrate as the guardian of peace and equity. "Paul meant to refer the precept respecting the power of magistrates (in Romans 13:8) to the law of love . . . as though he had said, 'When I require you to obey princes I require nothing more than what . . . is demanded by the law of love. . . . He then who introduces anarchy, violates love.' "[60] "Perfect justice would undoubtedly prevail among us, if we were as faithful in learning *active* charity (if we may use the expression) as we are skilful in teaching passive charity."[61]

When Calvin speaks of the "common humanity [which] would teach us with what humility and justice we ought to conduct ourselves toward each other,"[62] he does not confuse it with Christian love which is the fruit of the Spirit and faith in the regenerate.[63] The latter is "the highest degree of brotherly love." "Brotherly love is, indeed, extended to strangers, for we are all of the same flesh, and we are all created after the image of God; but because the image of God shines more brightly in those who have been regenerated, it is proper that the bond of love, among the disciples of Christ, should be far more close. In God brotherly love seeks its cause, from him it has its roots, and to him it is directed."[64] "If to injure our fellow-man is to pervert the order of nature, to injure our fellow Christian is to 'tear Jesus Christ in pieces.' "[65] On the other hand, Christian love always includes humanitarianism. "As the goodness of God extends to the whole world, so we ought to love all, even those who hate us."[66] Christian love, being grounded in the revealed law of God, in Jesus Christ and the Holy Spirit, is the criterion and guarantor of humanism. (See subsequent section on The Law of God and the Order of Nature).

The Order of Nature Expresses Itself in a Mutual Communication and Subjection

An extraordinarily valuable chapter in R. S. Wallace's book, *Calvin's Doctrine of the Christian Life,* is entitled, "Mutual Communication and Subjection Within the Order of Nature." With a wealth of quotations from Calvin's sermons and commentaries he has shown how the order of nature prevails in all human relationships. We will be content with a brief digest of Wallace's presentation.

"Language was created for the purpose of mutual instruction and encouragement," with the consequence that "all abuse of speech or language is a perversion of the order of nature, and its abuse is likewise a corruption of the order of nature"; as for example, the exaction of unjust usury from the poor.[68] Goods and services have been ordained for mutual communication. No man is self-sufficient: it is the order of nature that each must give and each must receive. No matter how clever and resourceful an individual may be each needs the help and services of his neighbor. The rich succor the poor and they in turn need the services of the poor.[69] Each must share in the responsibilities of society according to his calling in the interest of the common good.[70] Each must share in the burden of toil, for work is in accord with the order of nature.[71]

All communication one with another in love involves subjection one to another. "God has bound us so closely to one another that no one ought to exempt himself from subjection and wherever love reigns there is mutual servitude."[72] There is a "universal bond of subjection (*universale subjectionis vinculum*) which no one should try to avoid."[73] "The subjection of the inferior to the superior in the relationship of ruler to people, master to servant, husband to wife, child to parent is part of an inviolable order established by God the Father. Unless such order is observed and those in authority maintain their proper position and those under authority submit to those over them, then human society cannot be maintained."[74] "Natural sense itself dictates to us that we should obey rulers. If servants obey not their masters, the society of the human race is subverted altogether."[75] "Natural reason itself shows and dictates that reverence . . . is due to all lawful commands."[76] "All who rebel against a legitimate authority are as enemies of God and of nature."[77] Calvin even counsels individuals—"I am speaking all the while of private individuals"—to obey tyrants, though he approved action by constituted authorities, such as the three estates in their assemblies, "to withstand, in accordance with their duty, the fierce licentiousness of kings" and to protect the liberties of the people.[78] Similarly "the perpetual law of nature is not subverted by the sins of men; and therefore, however unworthy of honor a father may be . . . inasmuch as he is a father, he still retains his right over his children."[79]

Sometimes subjection to superiors is "contrary to the whole order of nature" and is due to the fall of man. But on the whole Calvin finds the origin and basis of all offices involving superiority and subordination not in the Fall, but in the order of nature. Such order is necessary, not only to avoid confusion, but to enable men to express true humanity.[80] The purpose of the State to guarantee the preservation of society corresponds to a naturally given instinct in man for society which is not extinguished by sin. And this instinct is directed against the selfish instinct for self-preservation. Aristotle's contention that the State has its origin in a natural social instinct is, as far as it goes, not unlike Calvin's view. The difference is that Calvin knows (from faith in God's Word) that the natural order itself has been created by God and is upheld by His providence. "Men can effect nothing, unless in so far as God stretches forth his hand to them, or rather makes use of them as His instruments."[81] Wherefore he taught that the State has been ordained "by divine providence," and not by natural instinct alone or because of "human perversity."[82]

At the same time the authority of superiors to inferiors—of rulers to their subjects, husbands to wives, parents to children, employers to employees—is not to be tyrannical and arbitrary. For the subjection is mutual—the superior to the inferior and *vice versa.* "For, when authority is granted to the elders, there is not given them the right or liberty of throwing off the bridle, but they are also themselves to be under due restraint, so that there may be a mutual subjection."[83] Commenting on Colossians 4:1, "Masters, treat your slaves justly and fairly," Calvin suggests that Paul used the Greek word *isotēta* to mean analogical or distributive right.[84] In the Commentary on II Corinthians 8:13 (*Corpus Reformatorum* L, 101), he ascribes the term to Aristotle, and explains: "He certainly does not mean that they should be equal in condition and station, but by this term he expresses that humanity and clemency and kind treatment that masters, in their turn, owe to their servants."[85] "Where love reigns, mutual services will be rendered. I do not except even kings and governors, whose very authority is held for the *service* of the community."[86] Princes are to "remember that their revenues are not so much their private chests as the treasuries of the entire people . . . which cannot be squandered or despoiled without manifest injustice. . . . These are almost the very blood of the people which it would be the harshest inhumanity not to spare."[87] Although the male enjoys a preeminence over the female, "they ought to be connected together by mutual benevolence, for the one cannot do without the other. If they be separated they are like the mutilated members of a mangled body. Let them, therefore, be connected with each other by the bond of mutual duty."[88] "The man who does not love his wife is a monster."[89] Wherefore "he who divorces his wife, tears from him, as it were, the half of himself. But nature does not allow any man to tear in pieces his own body."[90] Parents are to exercise kindness, gentleness and forbearance toward their children,[91] and provision for one's family is "a kind of duty which nature itself teaches; for they are (*storgai physikai*) natural affections. . . . The right of nature (*ius naturae*) is not altogether extinguished, so as to destroy the obligation of the older to govern the younger as committed to them by God, or at least to take care of them as far as they can."[92]

However, there are limitations to our duty to submit to authorities. Obedience to man must not become disobedience to God.[93] "Parents govern their children only under the supreme authority of God." The injunction to obey parents 'in the Lord' means that "if a father enjoins anything unrighteous, obedience is freely to be denied him."[94] Secondly, the distinctions between superiors and inferiors are political and civil, but "the government of the church admits nothing of this sort; for Christ allowed the pastors nothing more than to be ministers, and to abstain entirely from the exercise of authority."[95] Thirdly, all such civil distinctions are temporary and will be abolished in the coming Kingdom of God.[96]

The Order of Nature and Natural Rights

Josef Bohatec states that according to Calvin natural right (*ius naturae*) is derived from natural law, that is, the right required by the *lex naturae*.[97] This is correct in so far as Calvin sometimes identifies natural law with the objective order of nature. (See below, p. 173.) But from the contexts in which Calvin uses the terms it is clear that he sees natural rights grounded in the order of man's creaturely being. For instance, the right of honor (*ius honoris*) is said to be conferred to the eldest son by nature.[98] "What is natural cannot be abrogated by any consent or custom . . . since it flows from the fountain of nature itself, and is founded on the general principle of all laws, which is perpetual and inviolable."[99] And just because they are grounded in the order of nature, the *iura naturae* are said to be "indissoluble."[100] Natural rights include the right to life, liberty, and property. Life is an immutable good and whoever robs man of life robs him of what is sacred. Property rights are a natural right, for nature teaches us to regard possessions as if they were holy. Therefore landmarks should remain untouched.[101] Liberty is a great boon.[102] It is more than half of life, and to deprive a man of such a blessing is almost to destroy him.[103]

Natural Right and the Political Order

We have already seen that in Calvin's view the State has its roots in the order of nature. What concerns us here is the ordination of the State to safeguard natural rights and with them equity and humanity. The chief task of the State is to maintain peace that godliness and decency may be promoted.[104] This is done when the individual's right to freedom is protected by laws that are "stable" and "without variation."[105] Through the protection of just laws and rulers the subjective rights of individuals are raised to public rights. Thus freedom is the purpose of the use of force and the compulsion of laws serves freedom and preserves peace.[106] Conversely when the individual seeks to defend his own rights in the law-courts he defends the rights of the whole, the *"bonum publicum."*[107]

As a pre-condition for the preservation of society and human rights, Calvin insists upon the preservation of *order* by the State.[108] "This constrained and forced righteousness is necessary for the public community of men, for whose tranquillity the Lord herein provided when he took care that everything be not tumultuously confounded."[109] Consequently, in order to maintain order wars are judged 'lawful' (*legitima*). "Natural equity and the nature of the office dictate that princes must be armed not only to restrain the misdeeds of private individuals by judicial punishment, but also to defend by war the dominions entrusted to their safekeeping, if at any time they are under enemy attack."[110] "Although lawful war ought to be nothing else than an attempt to obtain peace, yet sometimes an engagement is unavoidable. . . . War, therefore, is not in itself to be condemned; for it is the means of preserving the commonwealth."[111] But war waged from greed or pride is a crime.[112] However, if rulers are forced to wage war, "let them not be carried away with headlong anger, or be seized with hatred, or burn with implacable severity. Let them also (as Augustine says) have pity on the common nature in the one whose special fault they are punishing. . . . Let them not (wage war) unless they are driven to it by extreme necessity. . . . Everything else ought to be tried before recourse is had to arms. Lastly . . . let (rulers) . . . be led by concern for the people alone."[113]

While the State has been ordained by God and armed with the sword for the purpose of protecting natural rights, the rights to life, liberty and property are not absolute. For the State may intervene in the sphere of individual rights in the interest of the welfare of the State. The State invades the personal right to property by taxation; the right to life by the requirement of military service.[114] However, the power of the State may not be exercised tyrannically; it is limited by justice and law. Thus citizens and the State are complementary in the interest of an order of justice binding upon both. The rights of the individual are not above the right of the State; the State does not absolutely decree concerning the rights of individuals. Calvin's well-known preference for an "aristocracy or a system compounded of aristocracy and democracy"[115] was due to his conviction that in this form of governing freedom would be best preserved.[116] True order prevails only where liberty is guaranteed. "The magistrates ought to apply themselves with the highest diligence to prevent the freedom (whose guardians they have been appointed) from being in any respect diminished, far less be violated."[117] For "nothing is more desirable than liberty."[118]

The Doctrine of Man: Man as Soul and Body

The Faculties of Reason and Will

We have seen, then, that man has been created in the image of God which consists in a vertical relation to God in Christ and in a horizontal relation of man to man. This is the good created order of human nature which persists in spite of sin and the Fall. Yet there is another sense in which man has been created in the image of God—his being constituted a soul and a body.

The soul is not the image but it is "the proper seat of God's image."[119] "Although the soul is not man, yet it is not absurd for man, in respect to his soul, to be called God's image. . . . The likeness of God extends to the whole excellence by which man's nature towers over all the kinds of living creatures."[120] "The human soul consists of two faculties, understanding and will. Let the office, moreover, of understanding be to distinguish between objects, as each seems worthy of approval or disapproval; while that of the will, to choose and follow what the understanding pronounces good, but to reject and flee what it disapproves."[121]

By means of these faculties man was created to know and serve God and also to know himself—the order of his nature—in relation to his fellow-man through the Word.[122] In this knowledge man is formed into the image of God and resembles God.[123] "The glory of God . . . peculiarly shines forth in human nature, where the mind, the will, and all the senses, represent the divine order."[124]

After Calvin has set forth in the *Institutes* the doctrine of original sin and its consequences, he returns to the question of the faculties of the soul to examine what they can now accomplish. (II, 2, 2). He concludes that "since reason, therefore, by which man distinguishes between good and evil, and by which he understands and judges, is a natural gift, it could not be completely wiped out, but it was partly weakened and partly corrupted. . . . Similarly the will, because it is inseparable from man's nature, did not perish, but was so bound to wicked desires that it cannot strive after the right."[125]

"When we so condemn human understanding for its perpetual blindness as to leave it no perception of any object whatever, we not only go against God's Word, but also run counter to the experience of common sense. For we see implanted in human nature some sort of desire to search out the truth to which man would not at all aspire if he had not already savored it. Human understanding then possesses some power of perception, since it is by nature captivated by love of truth. The lack of this endowment in brute animals proves their nature gross and irrational."[126]

Calvin proceeds to discuss the power of the understanding with respect to earthly things and to heavenly or spiritual things. In the former he includes "government, household management, all mechanical skills, and the liberal arts"; in the latter he includes the knowledge of God and His kingdom, of his fatherly favor in which our salvation consists, and of His will and law by which we are to frame our lives. He teaches that understanding with respect to arts and sciences is "inborn in human nature . . . [There is] a universal apprehension of reason and understanding by nature implanted in men."[127] "This prompted Plato to teach wrongly that such apprehension is nothing but recollection" whereas "every man ought to recognize in it the peculiar grace of God."[128] However, in regard to spiritual things "the greatest geniuses are blinder than moles."[129] "Human reason neither approaches, nor strives toward, nor even takes a straight aim at, this truth: to understand who the true God is or what sort of God he wishes to be toward us."[130]

Conscience as a Function of Reason: the Emergence of Natural Law

Here in connection with the faculty of understanding we observe Calvin's use of "conscience" and related terms. Conscience is the function of reason to make ethical judgments, to distinguish between just and unjust, man's "innate power to judge between good and evil" and which condemns man.[131] Strictly speaking, conscience is not the order of man's nature; rather it is the conscious awareness of that order, the testimony to and expression of that order. Similarly the *sensus naturae* and *communis sensus* dictate and teach what is according to man's social and moral being.[132] However, the innate sense of justice, natural feeling, is not confused with the natural or rather animal instincts of procreation, self-preservation, hunger, etc. Because these are purely instinctive and peculiar to animals who have no judgment or reason, they are to be sharply distinguished from moral sense. Calvin admits, of course, that animals with their instincts often put men to shame.[133] But the sense of justice belongs to man, the social animal, because beasts have no understanding for the ordering of society by law.[134] Moreover, conscience has its source, not in cosmic nature, the *natura rerum,* but in human nature.[135]

According to Calvin, conscience differs from the understanding in that it judges and convicts man.

> "For just as when through the mind and understanding men grasp a knowledge of things, and from this are said 'to know,' this is the source of the word 'knowledge,' so also when they have a sense of divine judgment as a witness joined to them, which does not allow them to hide their sins from being accused before the Judge's tribunal, this sense is called 'conscience.' "[136] "By the conscience of good deeds men support and comfort themselves; they who, in their conscience, know they have done evil, are tormented and troubled in themselves."[137] Conscience is "a certain knowledge of the law,"[138] that is, "certain conceptions of justice and uprightness naturally grafted in the minds of all men."[139] It is an "inward law engraved upon the hearts of all,"[140] that is, in the reason.

Here, then, we find the meaning of natural law in Calvin. It is true, as we have seen, that at times Calvin appears to identify natural law with the objective order of man's nature, and can say that nature or the order of nature, dictates and teaches. But usually he defines natural law as "that apprehension of the conscience which distinguishes sufficiently between just and unjust, and which deprives men of the excuse of ignorance while it proves them guilty by their own testimony."[141]

The Order of Nature Constant; Natural Law Variable

It is most necessary to observe the distinction Calvin makes between the order of nature and natural law. The order of nature —man's being with and for his fellow-man—is a constant that remains in spite of sin and the Fall. By contrast, natural law is man's variable and fallible apprehension of the order of his being. It is true that man can behave in an unsocial, antisocial and therefore inhuman way. Yet he does not cease to be a man. When he behaves inhumanly, he sins against his own good created order. He violates the order of his being. He acts "contrary to nature." Nevertheless, "since man is by nature a social animal, he tends through natural instinct (*naturae quoque instinctu*) to foster and preserve society."[142] Moreover, the faculties of reason and will are also constants of man's created nature. In spite of the Fall man remains a "rational animal." However, reason and will are not the order of human nature; they are the natural faculties by which man knows himself in relation to his fellow-man and acts as a "social animal." (Indeed, it is doubtful whether Calvin views man's reason and will apart from the I-Thou relationship in which he was created!). Moreover, although reason and will remain in fallen man, man's knowledge of himself, the apprehension of the order of his being which is natural law, is *not* constant. Sometimes it is in agreement with the order of nature and with the revealed law of God; at other times it fails and the natural law is shown to be "imperfect," "obscure" and "fallible." Failure to observe the distinction between the order of nature which is constant and natural law which is variable is the cause of widespread misunderstanding of Calvin's thought.

The Fallibility of Reason, Conscience and Natural Law an Effect of Original Sin

Calvin defines original sin as "the depravation of a nature previously good and pure"[143] and as "a hereditary depravity and corruption in our nature diffused in all parts of the soul, which first makes us liable to God's wrath, then also brings forth in us those works which Scripture calls 'works of the flesh' . . . or sins."[144] This depravity affects the whole man: all parts of the soul, not just a lower appetite but the reason and the heart.[145] However, Calvin is careful to point out that the depravity of man's nature is not be to attributed to God[146] or to created nature.

"Man is corrupted through natural vitiation, but a vitiation that did not flow from nature. We deny that it has flowed from nature in order to indicate that it is an adventitious quality which comes upon man rather than a substantial property which has been implanted from the beginning. Yet we call it 'natural' in order that no man may think that anyone obtains it through bad conduct since it holds all men fast by hereditary right."[147]

We have already seen above that according to Calvin reason has been "partly weakened and partly corrupted" through original sin, though it has not been "completely wiped out." Here we are concerned with the effect of sin upon conscience and natural law. Calvin admits that with respect to "knowing the rule for the right conduct of life . . . the human mind sometimes seems more acute. . . . If the Gentiles by nature have law righteousness engraved upon their minds, we surely cannot say that they are utterly blind as to the conduct of life."[148] "There exist in all men's minds universal impressions of a certain civic fair dealing and order. Hence no man is to be found who does not understand that every sort of human organization must be regulated by laws, and who does not comprehend the principles of those laws. Hence arises that unvarying consent of all nations and of individual mortals with regard to laws. For their seeds have, without teacher or lawgiver, been implanted in all men."[149] Moreover, this "original conception of equity" is not nullified by the fact that some men "fight against manifest reason" and "desire to overturn all law and right." "The fact remains that some seed of political order has been implanted in all men. And this is ample proof that in the arrangement of his life no man is without the light of reason."[150]

"But man is so shrouded in the darkness of errors that he hardly begins to grasp through this natural law what worship is acceptable to God. Surely he is very far removed from a true estimate of it. Besides this, he is so puffed up with haughtiness and ambition, and so blinded by self-love, that he is as yet unable to look upon himself and, as it were, to descend within himself, that he may humble and abase himself and confess his own miserable condition."[151]

The fallibility and insufficiency of natural law are exposed on the following grounds:

(a) The universal judgment discriminating between good and evil is not "sound and whole in every respect." The truth is not "discerned in individual instances."[152]

(b) "The intellect is very rarely deceived in general definition or in the essence of the thing; but it is illusory when it . . . applies the principle to particular cases."[153] Conscience calls evil what God's commandment calls evil, e.g. murder and adultery. But when ethical thought advances from the general rule to a particular case, man "forgets the general principle he has just laid down. . . . The adulterer will condemn adultery in general, but will privately flatter himself in his own adultery."

(c) Although in some cases the natural law does concur with the commandments of the Second Table, "it does not at all comply with the principal points of the First Table; such as putting our faith in God, giving due praise for his excellence and righteousness, calling upon his name and truly keeping the

Sabbath. What soul, relying upon natural perception, ever had an inkling that the lawful worship of God consists in these and like matters?"[154]

Moreover, "the first foundation of righteousness is the worship of God. When this is overthrown, all the remaining parts of righteousness, like the pieces of a shattered and fallen building, are mangled and scattered. . . . Not only is religion the chief part but the very soul, whereby the whole breathes and thrives. And apart from the fear of God men do not preserve equity and love among themselves. Therefore we call worship the beginning and foundation of righteousness. When it is removed whatever equity, continence or temperance men practice among themselves is in God's sight empty and worthless."[155] The virtues which deceive us by an empty show may have their praise in civil society and the common intercourse of life, but before the judgment-seat of God they will have no value to establish a claim to righteousness.[156]

(d) "Men have somewhat more understanding of the precepts of the Second Table because they are more closely concerned with the preservation of civil society among them. Yet even here one sometimes finds a failure to endure. A man . . . finds it utterly senseless to bear an unjust and excessively imperious domination, if only he can in some way throw it off. And this is the common judgment of human reason: the work of a servile and abject person is to bear it with patience; that of an honorable and free born man to shake it off. Nor do the philosophers consider the avenging of injuries to be a vice. But the Lord condemns this excessive haughtiness and enjoins upon his people a patience disgraceful in men's eyes. . . . Moreover the natural man refuses to be led to recognize the diseases of his lust."[157]

When reason, conscience and natural law conform to the order of nature and the revealed law of God, it is to be attributed to the special, preserving grace of God

Josef Bohatec, at the outset of his discussion of the extent of the effect of sin and the Fall, states that "nature is not completely corrupted by the Fall,"[158] since reason has not been wholly destroyed. This, however, is not a correct interpretation of Calvin's thought. In the very chapter of the *Institutes* to which Bohatec refers (II, 3), Calvin lays down the thesis from which he never deviates, namely, that "only damnable things come forth from man's corrupt nature," and that the "corruption of man's nature is such as to require total renewal of his mind and will."

Having laid down this categorical definition of man's total corruption, Calvin then introduces certain qualifications, which do not however invalidate his fundamental position. First, he grants that "not all these wicked traits appear in every man, yet . . . this hydra lurks in the breast of each."[159] Second: "In every age there have been persons who, guided by nature, have striven toward virtue throughout life. . . . They have by the very zeal of their honesty given proof that there was some purity in their nature." Calvin declares that he is not now discussing the question what merit these virtues have in God's sight. Rather that "these examples seem to warn against adjudging man's nature wholly corrupted." "But here it ought to occur to us that amid this corruption of nature there is some place for God's grace; not such grace as to cleanse it, but to restrain it inwardly." Thus Calvin makes a distinction between the grace of regeneration and the grace of preservation. God restrains unbelievers in order to preserve all that is. Thirdly, the restraint God imposes upon men does not remove the universal and total corruption because men are restrained by motives which are impure in themselves. "Some are restrained by shame . . . others by fear of the law . . . others because they consider an honest manner of life profitable . . . others by their excellence to keep the rest obedient to them. Thus God by his providence bridles perversity of nature, that it may not break forth into action; but he does not purge it within."[160] Fourthly, virtues in some men "are not common gifts of nature, but special graces of God, which he bestows variously and in a certain measure upon men otherwise wicked."[161] For example, in providing for the human race God "often endows with a heroic nature those destined to command," such as kings. This is the source of the qualities of great leaders celebrated in histories. But such virtues are defiled (a) by personal ambition and (b) because they are bereft of any "zeal to glorify God, the chief part of uprightness. As for the virtues that deceive us with their vain show, they shall have their praise in the political assembly and in common renown before men; but before the heavenly judgment-seat, they shall be of no value to acquire righteousness."[162] "Man cannot ascribe to himself even one single good work apart from God's grace."[163] Fifthly, man's natural endowments in the area of reason are special gifts of God's Spirit "which he distributes to whomever he wills for the common good of mankind."[164]

"If we regard the Spirit of God as the sole fountain of truth, we shall neither reject the truth itself, nor despise it wherever it shall appear, unless we wish to dishonor the Spirit of God. . . . What then? Shall we deny that the truth shone upon the ancient jurists who established civic order and discipline with such great equity? Shall we say that the philosophers were blind in their fine observation and artful description of nature? Shall we say that those men were devoid of understanding who conceived the art of disputation and taught us to speak reasonably? Shall we say that they are insane who developed medicine, devoting their labor to our benefit? What shall we say of all the mathematical sciences? Shall we consider them the ravings of madmen? No, we cannot read the writings of the ancients on these subjects without great admiration. We marvel at them because we are compelled to recognize how preeminent they are. But shall we count anything praiseworthy or noble without recognizing at the same time that it comes from God?"[165]

Farmers, cowherds or cobblers are not singled out with the title of "gods," because they have been called and approved of God to a particular way of living, but only those whom God has raised to a higher position and given authority.[166] Magistrates and kings are called "gods" because "they have a mandate from God, have been invested with divine authority, and are wholly God's representatives, in a manner, acting as his vicegerents."[167] They are granted exceptional privileges and stamped with a special mark.[168]

From the special elective character of rulers, by which they acquire the title "sons of God," Calvin lists kings along with prophets and teachers. They too acquire a sign of this election and of the gifts and blessings lent to them. Rulers also enjoy a special effect of the Spirit by which they possess a "heroic" or "princely virtue."[169] But when philosophers discourse with consummate skill upon political affairs, they omit "the principal point, which is that men, however much they may excel in wisdom and virtue . . . can effect nothing, except in so far as God stretches forth his hand to them, or rather makes use of them as his instruments."[170]

In Calvin's thought, therefore, a natural law operating through reason and conscience is not a constant, static law but a law that operates existentially and effectively when and where God bestows special gifts or graces of His Spirit whereby men know and act in accordance with the order of human nature under the restraint of God's preserving grace.

"To sum up: We see among all mankind that reason is proper to our nature; it distinguishes us from brute beasts, just as they by possessing feeling differ from inanimate things. Now, because some are born fools or stupid, that defect does not obscure the general grace of God. Rather, we are warned by that spectacle that we ought to ascribe what is left in us to God's kindness. For if he had not spared us, our fall would have entailed the destruction of our whole nature. Some men excel in keenness; others are superior in judgment; still others have a readier wit to learn this or that art. In this variety God commends his grace to us, lest anyone should claim as his own what flowed from the sheer bounty of God. For why is one person more excellent than another? Is it not to display in common nature God's special grace, which, in passing many by, declares itself bound to none? Besides this, God inspires special activities, in accordance with each man's calling."[171]

The Law of God and the Order of Nature

Only incidental reference has thus far been made to the law of God; attention has been concentrated on the doctrine of man. We have seen that man has been created in the image of God in and by the Word of God which is Jesus Christ. He exists in a vertical relation to God and in a horizontal relation to man. This is the order of human nature. It is a constant of man's creatureliness which persists in spite of sin and the Fall. The aspect of the order of nature with which we have been chiefly concerned in this paper is man's humanity: his existence with and for his fellow-man. Man's being is an I-Thou relationship; it is co-humanity. It is a free, loving relationship which expresses itself in mutual communication and subjection in all human relationships and in all forms of human society. It is the basis of natural rights and of the political order which God has ordained for the protection of those rights. Moreover, man has been created soul and body endowed by the Spirit with the faculties of reason, conscience and will by which man has a consciousness of the order of his own nature. The natural law is man's apprehension of the order of human nature, and by this law man judges and convicts himself. However, due to the effects of original sin, reason, conscience and natural law are fallible and insufficient. When and where they are sound and conform to the order of nature, it is due to the special, preserving grace of God and His Spirit.

In our discussion of the order of human nature, humanity, we have not forgotten that it always exists at the same time in a vertical relationship to God. Nor in our consideration of the natural order have we turned aside from Jesus Christ and Holy Scripture to some supposedly possible second and different source of the knowledge of man. The order of nature is created, established, and revealed in Jesus Christ. Nature is to be seen *within* grace; never outside or independent of grace.

The Eternal Law of God the Creator and the Temporal Order of the Creature

The law of God is addressed to man in his creatureliness. It encounters man in the natural order of his being. It meets man in his being with and for his fellow-man and, as body and soul, endowed with reason and will. God's law is addressed to His creature who is at once a social and rational animal. Wherefore God's law is to be sharply distinguished from the order of nature and from any immanent law of man's constitution, not to speak of any natural law. God's law is eternal and unchangeable. In the broadest sense it is the divine word or commandment by which He created and upholds the order of nature. "The law of God is . . . everlasting righteousness and truth. . . . All other rules of life, with whatever attractions they may appear to be recommended, are but a shadow, which quickly vanishes away."[172] "The whole order of nature depends solely upon the commandment or decree of God."[173]

Calvin often appears to teach in infralapsarian fashion that God's law was given as a consequence of man's creation and Fall,[174] and that "if Adam had stood upright . . . the very order of nature would have led us . . . to the primal and simple knowledge."[175] It is true that since the Fall, God's law does have the effect of giving us "a clearer witness of what was too obscure in the natural law" because of our "dullness" and "arrogance." But this does not mean that God's law was not prior to creation and given to man at his creation before the Fall. Commenting on the command God gave to Adam not to eat of the fruit of the tree of the knowledge of good and evil, Calvin writes:

"It seems, however, to some as if this did not accord with the judgment of Paul, when he teaches, that 'the law was not made for the righteous,' " (I Tim. 1:9). For if it be so, when Adam was yet innocent and upright, he had no need of a law. . . . But Paul does not deny that God, from the beginning, imposed a law upon man, for the purpose of maintaining the right due to himself. Should anyone bring, as an objection, another statement of Paul, where he asserts that the 'law is a minister of death,' (II Cor. 3:7), I answer, it is so accidentally, and from the corruption of our nature. But at the time of which we speak, a precept was given to man, whence he might know that God ruled over him."[176]

The Correspondence Between the Law of God and the Order of Nature

Although God's law is to be sharply distinguished from the created order of human nature, there is nevertheless a correspondence between them. God's law does not meet man in a vacuum or in a sort of neutral, independent sphere, but in man's creaturely being. The divine law is the 'vertical' which intersects the 'horizontal,' the order of nature. But this 'horizontal' is not alien to God; it is already his property. When the law entered our time and world, it came into its own.[177] As we have seen, the 'horizontal' has been created in the image of God and, in spite of its perversion through sin, is still constant. This explains why Calvin consistently teaches that there is a correspondence between the law of God and the order of nature, and even between the law of God and natural law, when the latter through the special preserving grace of God agrees with the former. This correspondence applies especially to the Second Table of the Decalogue. "There is a conformity between the Law of God and the order of nature which is engraven in all men."[178] "The law of nature, which is acknowledged by all nations . . . is enforced by the law of God."[179] In fact, Calvin can go the length of saying: "The law of God which we call the moral law is nothing else than a testimony of natural law and of that conscience which God has engraven upon the minds of men."[180]

However in view of what has already been said concerning the fallibility of conscience and natural law and the need for God's special, preserving grace, it is evident that Calvin did not mean that we could dispense with God's law and substitute a natural law. His point is that God's law is in harmony with the true order of man's creatureliness *which is itself known from God's law.*

The Superiority of the Law of God to Natural Law

The law of God clarifies and enforces natural law. "The Lord has provided us with a written law to give us a clearer witness of what was too obscure in the natural law."[181] "What God has naturally inscribed upon every heart. He would have written down, that its observance amongst the Israelites might be more sacred."[182]

The law of God, unlike natural law, includes the First Table of the Decalogue. This means not only that we are to love God as well as our neighbor but that without love of God and faith in Him there can be no true love of the neighbor.

Natural law does "not look to the goal that God's wisdom prescribes," namely, "to serve God," so that "even though men are God's instruments for the preservation of human society in righteousness, continence, friendship, temperance, fortitude, and prudence . . . by the very impurity of men's hearts these good works have been corrupted from their source. . . . For they are restrained from evil-doing not by genuine zeal for good but either by mere ambition or by self-love, or some other perverse motive."[183] "You will fruitlessly inculcate all those duties taught in this (Second) Table, unless your teaching has fear and reverence toward God as its foundation."[184] "Our soul should be entirely filled with the love of God. From this will flow the love of neighbor. . . . It would therefore be a mistake for anyone to believe that the law teaches nothing but some rudiments and preliminaries of righteousness . . . and does not also guide them to the true goal."[185]

"Does the essence of righteousness lie more in living innocently with men than in honoring God with piety?" Calvin asks. "Not at all! But because a man does not easily maintain love in all respects unless he earnestly fears God, here is proof also of his piety. . . . It is certain that the Law and the Prophets give first place to faith and whatever pertains to the lawful worship of God, relegating love to a subordinate position. But the Lord means that the law only enjoins us to observe right and equity toward men, that thereby we may become practised in witnessing to a pious fear of him."[186]

The law of God, in contrast to natural law, is a law of grace. Without going into a lengthy proof that Calvin taught that God's law includes in it the grace of Christ and is therefore a gracious, liberating, redemptive law, it will be sufficient for us to quote from his commentary on Psalm 19—one of the so-called "nature" Psalms—in which he specifically contrasts the law of God with "some knowledge of justice and uprightness . . . that God has put in the minds of men."

"But here a question of no small difficulty arises: for Paul seems entirely to overthrow these commendations of the law which David here recites. How can these things agree together: that the law restores the souls of men, while yet it is a dead and deadly letter? that it rejoices men's hearts, and yet, by bringing in the spirit of bondage, strikes them with terror? that it enlightens the eyes, and yet, by casting a veil before our minds, excludes the light which ought to penetrate within? But, in the first place, we must remember what I have shown you at the commencement, that David does not speak simply of the precepts of the Moral Law, but comprehends the whole covenant by which God had adopted the descendants of Abraham to be his peculiar people; and, therefore, to the Moral Law—the rule of living well—he joins the free promises of salvation, or rather Christ himself, in whom and upon whom this adoption was founded. But Paul, who had to deal with persons who perverted and abused the law, and separated it from the grace and the Spirit of Christ, refers to the ministry of Moses viewed merely by itself, and according to the letter. It is certain, that if the Spirit of Christ does not quicken the law, the law is not only unprofitable, but also deadly to its disciples. Without Christ there is in the law nothing but inexorable rigour, which adjudges all mankind to the wrath and curse of God. And farther, without Christ, there remains within us a rebelliousness of the flesh, which kindles in our hearts a hatred of God and of his law, and from this proceed the distressing bondage and awful terror of which the Apostle speaks."[187]

The law of God is the criterion of humanity and natural law. The sailors who shrank with horror from killing Jonah "had never known the doctrine of the law. Yet they were so taught by nature that they knew that the blood of men is dear and precious in the sight of God. And as to us, we ought not only to imitate these sailors, but to go far beyond them: for not only ought the law of nature to prevail among us, but also the law of God; for we hear what God had formerly pronounced with his own mouth, 'Whosoever sheddeth men's blood, shed shall his blood be.' (Gen. 9:6). And we know also why God undertakes to protect the life of men, and that is, because they have been created in his image. Whosoever then uses violence against the life of man, destroys, as far as he can, the image of the eternal God. Since it is so, ought not violence and cruelty to be regarded by us with double horror?"[188]

The Law of God is not Bound to the Order of Nature or Natural Law

The very chapter in the Book of Jonah which according to Calvin teaches that the law of God is the criterion of humanity illustrates the truth that God's law is not bound to the order of nature. It can sometimes require what is contrary to nature, as, for example, the command to cast Jonah into the sea, a command to which the sailors acceded with the greatest reluctance. "Do they here accuse God of tyranny, as though he confounded all things without any cause or reason?" asks Calvin. "By no means. They took this principle as granted,—that the will of God is right and just, yea whatever God has decreed is beyond doubt just."[189] Here, and also in his commentary on Abraham's sacrifice of Isaac, Calvin envisages what Kierkegaard later called a "teleological suspension of the ethical," that is, of natural law based on the order of nature. Nevertheless, whenever the law of God "inverts the order of nature," or contravenes it, it is not therefore capricious and meaningless. It is to be understood in the light of the history of the covenant of grace and of the expiation of sin through sacrifice, for which the order of nature was created, and in order that fallen human nature might be restored to the true order of nature. The inversion of nature is particularly manifest in God's work of election and calling.[190] It is "to teach us that the Church was produced and increased by divine power and grace, and not merely by natural means."[191] Joseph "errs in binding the grace of God to the accustomed order of nature: as if the Lord did not often purposely change the law of nature, to teach us that what he freely confers upon us, is entirely the result of his own will."[192] However, since the purpose of the inversion of the natural order is to attest to the restoration of fallen human nature, we may conclude that in the last analysis the correspondence between the law of God and the order of nature already described remains.

The Law of God, Natural Law and Positive Law

Because the law of God is the ground and revelation of the order of nature, because of its evident superiority to natural law, and because it is the criterion of natural law granted to believers, it follows that the law of God "is the true and eternal rule of righteousness, prescribed for men of all nations and times."[193] It is therefore the criterion not only of natural law but also of all positive, civil laws. This does not mean, however, that civil laws have to be framed in accordance with the political laws of Moses or that they may not vary in different lands and at different times. It means that "these must be in conformity to that perpetual rule of love" which is the principle of the Mosaic law.[194] Calvin never tires of inculcating the view that believers to whom God's law has been given are to frame their lives to it as the only rule of faith and life.

On the other hand, Calvin recognizes that the nations and their rulers devise laws in accordance with the "testimony of natural law and of that conscience which God has engraved upon the minds of men."[195] The equity revealed in God's law is prescribed in the natural law. "Hence, this equity alone must be the goal and the rule and limit of all laws."[196] The civil community lives from natural law in virtue of the special preserving grace of God. Yet Christians who live by faith in

God's revealed law are not to despise civil laws because they have been devised by unbelievers by means of natural reason and natural law. On the contrary, "whatever laws shall be framed to that rule [of equity] . . . there is no reason why we should disapprove of them."[197] Much rather we should attribute them to the kindness of God. "For if he had not spared us, our fall would have entailed the destruction of our whole nature."[198]

NOTES

[1] A paper delivered at the meeting of the American Society of Christian Ethics in Louisville, Ky., January 26–27, 1962.

[2] Josef Bohatec, *Calvin und das Recht,* 1934, p. 2 f.

[3] The English translation of these two pamphlets was published under the title, *Natural Theology,* London, Geoffrey Bles: The Centenary Press, 1946. Quotations have been taken from this English translation.

[4] *Ibid.* p. 37.

[5] *Ibid.*

[6] *Ibid.* p. 38.

[7] *Ibid.*

[8] *Ibid.* p. 39.

[9] *Ibid.*

[10] *Ibid.* p. 42 f.

[11] *Ibid.* p. 105.

[12] *Ibid.* p. 106.

[13] *Ibid.* p. 106 f.

[14] *Ibid.* p. 108.

[15] *Ibid.* p. 109.

[16] Gunter Gloede, *Theologia Naturalis bei Calvin.* Stuttgart, 1935.

[17] Peter Brunner, *Allgemeine und besondere Offenbarung in Calvins Institutio* in *Evangelische Theologie,* August 1934.

[18] Peter Barth, *"Das Problem der natürlichen Theologie bei Calvin," Theologische Existenz Heute,* No. 18, 1935.

[19] Wilhelm Niesel, *Die Theologie Calvins.* Munich 1938. E.T. *The Theology of Calvin.* Westminster Press, Philadelphia 1956.

[20] Cf. also my own article, "A Preliminary Aspect of Calvin's Epistemology," *University of Toronto Quarterly,* Vol. XIII, No. 4, July 1944.

[21] Comm. on Heb. 1:3, C.R. 55, 12. All quotations are taken from the *Ioannis Calvini Opera* in the *Corpus Reformatorum* (edited by G. Baum, E. Cunitz and E. Reuss, Brunswick, 1863–1900). Most of the translations from the commentaries have been taken from the *Calvin Translation Society* (Edinburgh, 1843–55); those from the *Institutes* from The Library of Christian Classics edition, Westminster Press, Philadelphia 1960.

[22] Comm. on Jn. 14:6, C.R. 47, 324. For a fuller discussion of the

sufficiency and uniqueness of the revelation in Christ, see R. S. Wallace, *Calvin's Doctrine of the Word and Sacrament,* pp. 61–70.

[23] *Inst.* II, 2, 22, C.R. 2, 203; II, 8, 1, C.R. 2, 267; Comm. on Rom. 2:15, C.R. 49, 38; *Inst.* II, 2, 24, C.R. 2, 186 f.

[24] John T. McNeill, *Natural Law in the Teaching of the Reformers,* in *Journal of Religion,* Vol. 26, 1946, p. 168. McNeill makes no reference to the debate about a natural knowledge of the divine will, and no attempt to relate natural law to theology except to state that "for Calvin it is of secondary interest in relation to his main doctrines . . . only because the realm of mundane affairs is, for him, subordinate to the realm of the supernatural. Within the mundane society, natural law is not secondary but controlling—and this because it is not earthly but divine in origin, engraved by God on all men's hearts" (p. 182).

[25] *Inst.* I, 1, 2, C.R. 2, 35.

[26] Comm. on Is. 6:5, C.R. 36, 132.

[27] Comm. on Jer. 9:23 f., C.R. 38, 50 f.

[28] Comm. on Gen. 2:9, C.R. 23, 38 f.; cf. Comm. on Lk. 11:27, C.R. 45, 349; Comm. on Jn. 1:3–4, C.R. 47, 4 ff., Comm. on Col. 1:16 f., C.R. 52, 85 f.

[29] *Inst.* I, 15, 4, C.R. 2, 138; cf. II, 12, 6, C.R. 2, 345. For an exhaustive treatment of Calvin's extraordinarily rich teaching concerning the *imago Dei,* see the four chapters in T. F. Torrance, *Calvin's Doctrine of Man,* pp. 35–82.

[30] *Inst.* II, 12, 6, C.R. 2, 345.

[31] Comm. on Jn. 17:22, C.R. 47, 388.

[32] *Opus cit.* p. 43. cf. Comm. on Rom. 2:11, C.R. 49, 36; *Inst.* III, 17, 5–6, C.R. 2, 593 f.

[33] Serm. on Deut. 5:28 f. cited by Torrance, *opus cit.* p. 45.

[34] Comm. on Psalm 29:9, C.R. 31, 290; Serm. on Job 38:12, C.R. 35, 378; 38:8, C.R. 35, 373; Comm. on Is. 1:3, C.R. 36, 30.

[35] Comm. on Is. 1:2, C.R. 36, 29.

[36] *Inst.* I, 14, 22, C.R. 2, 133; cf. I, 14, 2, C.R. 2, 118.

[37] Comm. on Psalm 8:6, C.R. 31, 95; cf. Comm. on Gen. 1:26, C.R. 23, 27.

[38] Comm. on Is. 1:3, C.R. 36, 30.

[39] Comm. on Is. 6:13, C.R. 36, 142.

[40] Arg. to Comm. on Gen. C.R. 23, 10.

[41] *Opus cit.* p. 23 f.

[42] Comm. on Gen. 2:18, C.R. 23, 46; cf. *Inst.* II, 2, 13, C.R. 2, 197.

[43] Comm. on Mt. 5:43, C.R. 45, 187.

[44] *Ibid.*

[45] *Inst.* III, 7, 6, C.R. 2, 510; cf. Serm. on Deut. 4:39, C.R. 26, 227; Serm. on I Tim. 2:1–2, C.R. 53, 128.

[46] Serm. on Gal. 6:9–11, C.R. 51, 105: cited by R. S. Wallace, *Calvin's Doctrine of the Christian Life,* p. 150.

[47] Comm. on Gen. 2:18, C.R. 23, 46.

[48] Comm. on Gen. 2:21, C.R. 23, 48.

[49] Comm. on Gen. 2:19, C.R. 23, 48.

[50] Comm. on Gen. 2:21, C.R. 23, 49; cf. Comm. on Gen. 1:27, C.R. 23, 28.

[51] Comm. on Gen. 2:18, C.R. 23, 46.
[52] *Ibid.*
[53] *Ibid.*
[54] *Ibid.*
[55] Comm. on Daniel 11:38–39, C.R. 41, 273; Comm. on Eph. 5:28, C.R. 51, 225.
[56] Comm. on Lk. 10:30, C.R. 45, 613.
[57] *Opus cit.* p. 150 f.; cf. Serm. on Gal. 6:9–11, C.R. 51, 100; Serm. on Deut. 2:1–7, C.R. 26, 9; Serm. on Gal. 5:14–18, C.R. 51, 19.
[58] Comm. on Gal. 5:14, C.R. 50, 251; cf. *Inst.* III, 7, 7; C.R. 2, 511 f.
[59] Comm. on Gal. 5:14, C.R. 50, 251; cf. Comm. on Jn. 13:35, C.R. 47, 319; *Inst.* II, 8, 54, C.R. 2, 305.
[60] Comm. on Rom. 13:8–10, C.R. 49, 252 ff.
[61] Comm. on Matt. 7:12, C.R. 45, 220. Bohatec has pointed out (*opus cit.*) that love is a decisive factor in Calvin's treatment of the commandments: in the Fifth (C.R. 26, 313; 24, 602), in the Sixth (C.R. 24, 612), in the Eighth (C.R. 24, 699), in the Ninth (C.R. 26, 363), and in the Tenth C.R. 2, 302).
[62] Comm. on Ps. 10:2, C.R. 31, 109; cf. Serm. on I Tim. 4:1–3, C.R. 53, 346.
[63] *Inst.* III, 2, 41, C.R. 2, 431 f.; Comm. on Jn. 13:34–35, C.R. 47, 318 f.; Comm. on I John 3:23–24; 4:12; 5:11.
[64] Comm. on Jn. 13:34, C.R. 47, 318.
[65] R. S. Wallace, *opus cit.* p. 152; cf. Serm. on Deut. 2:1–7, C.R. 26, 9.
[66] Comm. on Jn. 13:34, C.R. 47, 319.
[67] Serm. on Eph. 4:29–30, C.R. 51, 644.
[68] Serm. on I Tim. 6:9–11, C.R. 53, 581 f.
[69] Serm. on I Cor. 11:11–16, C.R. 49, 739; Comm. on Ez. 18:7, C.R. 40, 429.
[70] Comm. on I Cor. 7:20, C.R. 49, 415; Comm. on I Thess. 4:11, C.R. 52, 163.
[71] Comm. on Lk. 17:7, C.R. 45, 414.
[72] Comm. on Eph. 5:21, C.R. 51, 221.
[73] Comm. on Eph. 5:22, C.R. 51, 222.
[74] Wallace, *opus cit.* p. 158; cf. Serm. on Gal. 3:26–29, C.R. 50, 567 f.; Serm. on Deut. 5:10, C.R. 26, 310.
[75] Comm. on Exod. 20:12, C.R. 24, 605.
[76] Comm. on Deut. 17:12, C.R. 24, 358.
[77] Serm. on Deut. 5:16, C.R. 26, 320; cf. Comm. on Matt. 22:21, C.R. 45, 602.
[78] *Inst.* IV, 20, 26–31, C.R. 2, 1112–1118.
[79] Comm. on Exod. 20:12, C.R. 24, 603.
[80] Comm. on I Peter 5:5, C.R. 55, 287; Comm. on Exod. 20:12, C.R. 24, 602 f.; *Inst.* IV, 20, 3, C.R. 2, 1094.
[81] Comm. on Ps. 127:1, C.R. 32, 322.
[82] *Inst.* IV, 20, 4, C.R. 2, 1095.
[83] Comm. on I Peter 5:5, C.R. 55, 287; cf. Comm. on Eph. 5:22, C.R. 51, 222.
[84] Comm. on Col. 4:1, C.R. 52, 127.

[85] Cf. Comm. on Eph. 6:9, C.R. 51, 231 where Calvin adds that this law of analogy is "greatly misunderstood, because men do not try it by the law of love, which is the only true standard."

[86] Comm. on Eph. 5:21, C.R. 51, 126; cf. *Inst.* IV, 20, 29, C.R. 2, 1115.

[87] *Inst.* IV, 20, 13, C.R. 2, 1104.

[88] Comm. on I Cor. 11:11, C.R. 49, 477.

[89] Comm. on Eph. 5:28, C.R. 51, 225.

[90] Comm. on Matt. 19:4, C.R. 45, 529; cf. Comm. on Deut. 24:1, C.R. 24, 658; Comm. on I Cor. 7:10, C.R. 49, 410; Comm. on Gen. 2:24, C.R. 23, 50; Comm. on Exod. 21:1, C.R. 24, 701: "Nothing could be more opposed to nature than that a husband, forsaking his wife and children, should remove himself elsewhere. . . . There was then gross barbarity in this severance, whereby a man was disunited from half of himself and his own bowels."

[91] Comm. on Eph. 6:4, C.R. 51, 229.

[92] Comm. on I Tim. 5:8, C.R. 52, 309.

[93] *Inst.* IV, 20, 32, C.R. 2, 1116 f.; cf. Comm. on Matt. 22:21, C.R. 45, 602; cf. Comm. on Daniel 6:22, C.R. 41, 25.

[94] Comm. on Exod. 20:12, C.R. 24, 603.

[95] Comm. on Matt. 20:25, C.R. 45, 557.

[96] Comm. on I Cor. 15:24, C.R. 49, 547.

[97] *Opus. cit.* p. 10.

[98] Comm. on Gen. 48:17, C.R. 23, 585.

[99] Comm. on Lev. 18:6, C.R. 24, 662.

[100] Comm. on Deut. 24:1–4, C.R. 24, 657.

[101] Comm. on Deut. 19:14, C.R. 24, 676.

[102] Hom. on I Sam. 8:11–22, C.R. 29, 552 f.

[103] Comm. on Deut. 24:7, C.R. 24, 628.

[104] Comm. on I Tim. 2:2–3, C.R. 52, 267.

[105] Comm. on Dan. 6:9, C.R. 41, 8.

[106] *Inst.* IV, 20, 17, C.R. 2, 1107.

[107] *Inst.* IV, 20, 19 f., C.R. 2, 1108.

[108] Hom. on I Sam. 9:17–25, C.R. 29, 584; *Inst.* IV, 20, 9, C.R. 2, 1100.

[109] *Inst.* II, 7, 10, C.R. 2, 260.

[110] *Inst.* IV, 20, 11, C.R. 2, 1102.

[111] Comm. on Is. 3:4, C.R. 36, 83.

[112] Serm. on Deut. 2:1–7, C.R. 26, 12; Serm. on Deut. 20:2–9, C.R. 27, 609.

[113] *Inst.* IV, 20, 12, C.R. 2, 1103.

[114] Hom. on I Sam. 29:11–22, C.R. 29, 554.

[115] *Inst.* IV, 20, 8, C.R. 2, 1098.

[116] *Inst.* IV, 20, 8, C.R. 4, 1134.

[117] *Ibid.*

[118] Comm. on Gen. 39:2, C.R. 23, 502.

[119] *Inst.* I, 15, 3, C.R. 2, 136.

[120] *Ibid.* C.R. 2, 137 f.

[121] *Inst.* I, 15, 7, C.R. 2, 142; cf. I, 15, 8, C.R. 2, 142 f.: "God provided man's soul with a mind, by which to distinguish good from evil, right from

wrong. . . . To this he joined the will, under whose control is choice." Cf. also *Inst.* II, 2, 2, C.R. 2, 186.

[122] Arg. to Comm. on Gen.; *Inst.* II, 1, 3, C.R. 2, 177; I, 15, 1, C.R. 2, 134; Comm. on Ps. 147:19, C.R. 32, 431; Comm. on Acts 17:27 f., C.R. 48, 127 f.; Comm. on Jn. 1:4, C.R. 47, 5.

[123] Comm. on Jn. 17:3, C.R. 47, 376 f.; Comm. on Acts 17:28, C.R. 48, 418.

[124] Comm. on Gen. 1:26, C.R. 23, 27.

[125] *Inst.* II, 2, 12, C.R. 2, 196.

[126] *Ibid.*

[127] *Inst.* II, 2, 14, C.R. 2, 198.

[128] *Ibid.*

[129] *Inst.* II, 2, 18, C.R. 2, 200.

[130] *Ibid.*

[131] *Inst.* II, 2, 22, C.R. 2, 203 f.; cf. IV, 10, 3, C.R. 2, 869; I, 15, 2, C.R. 2, 135; Comm. on Rom. 2:15, C.R. 49, 38.

[132] Comm. on Exod. 20:12, C.R. 24, 605; 20:14, C.R. 24, 64; Comm. on Num. 3:5, C.R. 24, 444.

[133] Comm. on Is. 1:3, C.R. 36, 30.

[134] Serm. on Job 39:8–21, C.R. 35, 418 f.

[135] *Inst.* I, 5, 5, C.R. 2, 44 f.

[136] *Inst.* III, 19, 15, C.R. 2, 623; cf. II, 8, 1, C.R. 2, 266 f.; II, 2, 22, C.R. 2, 203 f.; IV, 10, 3, C.R. 2, 868 f.

[137] Comm. on Rom. 2:15, C.R. 49, 38.

[138] *Ibid.*

[139] Comm. on Rom. 2:14, C.R. 49, 37.

[140] *Inst.* II, 8, 1, C.R. 2, 267.

[141] *Inst.* II, 2, 22, C.R. 2, 204.

[142] *Inst.* II, 2, 13, C.R. 2, 197.

[143] *Inst.* II, 1, 5, C.R. 2, 180.

[144] *Inst.* II, 1, 8, C.R. 2, 182.

[145] *Inst.* II, 1, 9, C.R. 2, 183 f.

[146] *Inst.* II, 1, 10, C.R. 2, 184.

[147] *Inst.* II, 1, 11, C.R. 2, 184 f.

[148] *Inst.* II, 2, 22, C.R. 2, 203.

[149] *Inst.* II, 2, 13, C.R. 2, 197.

[150] *Ibid.*

[151] *Inst.* II, 8, 1, C.R. 2, 267.

[152] *Inst.* II, 2, 24, C.R. 2, 203 f.

[153] *Inst.* II, 2, 23, C.R. 2, 203.

[154] *Inst.* II, 2, 24, C.R. 2, 205.

[155] *Inst.* II, 8, 11, C.R. 2, 273 f.

[156] *Inst.* II, 3, 4, C.R. 2, 213.

[157] *Inst.* II, 2, 24, C.R. 2, 186 ff.

[158] *Opus cit.* p. 22.

[159] *Inst.* II, 3, 2, C.R. 2, 211.

[160] *Inst.* II, 3, 3, C.R. 2, 212.

[161] *Inst.* II, 3, 4, C.R. 2, 212 f.

[162] *Inst.* II, 3, 4, C.R. 2, 213.
[163] *Inst.* II, 3, 12, C.R. 2, 222.
[164] *Inst.* II, 2, 16, C.R. 2, 199.
[165] *Inst.* II, 2, 15, C.R. 2, 198.
[166] Comm. on Jn. 10:35, C.R. 47, 252; Comm. on Ps. 82:1, C.R. 31, 768; 45:6–7, C.R. 31, 451.
[167] *Inst.* IV, 20, 4, C.R. 2, 1095. Cf. Comm. on Dan. 5:18–19, C.R. 40, 712 where God's glory is said to be inscribed on kings.
[168] Serm. on Job 34:8, C.R. 35, 160; Serm. on Deut. 11:22–25, C.R. 27, 128.
[169] Comm. on Lk. 1:32, C.R. 45, 27; Comm. on Jer. 6:7, C.R. 38, 544; Comm. on Ps. 2:7, C.R. 31, 46.
[170] Comm. on Ps. 127:1, C.R. 32, 322.
[171] *Inst.* II, 2, 17, C.R. 2, 199 f. The editor of the Library of Christian Classics edition of the *Institutes* rightly appends the following footnote concerning the reference to "special grace" in this passage. "Neither common grace nor the special grace here mentioned has any relation to the salvation of its possessor. Special grace is a special endowment of capacity, virtue, or heroism by which a man is fitted to serve the divine purpose in this world, while he himself may remain in the common state of human depravity."
[172] Comm. on Ps. 119:142, C.R. 32, 279.
[173] Comm. on Ps. 119:91, C.R. 32, 254; cf. Comm. on Is. 40:8, C.R. 37, 12 f.; Comm. on Matt. 24:35, C.R. 45, 671: Christ's words are "more firm and stable than the entire structure of the world." The French version renders it: *que tout l'ordre de nature qui se voit au ciel et à la terre.*
[174] *Inst.* II, 8, 1, C.R. 2, 267; Comm. on Ez. 16:1–3, C.R. 40, 335; Serm. on Deut. 5:17, C.R. 26, 324.
[175] *Inst.* I, 2, 1, C.R. 2, 34.
[176] Comm. on Gen. 2:16, C.R. 23, 44 f.
[177] Comm. on Jn. 1:11, C.R. 47, 10: "There is no part of the world which the Son of God may not lawfully claim as his own property."
[178] Serm. on I Tim. 5:4–5, C.R. 53, 456 f.
[179] Comm. on Eph. 6:1, C.R. 51, 228.
[180] *Inst.* IV, 20, 16, C.R. 2, 1106; cf. II, 2, 13, C.R. 2, 196 f.
[181] *Inst.* II, 8, 1, C.R. 2, 267; cf. Comm. on Ez. 16:1–3, C.R. 40, 335; Comm. on Eph. 6:1, C.R. 51, 228.
[182] Comm. on Deut. 17:6; 19:15, C.R. 24, 627; Comm. on Rom. 2:15, C.R. 49, 38; Comm. on Ps. 19:7, C.R. 31, 199 f.; Comm. on Gen. 26:28, C.R. 23, 367 f.
[183] *Inst.* III, 14, 3, C.R. 2, 565.
[184] *Inst.* II, 8, 50, C.R. 2, 303.
[185] *Inst.* II, 8, 51, C.R. 2, 303.
[186] *Inst.* II, 8, 53, C.R. 2, 304; Cf. Comm. on Matt. 22:39, C.R. 45, 612.
[187] Comm. on Ps. 19:8, C.R. 31, 201.
[188] Comm. on Jonah 1:13–14, C.R. 43, 227.
[189] *Ibid.*
[190] Comm. on Gen. 16:1, C.R. 23, 222 f.; 18:11, C.R. 23, 253; 21:1, C.R. 23, 295 f.; 25:23, C.R. 23, 349 ff.
[191] Comm. on Gen. 25:20, C.R. 23, 347.

[192] Comm. on Gen. 48:17, C.R. 23, 586; cf. Comm. on Rom. 9:13, C.R. 49, 179.
[193] *Inst.* IV, 20, 15, C.R. 2, 1105.
[194] *Ibid.*
[195] *Inst.* IV, 20, 16, C.R. 2, 1106.
[196] *Ibid.*
[197] *Ibid.*
[198] *Inst.* II, 2, 17, C.R. 199.

CONTRACT AND STATUS IN RELIGION AND LAW

by

Leo Pfeffer

IT WAS just about a century ago that Sir Henry Maine published his classic *Ancient Law.* Reflecting current social Darwinism, the theme, or at least a major theme of the book was that the evolution of law from a primitive to an advanced civilization was manifested by progress from status to contract, a term used by him for obligations assumed by voluntary election. At least superficially, social history supported the theory. An early strand in the Bible asserted that God would visit the sins of the fathers upon the children to the third and fourth generation; later strands emphasized that the father would not die for the sins of his son nor the son for the sins of the father. Certainly, too, a relationship of employer and employee voluntarily entered into represents a more advanced level of civilization than one in which, through law, slave and master each acquire their status at birth.

For many reasons, Maine's theory proved attractive, but perhaps for none so much as its moral vindication of the exploding capitalist expansion of the 19th century. Adam Smith had supplied *laissez faire* with an economic basis, Darwin with a basis in biological science, Herbert Spencer with a base in social science, and Maine with one in the philosophy of law.

The industrial revolution made the institution of apprenticeship obsolete, and it was quite comforting for the industrialists to learn that they were in harmony with evolutionary progress when they replaced the relationship of status in individual apprenticeship with the relationship of contract in the mass employment of children for work in mills and mines. The customs of centuries had imposed severe restraints on the master's freedom in the treatment of his apprentices, but only the voluntary agreement of the contracting parties limited an industrialist's treatment of his workers. If the result was cruel exploitation of children and women, then this was undoubtedly unfortunate, but it was the price of advancing civilization and the industrialist did what he could to ameliorate the situation by making large financial gifts to charities and churches.

It was in the United States that the apotheosis of Maine's doctrine was achieved when, towards the end of the 19th century, the Supreme Court read into the Constitution not only Spencer's *Social Statics* but Maine's *Ancient Law.* Freedom of contract, the Court held, is one of the inalienable rights with which man is endowed by his Creator and for which we declared our independence of England and established our own constitutional republic.[1] In 1923 the Court held that Miss Lyons, an elevator operator in a building in Washington, D.C., was deprived of her constitutional liberties when Congress passed a minimum wage law which forbade her and her employer from contracting for her services at the rate of $35 a month.[2] As late as 1936 the Court held that "the state is without power by any form of legislation to prohibit, change or nullify contracts between employers and adult women workers as to the amount of wages to be paid."[3]

Neither freedom of contract nor Maine's *Ancient Law* could withstand the great depression of the thirties. The Supreme Court quickly realized that Miss Lyon's freedom to contract to work for $35 a month would have to yield to the need to assure to all a decent minimum standard of living. Nor could America survive in the 20th century without joining the rest of the civilized world in a new era of communal responsibility for individual welfare.[4] Whether Maine and the Supreme Court liked it or not, the welfare state was here to stay, and the welfare state and freedom of contract are simply incompatible.

The welfare state presents a serious dilemma to the liberal concerned both with individual freedom and social welfare. It encroaches upon areas which traditionally have been deemed to be within the domain of privacy and makes short shrift of individual freedom of choice. School attendance laws are compulsory; so too are social security laws, unemployment insurance laws, workmen's compensation laws, vaccination laws, water fluoridation programs, medicare, and often labor union membership. The direction the American welfare state is taking is hardly mistakable and the progress is irreversible.

Our concern here is with the conflict between the demands of the welfare state and of individual religious conscience. The issue has already reached the courts in a number of instances. An extreme Orthodox Jewish sect deemed it sinful for their children to study anything but the Torah. A prosecution for violation of the school attendance law was upheld notwithstanding their contention that its enforcement against them violated the freedom of religion guaranteed to them by the First Amendment of the Constitution.[5] Equally unsuccessful were similar challenges to fluoridation of a city's water supply[6] and to vaccination laws.[7] The courts have had no hesitation in ordering compulsory blood transfusions to save the lives of Jehovah's Witnesses' children over the objection of their parents that such transfusions were in sinful violation of the biblical command against consuming blood.[8] Indeed, the courts have issued the same orders for objecting adult Jehovah's Witnesses, overriding simultaneously freedom of contract and freedom of conscience.[9]

Yet, freedom of conscience occupies a high level in the

hierarchy of democratic values even in the welfare state of America. Government in all its branches, executive, legislative and judiciary, strives to accommodate the demands of social welfare to commands of religious conscience. The Supreme Court has ruled that while the welfare state may require that all children receive a basic secular education, it must allow parents the right to provide it through the medium of religiously oriented schools.[10] It has ruled that a Sabbatarian may not be denied the right to receive benefits under unemployment compensation laws because of his refusal, for reasons of religion, to accept an offer of employment requiring him to work on Saturdays.[11] It has held that jury service may not be forced upon a woman who takes literally the biblical command that one should not judge lest he be judged.[12] A number of state courts have ruled that zoning and town planning laws, a child of the welfare state, may not be applied to bar churches from moving into residential districts.[13]

Even more than the judiciary, the legislative and executive departments of American government have been solicitous of religious conscience. Religious groups, such as the Amish, have by law or acquiescence been exempted from compulsory participation in the social security program and from providing their children with more than a bare minimum of secular education. Conscientious objectors are exempt from military service and may be naturalized without undertaking to bear arms in defense of the nation. Many states excuse children of Christian Scientists from attending classes in which the germ theory of disease is taught, and in some states even from vaccination and x-ray requirements. Laws forbidding the unlicensed practice of medicine frequently exempt Christian Science practice and similar faith healing.

These instances, which can be multiplied, indicate that while there is a conflict between individual freedom of conscience and the commands which the welfare state imposes upon all who possess the status of citizen, American government will go far to preserve the integrity of free conscience even when it poses some threat to the concerns of the community. Nevertheless, where the threat to communal welfare is clear, immediate and grave, the Supreme Court has ruled often and unambiguously that societal needs are paramount. Henry Maine, to the contrary notwithstanding, in the 20th century welfare society, status is superior to contract.

Where, however, there is no conflict between conscience and community, Maine is entirely right; the progress of civilization is from status to contract. The distinction between compulsion in matters of communal welfare and freedom in matters of conscience which do not directly affect communal welfare was expressed some three centuries ago by Roger Williams in his famous letter to the Town of Providence:

> There goes many a ship to sea, with many hundred souls in one ship, whose weal and woe is common, and is a true picture of a commonwealth, or a human combination or society. It hath fallen out sometimes, that both papists and protestants, Jew and Turks, may be embarked in one ship; upon which supposal I affirm, that all the liberty of conscience, that ever I pleaded for, turns upon these two hinges—that none of the papists, protestants, Jews, or Turks, be forced to come to the ship's prayers or worship, not compelled from their own particular prayers or worship, if they practice any. I further add, that I never denied, that notwithstanding this liberty, the commander of this ship ought to command the ship's course, yea, and also command that justice, peace and sobriety, be kept and practiced, both among the seamen and all the passengers.

These "two hinges" may also be said to represent church and state and Williams' parable to represent the modern principle of the separation of church and state. In the domain of the state, compulsion is appropriate; in the domain of religion it is not. The separation of church and state represents advance in civilization for in a true sense it manifests the replacement of status by contract.

The struggle for the separation of church and state in the modern State of Israel is a struggle between status and contract in religion. The Brother Daniel case of a few years back illustrates this dramatically. The one fundamental statute of the State of Israel is the Law of Return. Under it, every Jew in the world (with a few exceptions, such as fugitives from justice) has the right to emigrate ("return") to Israel and reclaim his inherent citizenship. Brother Daniel had been born to Jewish parents in Europe but in adulthood converted to Roman Catholicism and was ordained as a priest. A few years ago he sought to reside in Israel as a citizen under the Law of Return, claiming that he was a Jew of the Catholic faith.

Under ancient Rabbinic law, the status of Judaism is acquired at birth by all persons born to Jewish mothers. Moreover, the status is immutable; notwithstanding purported conversion, there is no exit from Judaism. Under Rabbinic law, therefore, Brother Daniel was a Jew, entitled to avail himself of the provisions of the Law of Return. The Supreme Court of Israel, however, rejected Rabbinic law and ruled that the statute used the term "Jew" in the sense that was generally understood by the people, and in popular usage the term does not encompass one who converted to and became a priest in the Catholic religion.

Despite this decision, status rather than contract is the norm of church-state relations in Israel. There is no civil marriage; every person possesses the status of some religion and, unless he wishes to fly to Cyprus or some other nearby country, must be married by a clergyman of the particular religion ascribed to him by the law of the state. A Christian may work or keep his business open on Saturday, provided the abstains from work or business on Sunday, and a Moslem can do the same if he rests on Friday. But one who is born to a Jewish mother, even if he is an atheist, must observe Saturday as his day of rest. A man born into a family named Cohen, Kaplan or Katz, or otherwise identifiable as presumably descending from Aaron, the first priest, cannot lawfully marry a divorced woman (Lev. 21:7). There is no exit from the status of *kohen* any more than from the status of Jew.

In the western world, it is the Roman Catholic Church which is the most powerful defender of status in the area of religion. It may be that the recent schema on religious liberty issued by the Vatican Council will mark the beginning of a change in Catholic doctrine. At present, however, there is no indication of any change in long-standing orthodox Catholic teaching that religion is a matter of status, that a child born to a Catholic mother is subject to the jurisdiction and discipline of the Catholic Church and that the Catholic status, acquired by baptism, is immutable.

In the United States, this Judaeo-Catholic doctrine is challenged by Protestantism (and secularism). The Protestant principle is that religion is a matter not of status but of election (contract, in Maine's terminology). Religion cannot be thrust upon a person; it must be voluntarily assumed and can be voluntarily cast off. Voluntarism is what Winthrop Hudson called the great tradition of the American churches.

This difference in approach is reflected in religious statistics and, incidentally, shows how misleading if not meaningless religious statistics can be. The estimated population of the United States today is about 195 million. The Roman Catholic Church claims about 46 million, and Jewry claims about five and a half million. Assuming some million or two for the membership of such minority religions as Islam, Buddhism and Ethical Culture, there would seem to be some 140 million Protestants in the United States.* American Protestantism, however, claims less than half this amount, some 69 million. The explanation for the discrepancy lies in the fact that Catholicism and Judaism include in their figures all persons born

* Orthodox Jewry adopts this approach. Taking the base figure of 5½ million, it subtracts the million claimed by Reform and the million and a quarter claimed by Conservatism, and claims for itself the balance of some three million.

to Catholic or Jewish mothers from the moment of birth and irrespective of whether they maintain any relationship to churches or synagogues. Protestantism, on the other hand, claims only those who have reached an age when they can make a meaningful election and actually elect Protestantism by some affirmative expression or act.

The same approach of elevating status over election or contract is manifested in the demand, largely Catholic, that a question on religion be included in the decennial census conducted by the Federal government. Religion, in this view, is a matter of status, like age, sex and marital status, and should be counted and recorded the same way.

Another manifestation is Catholic Church hostility to nonsectarian or even public welfare institutions. Orphan asylums, children's homes, homes for the aged and hospitals should be Protestant, Catholic or Jewish and all persons seeking welfare assistance should obtain it at the institution of their religion. (In the Canadian province of Quebec, this philosophy has governed the educational system. There are as yet no nonsectarian public schools in the province, only Catholic schools and Protestant schools, the latter accepting all non-Catholic children.)

One consequence of this approach is the situation in New York City in respect to foundlings. According to W. S. Gilbert in *Iolanthe,* every English child is born either a Liberal or a Conservative. Up to some fifteen years ago, every child born in New York was either a Protestant or Catholic. By agreement between the two church bodies and the city, foundlings were turned over alternately to Protestant and Catholic adoption agencies. Jewish protests resulted in a liberalization of the procedure, and today every third white foundling goes to the Jewish adoption agency. (Negro foundlings are still divided equally between the Protestant and Catholic agencies.) Nonsectarian adoption agencies receive no foundlings, presumably because nobody is born nonsectarianly.

Another consequence of the status approach to religion was

the Goldman case about a decade ago. It involved twins born out of wedlock to a Catholic mother, who, being unable to care for them, gave them to the Goldmans, a childless Jewish couple in Lynn, Massachusetts, to be raised as their children. When the couple had had the twins for three years, they presented to the appropriate court a petition for their legal adoption. The twins' mother signed an affidavit in which she stated that she consented to the adoption, knowing that the Goldmans were Jewish and would bring up the twins as Jews. The judge, although he found that the Goldmans were in all respects fit and proper and would give the twins parental affection and a good home, nevertheless refused to allow the adoption because of the difference in religions. He ruled that even though the twins had never been baptized, they were Catholic since they had been born to a Catholic mother, and that this status could not be changed, at least until the children reached maturity and changed it themselves.

The ruling was affirmed by the highest court in Massachusetts, and the United States Supreme Court refused to review the decision, although probably on technical grounds.[14] After the legal proceedings were ended, the Massachusetts Department of Public Welfare sought to compel the Goldmans to surrender the twins so that they might be placed in a Catholic institution. The Goldmans, upon hearing of the Department's intentions, abandoned their home, business, and nonmobile assets and departed with the twins to establish a new home in another state. The Department indicated that it would not let the matter drop but would seek to extradite the Goldmans and thus recover the twins so that they might be placed in a Catholic institution. Apparently, however, it was unable to trace the Goldmans or the twins, who presumably are today living together somewhere as a family unit.

The First Amendment to the Federal Constitution rejects status in religion insofar as government and law are concerned.

It rejects the concepts of religion by inheritance and no-exit. The words "Congress shall make no law respecting an establishment of religion or prohibiting the free exercise thereof," mean that under law entry into religion must be voluntary and exit free. They mean that in our democracy election, not status is the only religious test that will be recognized. It is for this reason that a great American jurist, David Dudley Field, though speaking hyperbolically nevertheless expressed substantial truth when he said in 1893 that "the greatest achievement ever made in the course of human progress is the total and final separation of church and state."

NOTES

[1] Lochner v. New York, 198 U.S. 45 (1905).

[2] Adkins's v. Children's Hospital, 261 U.S. 255 (1923).

[3] Morehead v. New York ex rel. Tipaldo, 298 U.S. 587 (1936).

[4] West Coast Hotel Co. v. Parrish, 300 U.S. 379 (1937).

[5] Donner v. New York, 342 U.S. 884 (1951).

[6] Birnel v. Town of Firecrest, 361 U.S. 10 (1959); Kraus v. City of Cleveland, 351 U.S. 935 (1956).

[7] Jacobson v. Massachusetts, 197 U.S. 11 (1905).

[8] People ex rel Wallace v. Labrenz, 344 U.S. 824 (1952).

[9] Application of Georgetown College, 331 F. 2d 1000 (1964); Raleigh Fitkin Hospital v. Anderson, 201 A. 2d 537 (N.J. 1964).

[10] Pierce v. Society of Sisters, 268 U.S. 510 (1925).

[11] Sherbert v. Verner, 374 U.S. 398 (1963).

[12] In re Jenison, 375 U.S. 14 (1963).

[13] City of Sherman v. Simms, 143 Tex. 115 (1944); Ellsworth v. Gercke, 62 Ariz. 198 (1945); Roman Catholic Archbishop v. Baker, 140 Oreg. 600 (1932).

[14] Goldman v. Fogarty, 348 U.S. 942 (1955).

SUBSIDIARITY AND THE ECUMENICAL ESTABLISHMENT

by

Dean M. Kelley

WHETHER we go our separate ways or go together, the religious bodies and their related instrumentalities of education and welfare pose a dilemma for our society which will probably be resolved during this decade—by the concatenation of events if not by a more reflective process. And the outcome will shape the structures of our society for generations to come.

The dilemma has been sharpening for some time, and presses us most clearly in the anti-poverty program. It was summed up recently at a meeting of religious leaders with the top executives of the Office of Economic Opportunity, where a Roman Catholic spokesman voiced distress about a new rubric in the manual of the Community Action Program. The new rubric advised community action agencies applying for federal funds to utilize public agencies wherever possible for their operations, and if they utilized private agencies they must justify the necessity.

With plaintive restraint, the Monsignor reminded the federal administrators that the cooperation of the churches in the war against poverty had been besought by government, and the churches had responded favorably—only to find themselves now treated like country cousins! "Why do you put us in the position of being the last resort?" he remonstrated. "Do you want our help or don't you?" Some of the church leaders present seemed to nod in agreement. Others wondered at the logic of his argument.

The restriction in the handbook applied only to choice of "subcontractors" to be employed with government funds in community action programs. It did not apply to persons or groups volunteering their efforts to alleviate human need. It did not apply to persons or groups supporting or criticizing the programs proposed as remedies to poverty. All these things the churches and their members could do freely, forthrightly, without hindrance or limitation. The Monsignor seemed to some to be saying that the churches were not clamoring to be in the forefront of the ranks of *volunteers.* What they wanted was their share of the *money.* If they couldn't have first chance, or at least equal chance, at the tangible goodies, they wouldn't play.

Actually, the Monsignor did not threaten; he spoke more in sorrow than in anger; and back of his comment was a concept of social order that has a long and distinguished history, and which has recently been formulated in the "doctrine of subsidiarity." As stated in one of the social encyclicals of Pope Pius XI:

> [It is] unjust and a gravely harmful disturbance of right order to turn over to a greater society of higher rank functions and services which can be performed by lesser bodies on a lower plane.[1]

This means that what a family can do for itself, no higher or greater body should do for it. What voluntary associations of families can do for themselves, no governmental body should try to do. What a local and lower level of government can accomplish, no higher and broader level of government should support or displace.

Many Americans would agree on this general principle, but there is not always agreement on how it should be applied. Some social needs and services are too broadly inclusive to be handled on any local or voluntary level—the postal service or Social Security, for instance. In education and welfare, however, many believe that government should not displace or compete with the voluntary organizations—hospitals, orphanages, old peoples' homes—which citizens have set up. Instead, they believe that government should work through these existing voluntary "subsidiary" agencies. Thus, the voluntary agencies become administrators of tax funds and intermediaries between government and the people.

This philosophy has become increasingly attractive to many legislators and administrators in Washington, since it offers a way to get jobs done without appearing to exercise "federal control" or to expand the bureaucracy of government. It has also a persuasive logic: since the members of these voluntary private groups pay taxes for health care or education or whatever, why should government not make available to those citizens through *their own chosen voluntary agency* the services they have paid for? Besides, since many free-will contributions are made to these voluntary agencies for their humane and edifying works, such contributions enable such agencies to offer comparable services at less cost than public agencies can.

For instance, as medical care becomes more and more expensive, and government is expected to help meet its costs, at least for the disadvantaged members of society, should the government build a big new public hospital in a community where several small voluntary hospitals are trying to meet the need? Or should government utilize existing facilities, improving and expanding them until they can provide the total medical care for the community? The Hill-Burton Hospital Construction Act represents a decision of public policy that federal funds may be used in the latter pattern.

Many people feel that neither private nor public entities should enjoy a monopoly in our society, but that in "antagonistic cooperation" or friendly competition they keep each other "on their toes." We may differ in our views about the proper "mix" between public and private in various fields, but few of us would want either completely eliminated. This rightful concern has led to a lot of deceptive sloganeering which implies that church-related colleges or church-related hospitals are the last remaining bulwark against monolithic, monopolistic creeping-welfare-state-socialism, and if the churches don't get tax aid for their institutions on a par with the tax aid given state institutions, the State will just "take over" the fields of education and welfare!

It is strange that the Gospel of Adam Smith should be subject to this latter day development of doctrine. He would probably have felt that the proper application of his doctrine to the host of voluntary welfare agencies would not involve the taxing power at all, but that all welfare should be limited to "charity" freely given by individuals. But once government has entered the welfare field, it possesses an engine of such power that voluntary efforts seem feeble in comparison, and cannot successfully compete. So far as money is concerned, this may be true. So far as human concern and sacrificial service are needed, however, tax money alone cannot buy it or deliver it. Only the dedication of the human heart can produce that—and it still remains the greatest power in the world. What we have not yet determined is the connection between taxation and dedication.

A fatal fallacy in the church-or-state bugaboo is the excluded middle. There are not *two* possible categories of welfare institutions—governmental and church-related, but *three.* Between the institutions belonging to the public and those related to the churches lies the broad range of *private nonsectarian institutions* of which Harvard, Yale and Princeton are examples. Although founded by churches for religious purposes, they are no longer effectively church-related, but have become nonsectarian—"secularized"! The same thing has happened and is happening and will happen to church-related institutions of all kinds as they seek to appeal to and serve a broader constituency than the church which established them. As they rely increasingly for their support upon the general public, they seek to become increasingly what that public envisions as a "good general hospital" or a "good liberal arts college." They resist strenuously any effort to differentiate them from the other institutions in the same field, and seek to be considered and treated as much as possible like "one of the boys."

The churches, however, are loath to lose their institutions, and some of them have tried to retain a close control over the personnel and program of the agencies they have set up to fulfill their mission. Some boast that they have been able to utilize various forms of federal aid without suffering any form of federal control. This blithe romanticism was clearly voiced by the president of a great university which is owned outright by a major denomination. Although he has built several dormitories with federal loans, he insists that there are "no strings attached." "Otherwise I wouldn't have accepted the loans," he announces. Apparently he has not read the fine print reflecting the President's Executive Order on nondiscrimination in federally-financed housing,[2] which stipulates that he cannot bar from his dormitories any qualified student on grounds of race, religion or national origin. Maybe he just won't admit them to classes in the university!

The moral of this illustration is that money does not come with "no strings attached"—even when it seems to be unentangled. The strings may be long rather than short, hidden rather than visible, agreeable rather than onerous, but they are there. And in the case of tax money, they are enforceable by law. Congress is writing into education and welfare laws the condition that tax money cannot be used for the building of "religious structures" or for the inculcation of sectarian doctrine. Although this is a minimal protection against "establishment of religion," it can become a genuine hindrance to the churches in fulfilling their mission through the institutions they have founded for that purpose. Certainly, part of their purpose is the healing of human ills or the educating of citizens apart from all proselytizing or institutional advantage. But they are no longer fully able to determine whether their (tax-aided) institutions can do more than that in attaining distinctly religious objectives.

There are those who claim—with some justice—that just because government wishes to "purchase" needed "services" from a church-related institution, it does not "buy" the whole institution. To a certain extent this is true. But when government purchases 75% or 80% of the total output of services of an institution, it may actually have "bought" the institution without intending it. If the choice were put to them in take-it-or-leave-it terms, the directors of the institution might cut off the flow of government largesse and go their own independent way, but it never is put so clearly. The institution is seldom challenged to reject a policy of government and go it alone. Rather, the institution and its administrators are not inclined to look critically upon the source of main support—they identify with and accommodate themselves to its operation—for they are *part* of it.

The alternative to governmental control of the church-related programs and institutions which it aids is for government simply to turn over to the institutions their "share" of the tax appropriations with "no questions asked." Presumably the tax resources available for education or welfare could be divided among a number of church-related agencies so that each could serve the needs of its own constituents. That would be full-blown subsidiarity, such as is practiced in certain European nations, especially in the Netherlands.[3] Such a pattern, however, would require a major revision of many American traditions now older than many foreign governments, such as public accountability and control of public funds.

The big problem with subsidiarity, however, is that it assumes everybody belongs to one of the subsidiary associations which act as administrative agencies for government. But in this country there are many people who belong to very small religious groups, or to none at all. Where do they go for *their* services? When this problem confronted the Jews of Quebec, they were generously admitted to the Protestant schools[4]—which assumes either that education is not as significant religiously to Jews as it is to Roman Catholics (for instance), or that the religious content of the Protestant schools is so minimal or so innocuous as to cause no offense or inconvenience to non-Protestants—either or both of which may be true.

No one likes to be a permanent guest in somebody else's house, and no citizen wants to be obliged to go to someone else's school or hospital if he can go to his own. But what if there is no school or hospital of "his own" even though he is paying taxes for education or welfare? *No citizen should have to go to or through a church or church agency to obtain the civic benefits to which he is entitled by virtue of his citizenship and payment of taxes.* By what right may a church or church agency deny to any citizen the services his taxes pay for, or employment provided in the same way? Can a church hospital refuse to employ nurses, attendants and physicians of faiths other than their own, or of no faith, when the funds out of which it pays its employees, and the funds which built its pavilions, come largely out of taxes paid under compulsion of law by all citizens?

"Subsidiarity" assumes that everyone belongs to one or another of the groups through which government is expected to channel its services. In actuality, many of those who need such services most are left out, or must submit to sectarian teaching, practices, and atmosphere.

This question was posed to the Fourth Circuit Court of Appeals in respect to race when a private hospital refused to admit Negro physicians to its staff. The court, in *Simkins v. Moses H. Cone Memorial Hospital,*[5] ruled that because the hospital had been built in part with Hill-Burton funds, it was no longer a "private" hospital, but participated sufficiently in the action of the state that it could no longer enjoy the luxury of selectivity on the basis of race in admitting physicians to practice in its wards. How would a court decide a similar case involving religion? Church-related institutions must ponder the implications of becoming no longer private but somehow "public" when they seek and accept public funds.

Another problem with "subsidiarity" is that important decisions on how tax resources will be used are made by the administrators of private agencies—persons not readily amenable to the public. Often without intending to do so, or realizing what they are doing, they may change the impact of a tax-supported program until it is scarcely recognizable by the legislature which appropriated the money. And even where a legal recourse is theoretically available, what government agency wants to take a church to court?

It is presumably because of such considerations as those just mentioned that the Office of Economic Opportunity had expressed a preference for public rather than church related subcontractors.[6] And the clergyman who objected probably did so in part because it offended his sense of "subsidiarity"—that government should work through existing voluntary groups rather than displacing them—even if they are churches.

But perhaps there was another element in his objection which should interest us more. Perhaps he felt that the churches were being by-passed not only or mainly as administrators of public funds, but as determiners of public policy. Although citizens are not excluded from participation or leadership in the community action organization even if they are clergymen, and although church members and even churches can volunteer their services to the poor freely, he may have felt that their place in the forefront of the war on poverty was challenged.

At present, the anti-poverty program presents a very unusual approach to the subsidization by the federal government of social change on local, state and regional levels. Despairing of the responsiveness or effectiveness of some duly elected municipal governments, Congress and the Administration apparently contemplate encouraging and legitimating certain voluntary forces of ferment by means of various by-passes around City Hall. Recently a couple of mayors denounced the anti-poverty program as a fomenter of class strife in their communities. It is not fomenting strife; the strife is already present in our slums, as Mayor Yorty discovered in the Watts district of Los Angeles in 1965. The federal administration is simply seeking to canalize that strife into productive channels that will not be rigidified or obstructed by the arteriosclerosis of various big-city political machines. It is trying to facilitate peaceable revolution in order to forestall violent revolution.

Some very significant questions are thereby thrust upon us about our accepted assumptions of democracy. Presumably public funds are subject to public control through public officials on the grounds that they are amenable to the electorate. If they do not use the taxing power to accomplish what the people want, the people can "turn the rascals out." It may not be easy to do, but it can be and has been done.

The Administration of the Anti-Poverty Program now sets up in every big city a Community Action Program, in which the poor shall have a significant voice in the spending of federal funds designed to aid them. In many cities the mayors view this as a threat to their political control or democratic accountability—whichever way we wish to put it—and they are not far wrong.

Some of us discussed this with Donald Baker, General Counsel of the Office of Economic Opportunity, asking whether the co-opting of miscellaneous private individuals onto a board administering public funds did not leave the community no recourse at the polls to control the selection of those who determined their public affairs. Why should the solution to political problems be taken out of the hands of the duly-elected and ostensibly accountable public officials and given to an aggregation of assorted citizens whose mode of selection, term of office, and legal accountability is not stipulated in the law?

Mr. Baker replied in effect that the municipal machinery is simply not serving the poor in many cities and it is necessary to find a way around that machinery to the powerless slum-dwellers if poverty is to be eliminated. This by-pass in our political structure is thus conceived to be somehow more "democratic" than the democratic process.

The community consortium of co-opted individuals is designed to facilitate the shifting and redistribution of social and political power without the tedious methods of political "reform" movements, so long to make ready, so soon to collapse after the rascals have been thrown out. Does this suggest some defect in the pattern of democratic government we have set up? Does it lack self-corrective mechanisms on the municipal level which would enable the citizenry to reassert their will over unresponsive officials? Or has the management of our decaying cities become so hopeless that the old theories no longer apply, and we must jury-rig our crumbling transit systems and hospitals and mental institutions? The answer is not clear, at least to me, and I pose it simply as the background for a new conundrum in the area with which I am more familiar: the Ecumenical Establishment.

The churches (and synagogues) have always been concerned about the poor and are now concerned in the war on poverty. They have aided the poor when no other institution would, and they feel a historic solicitude for the betterment of the poor that inspires a certain sense of precedence over Johnny-come-lately's on the poverty scene—such as government. "We were here first," the churches seem to say (and they were); "you can't cut us out now!"

In less sanctified circles, such a response might sound like a "vested interest" in the poor. Social welfare professionals are sometimes criticized for perpetuating or at least institutionalizing poverty, but let us not apply such criticism to the churches! Let us rather consider the churches' avowed selfless concern for the poor at its face value, and concede that the churches are likely to be less directly interested in their own institutional aggrandizement than City Hall. What part are they properly to play in the war on poverty and the civil rights struggle and other social causes?

Some church leaders see their role in remedying poverty as continuous with what they have always done, binding up the wounds of society's victims, only now with government help, distributed proportionately to the several religious bodies in the pattern of "subsidiarity."

Others feel that the churches' part should be far more dynamic. Rather than helping to make poverty palatable and thus perpetuating it, they say, the churches should help end it. Rather than comforting victims (and reassuring the victimizers?) the churches should discomfit everyone until the social structure which permits or produces poverty is changed—not a gentle or easy task. This latter counsel takes the form in some cities of seeming to intensify civil strife. Churches and councils of churches in Rochester and elsewhere have hired Saul Alinsky to come in and "stir up trouble" on behalf of the poor—or so it looks to City Hall!

"If there are no other institutions to help organize the poor and to counterbalance City Hall, *we'll* do it," these churchmen seem to say. And maybe they are right. Perhaps that is the only really effective way to end poverty. But it poses some problems for the churches and for society.

However high and selfless the motives of church leaders, and however much the poor may need and welcome and benefit by their help, the churches are still mostly human, and prone to err, particularly to err in the lack of self-criticism and correction. Crusades in time can produce some rather unlovely leaders, who see no value but their Cause, no limitations to its warfare, no harm but in its loss. There is the possibility that some of the self-appointed saviors of the Poor might become so caught up in the fight as to grow as inattentive to the plight of individual poor persons as the politicians they are trying to unseat! This need not be too dangerous, so long as the crusading churchmen remain private citizens, leading voluntary movements for reform. But when they become part of the political structure, the problem is more serious, and the peril of "establishment of religion" begins to appear.

For purposes of this discussion, let us define "establishment of religion" as the grafting of religious organization into the power structure of society, for example, by granting civil authority to religious functionaries (as such), or giving the civil magistrate jurisdiction over matters of religion, or supporting religious institutions or activities by the taxing power, or imposing religious tests or regulations upon citizens as a condition of their participation in civic life. "Disestablishment" is the condition in which the structures of religion and government are independent.

This does not mean that church members—even clergymen—do not have full right to speak and vote as citizens, even to hold public office, provided they do not determine policy in both structures at the same time. It does not mean that churches may not cooperate with government as long as they do so voluntarily and with their own resources. This does not mean that government may not utilize the facilities, structures and services of churches in emergencies of human need, so long as it does not continue to do so when the emergency is no longer present, or until its efforts become "systematic" state action. (When something happens once or twice it is not "systematic" and therefore not "establishment": when it becomes regular, recurrent, accepted, then it is "systematic" establishment.)

Back in the days of the beginning of this nation, James

Madison and other architects of disestablishment felt that the "multiplicity of sects" made the First Amendment necessary and lent it strength. As long as religious groups were relatively equal and in hot competition with one another, the rights and liberties of citizens were safer and the civil government was less likely to be subjected to ecclesiastical interference or control. Even a system of "subsidiarity" could not be too damaging if the resources of society were distributed among *competing* sects.

But the development of modern ecumenicity has changed all that. Today Roman Catholics, Protestants and Jews are prepared to work closely together in support of civil rights, in concern for peace, and in the war on poverty.

Suppose there were a top-level interreligious committee on the elimination of poverty, composed of 50 or 60 of the top leaders of the three major faith-groups. This "summit" group would be able to command national respect and attention, to focus moral concern upon recalcitrant problems in the area of poverty, and to mobilize support for national efforts to eliminate it.

All of this would be laudable as long as it did not move beyond the "voluntary" realm and become "official"—that is, exercise the power or authority of government, or exert power and authority over government. *That way "establishment" lies.* "Establishment" is not wrong because it violates the First Amendment, but because it damages freedom of religion and the integrity of civil society, as well as of the church. The First Amendment is not true because it is in the Constitution; it is in the Constitution because it is *true.* It points to some enduring and long-range realities of human experience which we might otherwise lose sight of in pursuit of short-range goals, and we violate it at our peril.

It is my conviction that any condition which partakes of the nature of "establishment" will harm civil society and the churches *in the long run,* and will restrict the religious liberty of citizens. If it *doesn't* have such evil consequences, the First Amendment is mistaken, a hollow formalism, a needless hindrance to the Great Society, and should be repealed. But we must not expect to see the evil consequences immediately. It took centuries for Constantinianism to show its faults and more centuries to reverse them. But the validities of history should not be so readily lost to sight. Rather we should be asking ourselves, "To what hazards of the modern world does the First Amendment point today?"

My contention is that it suggests caution in accepting or appointing ourselves to the role of the leader of cooperating religious groups as *surrogates for government* in the saving of the poor. What makes "politicians" what they are—for better or worse—is acting as brokers of civil power, and when churches undertake that activity, they become thereby the same thing as those they replace. Men and institutions are shaped not so much by what they believe they are as by what they do, what they live on and by, what function they perform in life's transactions.

A church which performs governmental functions is to that extent a government, whatever it may call itself, and to that extent (I can maintain this in another paper which would be longer than this one) unfits itself to be a church, which has as church its own unique and indispensable service to perform for society as important as that of government.

What does this contention suggest about the emerging Ecumenical Establishment? That it has a unique opportunity to help shape modern society more the way it ought to be—IF it does not yield to the temptation to exercise rule or authority over the kingdoms of the world.

Suppose that in a given community the leaders of religious bodies—not separately, but together—decide that City Hall is oppressing the poor. Suppose that they thereupon cooperate to offer an alternative structure of civil succor to the poor. Suppose they jointly form a body which obtains federal funds and with them sets up a whole range of services which it administers for the benefit of the poor independently of City Hall—health care centers, headstart programs, mental health clinics, elementary schools, employment retraining, homes for the aged—the whole works. Suppose they provide legal aid to the poor with which to secure their rights from City Hall. Suppose that with this help from the ecumenical anti-poverty body the poor are freed from the oppression of City Hall, and become dependent instead upon the new surrogate for government, the pillars of the several main religious bodies.

Having no terms of office or amenability to the electorate, bearing a joint (and perhaps diminishing) prestige that makes them unassailable, if their works take form and fallibility from their political function, and they become in operation increasingly like City Hall, *how will you turn* THOSE *rascals out?*

NOTES

[1] From *Quadragesimo Anno,* Par. 79.

[2] Executive Order No. 11063.

[3] Cf. Reller, Theodore L., "Public Funds for Religious Education: Canada, England and the Netherlands" in Giannella, ed. *Religion and the Public Order 1965,* Chicago: University of Chicago Press, 1964, pp. 181–191.

[4] *Ibid.,* p. 174.

[5] *Simkins* v. *Moses H. Cone Memorial Hospital,* F(2d) 959 (4 Cir., 1963), Cert. denied, 376, U.S. 938.

[6] *Community Action Program Guide,* Vol. 1 "Instructions for Applicants," p. 19, No. 9b, Office of Economic Opportunity, 1965.

RELIGION AND CONSCIENCE IN CONSTITUTIONAL LAW

by

Elwyn A. Smith

THE immense public attention attracted by the education cases before the Supreme Court since 1947 has left the impression that the Court's concern to frustrate the establishment of religion in one form or another has come to outweigh its concern for freedom of exercise. Justice Potter Stewart, dissenting in *Schempp*,[1] showed concern, for example, for the freedom of children (and their parents) who wished to open the school day with a non-sectarian prayer. Cases subsequent to *Engel v. Vitale*[2] and *Schempp*, however, should satisfy the critics of the Court that this is not the case. In *Sherbert v. Verner*[3] the Court treated religion uniquely as a criterion, contrary to the interpretation put on the "neutrality" concept of the *Schempp* decision by some commentators;[4] and in *United States v. Seeger*[5] has carried concern for protection of objectors to war pleading religious grounds to new lengths through its construction of the Universal Military Training and Service Act of 1951.[6]

The persistent problem of the relation of civil authority to religion was given its American form by the First Amendment itself. The history of European conflict reflected in colonial American history explains the naming of religion at the very head of the Bill of Rights, as well as the forbidding of religious tests for public office in Article 6, Clause 3 of the Constitution. Thus the Constitution *ipso facto* forced on public authority the need to recognize religion in some determinate fashion for the purposes of law: "Neither government nor this Court can or should ignore the significance of the fact that a vast portion of our people believe in and worship God," wrote Justice Goldberg in *Schempp,* Justice Harlan consenting. "Government must inevitably take cognizance of the existence of religion and, indeed, under certain circumstances, the First Amendment requires it to do so."[7] Yet the burden of that Amendment is to require that government shall not intrude on religion, either by favoring or disfavoring it. Definitions of religion, however limited or ingenious, always risk infringing this fundamental constitutional protection of religious liberty. The *Seeger* case brought the Supreme Court into direct confrontation with this problem.

Defining religion is nothing new; court opinions at many levels are abundantly furnished with definitions. The way was easier when the United States was overwhelmingly Christian and dominantly Protestant. In the less stressful year of 1844 Justice Story could write: "It is also said, and truly, that the Christian religion is a part of the common law of Pennsylvania."[8] Justice Brewer could say in 1892: "These [numerous citations] and other matters which might be noticed add a volume of unofficial declarations to the mass of organic utterances that this is a Christian nation."[9] "Religion" was generally assumed to be Christianity and conscientious objectors came almost entirely from the membership of specific peace sects.[10] *Seeger* stands at the modern end of that history and boldly deals with the fact that the traditional assumptions about religion have been obsolete for some time.

Similarly, the assumptions conventionally made about "conscience" have changed. From the beginning of American history religion and conscience have been conjoined. Black's rule that words must be used in their accepted sense[11] has been loyally observed by American jurisprudents. Although amply evident in colonial times,[12] the association of religion and conscience was definitively injected into American Constitutional discussion by James Madison. "The religion of every man must be left to the conviction and conscience of every man; and it is the right of every man to exercise it as these may dictate."[13] Madison's original version of the Bill of Rights read in part as follows: "The civil rights of none shall be abridged on account of religious belief or worship . . . nor shall the full and equal rights of conscience be in any manner, or on any pretext infringed. . . ."[14] The version passed by the House read: "That Congress shall make no law establishing religion or to prevent the free exercise thereof, or to infringe the rights of conscience." The last clause was finally abandoned not because the framers saw a fundamental difference between rights of religion and those of conscience but because the latter seemed amply safeguarded by the religion clauses.[15]

The phrase of the *Memorial and Remonstrance* was to be repeated *ad infinitum:* ". . . the free exercise of religion according to the dictates of conscience." Whether this should be read to mean that anything dictated by conscience should automatically be regarded as religion by the law was a problem reserved to modern times; the Founding Fathers made the assumption that conscience is a forum in man reserved to deity. On that view, government intrusion on conscience infringes the rights of God in man. Madison said in the *Memorial:* "It is the duty of every man to render to the Creator such homage and such only as he believes to be acceptable to him. This duty is precedent both in order of time and degree of obligation to the claims of Civil Society." He spoke of free exercise according to the dictates of conscience as a "gift of nature" and a "fundamental right." The notion that the imperative of conscience might proceed not from divine authority but from the mind's ingestion of social custom, psychological conditioning, or non-religious philosophical training is not reflected in these early documents.[16]

The assumed relation of conscience to deity prevailed even when certain justices used expressions capable of a more secular interpretation. "The state has a perfect right to prohibit polygamy," wrote Justice Bradley in 1890, "and all other open offenses against the enlightened sentiment of mankind, notwithstanding the pretense of religious conviction by which they may be advocated and practised."[17] "Enlightened general sentiment" was understood by his generation to be the product of Christianity. Without that presupposition, Justice Bradley might have been here announcing a concept of secular conscience. As it was, the claim to be "religious" advanced by the Mormons was vitiated, in his view, by its violation of common sentiment. It was barbarism, not religion. Justice Bradley could not conceive that polygamy might be advocated in good conscience.

II

Legal thought has assumed for some time that conscientious objection to war must proceed from one of three sources: "religious" objection; "ethical" or "moral" objection; or "political" and "sociological" (and lately "philosophical") objection.[18] The grip of this venerable preconception is evident in the draft law of 1951 and in the government's brief in the *Seeger* case. But what is the relation of "conscience" or "conscientiousness" to these three areas in which objection to war may be made? A man may have conscientious scruples in any or all of these classes. The draft laws of the United States have never exempted men whose political objections to war were conscientiously held; yet conscience ordinarily figures in some way in political decisions. The earlier technique of requiring that the claimant for exemption show that he is a member of a historic peace church, abandoned in the 1940 law, was not intended to eliminate the role of conscience. A man may fall in any or all the three above classes of objection to war in good conscience and not be the member of such a sect. "Conscience" is clearly a broader term than religion.[19]

On the other hand, popular assumption, traditional Christian theology, and the law agree in feeling that the imperative character of conscience reflects an origin that is more than human. The dilemma is neatly posed by the government's brief in *Seeger.* "In *Torcaso,* the Court speaks of non-believers and of believers in religion who do not believe in the existence of God. Surely 'non-believers' does not mean people without conscience. Instead, non-believers, in the opinion as in common usage, means those people who recognize no authority above the obligation of man to his fellow man. In contrast, the Court clearly labelled as religious those who do not believe in God within the normal meaning of that word but who do believe that man has definite obligations to a force superior to himself."[20] From such reasoning it is only a short step to the view that anyone who feels a "definite sense of obligation" is, whether he knows and acknowledges it or not, responding to a "force superior to himself."

To identify religion with conscience and to grant exemption to any individual who might feel a pang of conscience would create havoc, it has been uniformly felt by American legislators. There are several ways out: to cut back on the latitude granted to conscientious objection held individually in favor of a group identity (as provided in the Draft Law of 1917, for example); to separate religious scruples from those that are conscientious but not religious by a *tour de force* of definition; to accept conscientious objection based on religious (or on religious and ethical) grounds but exclude conscientiously held political objection (in effect, establishing a distinction between "religious" and "secular" conscience); or to accept all sincere objection. In making such choices, legislatures and courts must balance private right and/or privilege with the public interest.

The blending of religious and ethical objections poses no problem if a religious element as recognized by law dominates. The problem is posed when the objector claims to be religious and ethical but does not conform to the going understanding of "religion." *Hamilton v. Regents of the University of California*[21] was the sort of case for which the law was prepared. "Appellants as members of [the Methodist Episcopal] Church accept and feel themselves morally, religiously, and conscientiously bound by its tenets and disciplines. . . . Each is a follower of the teachings of Jesus Christ: each accepts as a guide His teachings and those of the Bible, and holds as a part of his religious and conscientious belief that war [is] immoral, wrong, and contrary to the letter and spirit of his teaching and the precepts of the Christian religion." The Court rejected the appeal for relief from required service in the R.O.T.C. not because of any misalignment of religion, morality, and conscience, but because students at the University had freely chosen to enroll and were held to have freely opted for all the requirements of the school.

These objectors to R.O.T.C. had protested as individuals. What weight should be given a private state of mind? Concurring in *Hamilton,* Justice Cardozo remarked: "Never in our history has the notion been accepted or even, it is believed, advanced, that acts . . . indirectly related to service in camp or field are so tied to the practice of religion as to be exempt, in law or in morals, from regulation by the state. . . . The conscientious objector, if his liberties were to be thus extended, might refuse to contribute taxes in furtherance of a war, whether for attack or for defense, or in furtherance of any other end condemned by his conscience as irreligious or immoral. The right of private judgment has never yet been so exalted above the powers and the compulsion of the agencies of government."

The scruples of these youths were religiously based, church-supported, ethical, and conscientious, but the field in which they wanted them applied went far beyond exemption from military conscription for combatant service. This created a problem. No matter how religious, how moral, how conscientious, how fully identified with a church, there are limits. In exercise of private judgment, whether religious or not, a claimant cannot expect protection which jeopardizes the nation; neither the draft legislation nor the Constitution provide it. Even the authority that arises from the presumption that it is God who is heard in the conscience still cannot justify endangering the nation. It seems fair to see here an unspoken assumption about the nature of conscience: that it is not only a divine voice in man but also "secular," since it has a serious impact upon such secular affairs as the national safety; and that its "religious" element exists in tandem with an ineradicable secular quality derived from the existence of man in a secular environment. The latter circumstance justifies prudential limitations upon the field of exemption from national service.

The exact weight which should be granted to a purely private state of the moral mind as against the public interest was fully canvassed in the flag salute cases: *Minersville v. Gobitis* (1940) and *Board of Education v. Barnette* (1943).[22] In both cases, Justice Frankfurter took the position that the public weal overruled private scruples arising from the objectors' religion; but in *Barnette* the Court reversed *Gobitis* and ruled for the objectors on the ground that refusal to salute the flag did not amount to "grave danger to the nation," that an enforced ceremonial was "more likely to defeat than to serve its high purpose," and that such a requirement was a "handy implement for disguised religious persecution." Concurring, Justice Murphy declared flatly that the right to choose and believe as one wished "according to the dictates of conscience"—on an entirely personal basis—was "a right which the Constitution specifically shelters." Still, the ambit of the case was fixed by the principle of danger to the nation.

III

The intermixture of these elements in *United States v. Macintosh*[23] gives it particular interest for this inquiry. Professor D. C. Macintosh of the Yale Divinity School was an applicant for citizenship, not a pacifist, and did not represent himself as a conscientious objector to war in all circumstances.[24] He affirmed that "the individual citizen should have the right respectfully to withhold from the government military services . . . when his best moral judgment would compel him to do so." The question was military service, the critical issue (by contrast with marginal services, such as R.O.T.C. training in the *Hamilton* case), although it was not a draft exemption question being decided in time of war. Private judgment not specifically associated with a "peace church" figured centrally; as did moral conviction and, of course, conscience. There was one further element: Professor Macintosh's scruples were directly associated with his religious convictions, which were wholly traditional in that they spoke expressly of "the will of God," in contrast with the problem posed to the Second Circuit Court of Appeals by *Kauten* and other similar cases.[25] Professor Macintosh "could not put allegiance to the government of any country before allegiance to the will of God."

Macintosh was denied citizenship. The Court feared intrusion of private judgment into the sphere of the state. The war power of the state includes "the power, in the last extremity, to compel the armed service of any citizen in the land, without regard to his objections or his views in respect of the justice or morality of the particular war or of war in general." These scruples, even though based on a religion that spoke expressly of "God" as well as morality and political judgment, were firmly classified as a matter of private judgment. "When he speaks of putting his allegiance to the will of God above his allegiance to the government . . . he means to make his own interpretation of the will of God the decisive test. . . ." Peremptorily to have dismissed Professor Macintosh's scruples, which conformed perfectly to the traditional American understanding of the form of conscience protected by the law, as belonging to the sphere of private judgment was a refusal to give their religious character its customary weight. In effect, the decision classified his objections as political rather than religious.

It had never before been a problem to the law that a man's religion involved "his own interpretation of the will of God"; on the contrary, it had always been understood that an inevitable privacy was inextricably involved with the character of religion. By dealing with Professor Macintosh's scruples without regard to the religious weight they bore, by treating them simply as political, the Court identified his conscience as secular. Later courts repeatedly faced the same combination of religious, moral, and political scruples; but they gave the former the dominant weight once they were validated as sincerely operative in the mind of the objector. Only when conscience was found not to be associated with religion but only with political, sociological, and, more ambiguously, with philosophical objections was it set aside.

Chief Justice Hughes' dissent foreshadowed the reversal of the Court's position in *Girouard v. United States.*[26] Against the *Macintosh* majority, Hughes announced the fundamental and historical position developed to that date. "When one's belief collides with the power of the state, the latter is supreme within its sphere and submission or punishment follows. But in the forum of conscience, duty to a moral power higher than the state has always been maintained. . . . The essence of religion is belief in a relation to God involving duties superior to those arising from any human relation." This is not the first time that a

Supreme Court justice had launched into a definition of religion, as Justice Hughes pointed out, quoting *Davis v. Beason.*[27] "The term 'religion' has reference to one's views of his relations to his Creator and to the obligations they impose of reverence for his being and character and of obedience to his will." Chief Justice Hughes commented: "Freedom of conscience itself implies respect for an innate conviction of paramount duty. The battle for religious liberty has been fought and won with respect to religious beliefs and practices which are not in conflict with good order, upon the very ground of the supremacy of conscience within its proper field."

Consistently with this thinking, Justice Douglas, writing for the majority in *Girouard,* wrote: "The struggle for religious liberty has through the centuries been an effort to accommodate the demands of the State to the conscience of the individual. The victory for freedom of thought recorded in our Bill of Rights recognizes that in the domain of conscience there is a moral power higher than the State." Madison had not fixed on membership in a pacifist sect as a criterion of true religiousness or true conscientiousness; neither did Hughes or Douglas. The issue was re-established on its original ground of the individual conscience alone in the draft laws of 1940, 1948 and 1951. The familiar assumptions of individual decision and response to "higher power" continued to be made.

Conscience as a "forum" separates out a distinct sphere in the mind of man in which an authority higher than his own or his fellow-man's operates commandingly. Justice Clark spoke of an "inviolable citadel of the individual heart and mind" in *Schempp* in 1963. The problem for Hughes and later courts was this: does individual decision to refuse obedience to a draft call fall within the legally protected "proper field" of conscience; or do claims for exemption fall outside it? What are the bounds of that "proper field"? Religion? If so, what are the bounds of religion? What about morals? The same question may be asked.

Must the operation of conscience always be disallowed when the claimant advances political objections to national service in the absence of "religious" reasons?

IV

Congress had wrestled with these problems through a succession of draft laws. This history has been well reviewed.[28] While the intimacy of religion and conscience suggested to the Founders that freedom for the operation of the latter was encompassed in the protections of the First Amendment, the particular problem of conscientious objection remained to be dealt with by statute. "The fact that Congress moved into the field of conscientious objection as early as 1811 indicates that the generation closest to the Founding Fathers did not feel that the First Amendment secured the rights of conscientious objectors."[29] Thus began the long struggle to define the ground and sphere of statutory protection for *bona fide* conscientious objection to national service. We shall deal here with changes between the draft laws of 1917 and 1951 as they illuminate the evolution of thought that led in the direction of *Seeger.*[30]

The Draft Act of 1917[31] provided exemption to conscientious objectors who were affiliated with a "well-recognized religious sect or organization [then] organized and existing and whose existing creed or principles [forbade] its members to participate in war in any form. . . ."[32] This rule was superceded in the 1940 Draft Law[33] by the provision that exemption was open to those whose objection to war was based on "religious training and belief." As the Supreme Court pointed out in *Seeger,* "the Congress recognized that one might be religious without belonging to an organized church" and thus oppose war conscientiously. The obverse of this needs also to be noted, as it was in *United States v. Simmons:*[34] "affiliation with a particular religious sect does not *per se* entitle a registrant to objector status. The duty imposed on the [draft] board is to determine subjectively and objectively the sincerity of the individual's belief, not the nature of the teachings of any religious faith."[35] Nevertheless, the affiliation of a professed objector with a church either teaching pacifism or if non-pacifist, testifying to its confidence in objecting members continued to be important, as indicated by the actions of numerous major American denominations[36] and of the United States District Court which wrote in *United States v. Hein:*[37] "[If] each case [were to] be determined on whether the individual himself was a conscientious objector . . . that would open the door to chaos and fraud."[38] This judicial observation notwithstanding, the traditional emphasis on the entitlement of the individual to a personal view, the uniform acceptance of the standard of sincerity, and the manifest impropriety of exempting whole classes of draft age men according to religious affiliation alone rather than personal attitude continued to demand that draft boards and courts judge the objector's own views. The draft laws of 1940, 1948, and 1951 at once broadened and narrowed the law: they broadened the exemption provision to include sincere and religiously motivated objectors not members of peace churches; they limited it to just those members of peace churches who personally objected to war on grounds of "religious training and belief." Presumably a Mennonite or Quaker who objected to war largely on political grounds would have had a stronger claim to exemption under the 1917 statute than under those that followed.

Before the draft law of 1948 was drawn, the celebrated contest between the Second and Ninth Circuit Courts of Appeal broke out, symbolized by the conflict between *Berman v. United States,*[39] expressing the thought of the Ninth Circuit, and *United States v. Kauten,*[40] containing a line of thinking spelled out by the Second Circuit Court not only there but also in *United States ex rel. Phillips v. Downer.*[41] (The Supreme Court denied certiorari in this case (375 US 930) and *United States ex rel. Reel v. Badt.*[42]) There was a substantive difference between the conservative construction placed on the 1940 draft law by the Ninth Circuit Court when it contended in *Berman* that if "the exemption from military service written into the [1940] statute runs to all who sincerely entertain conscientious objection to participation in war . . . the phrase 'by reason of religious training and belief' would have no practical effect whatever."[43] As the *Brief for the United States* in *Seeger* pointed out, the Ninth Circuit Court concluded that the defining phrase "was written into the statute for the specific purpose of distinguishing between a conscientious social belief, or a sincere devotion to a high moralistic philosophy, and one based upon an individual's belief in his responsibility to an authority higher and beyond any worldly one."[44]

The Ninth Circuit Court quoted Chief Justice Hughes' dissent in *Macintosh,* defining religion: "The essence of religion is belief in a relation to God involving duties superior to those arising from any human relation." The key point in debate between the two courts hinged on the scope of the word "religion." Hughes associated it with belief in "God"—not a philosophical "godness" or "supreme being." The required sense of obligation was larger than the natural sense of duty between men; it must point to the supernatural. "Religion" to Hughes and most of his generation involved the supernatural. If this point were preserved, some latitude of definition might be permitted. If, for example, the term "Supreme Being" were understood to preserve the suggestion of the supernatural, its use would remain consistent with Hughes' intention. The same applied to conscience: if a sense of obligation is construed to reflect a command from beyond the natural sphere—mutual human obligation is "natural"—then precisely *that* objector was entitled to exemption. Political objection reflects that conscience which arises from a wholly natural sense of obligation; politics is secular; so it is a secular conscience. Religious conscience is aroused by an authority dictating obligations "superior to those arising from any human relation"—political, social, familial, intellectual. The world view that distinguishes natural from supernatural is axiomatic to the thinking of the Ninth Circuit Court. In *Berman* it spoke explicitly of "an authority higher and beyond any worldly one."

The point at which Judge Augustus Hand attacked the problem was defined by R. G. Phillips in *United States ex rel. Phillips v. Downer, Col.*[45] Phillips believed that "war is ethically and invariably wrong." He stated: "my opposition to war rested on basic ethical and humanitarian grounds, essentially religious in character." Again, he spoke of "a general humanitarian concept which is essentially religious in character."[46] This kind of language short-circuited the wires of legal tradition. On the familiar assumptions, it was nonsense to term a basically humanitarian scruple "religious." The draft law of 1940 was not intended to exempt such cases. But the reality faced by Judge Hand was that the common meaning of "religion" had already broadened well before 1940. Well known as his phrases are to students of this problem, they require quotation here.

> It is unnecessary to attempt a definition of religion; the content of the term is found in the history of the human race and is incapable of compression into a few words. Religious belief arises from a sense of the inadequacy of reason as a means of relating the individual to his fellowmen and to his universe—a sense common to men in the most primitive and in the most highly civilized societies. It accepts the aid of logic but refuses to be limited by it. It is a belief finding expression in a conscience which categorically requires the believer to disregard elementary self-interest and to accept martyrdom in preference to transgressing its tenets. A religious obligation forbade Socrates, even in order to escape condemnation, to decide questions without favor to anyone and only according to law. Recognition of this obligation moved the Greek poet Menander to write almost twenty-four hundred years ago: 'Conscience is a God to all mortals'; impelled Socrates to obey the voice of his 'Daimon' and led Wordsworth to characterize 'Duty' as the 'Stern Daughter of the Voice of God.'
>
> There is a distinction between a course of reasoning resulting in a

conviction that a particular war is inexpedient or disastrous and a conscientious objection to participation in any war under any circumstances. The latter, and not the former, may be the basis of exemption under the Act. The former is usually a political objection, while the latter, we think, may justly be regarded as a response of the individual to an inward mentor, call it conscience or God, that is for many persons at the present time the equivalent of what has always been thought a religious impulse.[47]

From these and other considerations Judge Hand ruled that Congress intended to "take into account the characteristics of a skeptical generation" not disposed to divide all being into natural and supernatural; and that it intended to make "the existence of a conscientious scruple against war in any form, rather than allegiance to a definite religious group or creed, the basis of exemption."

We think that the *Brief for the United States* in *Seeger* proved its contention that the Congress did not intend so much as this, even though the Supreme Court argued that the Congress' reference to *Berman* "might mean a number of things." Clearly the Congress did avoid the issue between the viewpoints of *Kauten* in the Second Circuit and *Berman* in the Ninth, as the Supreme Court asserted. That is one reason this question came to the Supreme Court in *Seeger*. The Court noted that the above remarks of Judge Hand did not mean that Kauten should be exempt since his objections were exclusively political. But the reasoning in *Kauten* had far larger implications. Suppose Kauten, an atheist, instead of objecting only to some wars on political grounds had categorically refused to participate in war in any form, professing conscientious scruples. Would he not be exempt on Judge Hand's reasoning? His political objections would be superseded by the more deeply rooted ground of his objection. As Judge Hand saw it, it is the *categorical* quality of an inward command that merits its recognition by the draft legislation.

This viewpoint faced the fact that there has occurred a breakdown of the world view that is fundamental to the present draft laws. The law is not happy to find that it has erected statutes on theological foundations. The assumption of the national draft law is that there exists a clear division between the natural and the supernatural in the sphere of being. This leads to the further assumption that objectors to war may be divided between adherents of "natural," "secular" objection to war and adherents of "supernatural," "religious" objections. It is further assumed that authentic objectors will ordinarily fall in the latter class, with the effect that justice will be done to the nation's reluctance to force men of conscience to violate their convictions. The trouble is that many persons of profound and honest conviction have abandoned the natural-supernatural view of the universe. Secular conscience is as sincere and often far better taught than the Mennonite farmer or sophisticated Quaker whose exemption from military service has never been disputed in the United States. Most secular conscientious objectors do not regard themselves as irreligious and few are atheists; typically they are agnostic, a "skeptical generation." They have been trained not to affirm what they cannot know, whether their knowledge is scientific or intuitive. They do not deny God; but they cannot affirm him. To them "religion" is an ideal of mankind.

In *Kauten, Phillips,* and *Badt* the draft law of 1940 was confronted with a class of persons with whom it was not equipped to deal. The same was true of the Jehovah's Witnesses: they refused conscientious objector status and claimed to be ministers but were not, according to accepted standards. They composed the largest single class of persons convicted under the law of 1940.[48] The obvious solution is legislative: the Congress should write a new law taking account of these strange classes of objectors in a manner consistent with the Madisonian tradition and its evolution in American law. The Congress did write new laws in 1948 and 1951. But they reveal no alteration aimed to relieve the problem posed by the Jehovah's Witnesses even though they did not altogether ignore the philosophical conflict exposed by the two circuit courts. In 1948 Congress changed "God" (the language of Hughes in *Macintosh*) to "Supreme Being," while retaining the fundamental theological substructure of the earlier law. This it made plain when it defined "religious training and belief," the admissible reason for conscientious objection, as "an individual's belief in a Supreme Being involving duties superior to those arising from any human relation, but [not including] essentially political, sociological, or philosophical views or a merely personal moral code." It further asserted its intention to "reinact . . . substantially the same provisions" for exemption as contained in the 1940 law.[49] The laws of 1948 and 1951 make the same assumptions as the Ninth Circuit Court in the *Berman* decision, not those propounded by Judge Hand in *Kauten, Phillips,* and *Badt.*

V

The Congress having maintained the older position, the problem continued to come into the courts. The Supreme Court may have indicated general agreement with the point of view of the Second Circuit when it refused certiorari in earlier appeals from its judgment,[50] but the *Seeger* decision was deliberately limited. Since none of the three men before it was an atheist, its decision did not reach that question. Second, it excluded claims made on the basis of the First Amendment, even though Judge Hand had written in his judgment on *Seeger:* "[Congress] has transgressed the limits imposed by the Constitution . . ." in limiting the exemption privilege to believers in a Supreme Being and excluding other sorts of religious people. The Supreme Court was nevertheless moved by Judge Hand's remark that "for Daniel Seeger, the stern and moral voice of conscience occupies that hallowed place in the hearts and minds of men which was traditionally reserved for the commandments of God," as its test indicates.[51]

Because the *Kauten* dicta pose the problem more radically than did Seeger, Jakobson, and Peter, there is a balance of thinking in Judge Hand's opinion which has not been adjudicated but may yet have to be taken into account, if a claim to exemption by a professed atheist should reach the Supreme Court.

After *Kauten* came the *Torcaso* decision. In his opinion on *Seeger,* Judge Hand wrote: "Our decision in *Kauten* was the precursor of *Torcaso. . . .* Today a pervading commitment to a moral ideal is for many the equivalent of what was historically considered the response to divine commands. . . ."[52] *Torcaso v. Watkins,*[53] it will be remembered, ruled that a notary public could not, under the Establishment Clause of the First Amendment, be required to take an oath which required belief in God. "Neither a State nor the Federal Government," wrote the Court, "can constitutionally . . . aid those religions founded on different beliefs." Actually, two issues are presented here: one posed by religions that do not believe in "God" or a "Supreme Being" but do affirm the transcendental—Justice Douglas cited Buddhism, Hinduism, and others in his concurring opinion in *Seeger* —and another posed by deeply felt religiousness that is not associated with a recognized historical religion and does not claim a transcendental reference. The change in the draft law between 1940 and 1948 represents an accommodation of the law to American believers in the transcendent whose faith is not modelled on the Judaeo-Christian tradition; e.g., the 80,000 Buddhist Americans. It cannot be construed as an adaptation to Judge Hand's viewpoint. The government brief in *Seeger* demonstrated that the Congress specifically rejected proposals that this more extensive adaptation should be introduced into the law.[54]

Torcaso said nothing about atheism; it denied only government power to favor religions "based on belief in the existence of God as against those religions founded on different beliefs." In this frame of reference, "atheism" is not a "religion founded on other beliefs." The "other beliefs" intended in that phrase affirm the transcendental. *Torcaso,* therefore, remained within the ambit of the natural-supernatural distinction. *Kauten,* on the other hand, did not. Here is the significant issue; on this point hangs the significance of *Seeger* for the law's understanding of religion and conscience.

The term "atheist" may be understood not synonymously with "nihilist," "anarchist," or "bloody revolutionary" but to denote a man who denies the existence of God, any Supreme Being, and even the reality of the transcendent. Such a view would distinguish him from Buddhist and Hindu as well as from Jew, Christian, and Moslem. An atheist's claim to exemption on ground of conscientious objection to war would rest exclusively on humanitarian grounds. It might be as deeply felt as any man's; it would be moral, if it be conceded that one who denies God but affirms man may be moral; and it would doubtless be as fully intertwined with political, sociological, and philosophical views as a modern Quaker's. Kauten himself was an atheist but he did not oppose war as such; rather he claimed exemption on ground of "a course of reasoning resulting in a conviction that a particular war is inexpedient or disastrous. . . ." Not doubting his good conscience, Judge Hand saw a difference between earnestness in political conviction and "a conscientious objection to participation in any war under any circumstances" and disallowed his claim. The outcome would have been different, we suppose, if this atheist had objected categorically, conscientiously, and sincerely to war in any form. Kauten would then have been responding to the "inward mentor" of Judge Hand's opinion, which for purposes of law would have been equivalent to a "religious impulse."

The *Brief for the Government* argued the danger of too close an identification of religion and conscience. "If religion includes conscience, the First Amendment would be expanded beyond anything either the framers or this Court ever suggested. It would mean that a wide variety of governmental regulations would raise First Amendment issues whenever they happened to conflict with action taken by persons which was based on philosophical and moral views. For example, a man may have a strong philosophical belief that labor unions are evil. Surely, a free-exercise-of-religion question is not raised if he refuses to bargain with a union in his plant."[55] Attorneys for the government proposed to resolve this *reductio ad absurdum* by distinguishing between religious and non-religious objectors along familiar lines: a Jew refuses to eat pork on ground that God has forbidden it; Seeger, Jakobson, and Britt object to war "entirely on the basis of their own reasoning."

Judge Hand's response to the above argument, we suppose, would be to grant exemption to anyone whose objection to war is comprehensive, categorical, and sincere. No extension of the First Amendment along lines envisioned in the above Brief would figure. No vague new "religion" would be added to those that contemplate God, a Supreme Being, or transcendence, whatever that might mean. Rather "religiousness" would be respected by the law—if a word cognate to "religion" need be retained. Sincerity and thoroughness of conviction would be the actual criteria. Judge Hand's argument leads to the British Act of 1939.[56]

How far did *Seeger* go in this direction?

The Justices posed the question of the case in a way that immediately goes beyond narrow construction of the terminology of the 1948 and 1951 laws. "Our question . . . is the narrow one: Does the term 'Supreme Being' as used in [section] 6(j) [of the Universal Military Training and Service Act of 1951] mean the orthodox God or the broader concept of a power or being, or a faith 'to which all else is subordinate or upon which all else is ultimately dependent?' " The word "being" is used here not in the upper case sense of synonymity with "God" but in the philosophical sense: "there are those who think of God as the depth of our being." To Hinduism, "God" is "transcendental reality." Already we are deep in the territory of philosophy, one of the three areas deliberately excluded by the draft law when it said that "religious training and belief" excluded "essentially political, sociological, or philosophical views or a merely personal moral code."

A first issue lies in the question: were Seeger's beliefs "essentially . . . philosophical"? "At trial Seeger's Counsel admitted that Seeger's belief was not in relation to a Supreme Being as commonly understood. . . ." He believed "in a devotion to goodness and virtue for their own sakes, and a religious faith in a purely ethical creed." He affirmed "ethical belief in intellectual and moral integrity 'without belief in God except in the remotest sense.'" Jakobson came a little closer to the Judaeo-Christian tradition in its familiar American form: "he believed in a 'Supreme Being' who was 'Creator of Man' in the sense of being 'ultimately responsible for the existence' of man and who was 'the Supreme Reality' of which 'the existence of man is the result.'" Jakobson defined religion as the "sum and essence of one's basic attitudes to the fundamental problems of human existence." Forest Britt Peter (no. 29) quoted John Haynes Holmes' definition of religion as "the consciousness of some power manifest in nature which helps man in the ordering of his life in harmony with its demands . . . [It] is the supreme expression of human nature; it is man thinking his highest, feeling his deepest, and living his best." All these registrants gave evidence of having read and been formed in their thinking by literature clearly religious by traditional standards.

These men had adopted a viewpoint at once philosophical and religious, affirming a principle of transcendence quite different from the natural-supernatural dichotomy of Chief Justice Hughes' generation. That transcendence, even Jakobson's novel definition of the Supreme Being, is continuous with human existence, not clearly distinct from it; while clear separation of spheres is fundamental to the traditional religious dichotomy. Because these men adhered to a concept of the transcendent, they were not termed atheists, although on traditional western theological views of God, they might have been. The ground of their conscientious objection could not, however, be termed "religious" as against "philosophical." The decision for Seeger in the Circuit and Supreme Courts had the effect of bringing together, for purposes of law, the concept of "religious belief" with any philosophy which acknowledges transcendent reality, whether qualitatively different from humanity or continuous with it.

The Supreme Court formally cut free of the theology of the draft law by declaring that the Congress could not have intended any "picking and choosing among religious beliefs." That phrase was really a *tour de force.* Read one way, it might mean: In view of its respect for the First Amendment, the Congress could not have intended to make any decision between a monistic view of the cosmos (excluding it as "philosophy") and a dichotomous view of the cosmos (declaring the natural-supernatural division of reality essential to legal definition of "religion"). Read less exactly: Since some religious beliefs are also philosophical, we cannot believe the Congress intended to disallow those customarily expressed philosophically. In any case, the Court chose the broader interpretation of "religion," consistently with Judge Hand.

The exclusion in 1951 of objectors pleading only a "merely personal moral code" was handled similarly. We have noted that thinking on conscientious objection has traditionally postulated three basic grounds: religious; ethical and moral; and practical —political and sociological. "A merely personal moral code" must be understood as referring to the second of these. "The use by Congress of the words 'merely personal,' " wrote the Court, "seems to us to restrict the exception [which would deny the registrant deferment] to a moral code which is not only personal but which is the sole basis for the registrant's belief and is in no way related to a Supreme Being."

The fact that religious and philosophical views are held "personally" is not relevant as a factor of exclusion: it has long been assumed that such views are so held. The special meaning of the phrase derives from the second class of traditional supporting grounds for conscientious objection. The excluded "moral code" is one which denies all reference to transcendent authority.

If this is a correct construction of this text, the Court meant business when it remarked that "the question is not one between theistic and atheistic beliefs. We do not deal with or intimate any decision on that situation in this case." This is a decision only about the application of the statute to different sorts of theists, including philosophical transcendentalists. "Theists" include any who affirm man's own self-transcendence; these are exempt under the terms of Section 6(j) of the draft law. But the *Seeger* decision cannot be read to exempt atheists if by atheist is meant an objector who denies all religious doctrines or secular philosophies of the transcendent. That question is not only formally but substantively excluded.[57]

The reasoning summarized to this point enabled the Supreme Court to avoid judgment on the First Point of the *Brief for the Respondent:* "Section 6(j) of the Universal Military Training and Service Act (50 U.S.C.A., App. no. 456(j), as amended by Congress in 1948 by the insertion of the 'Supreme Being' provision, is invalid, as in violation of the 'religion' clauses of the First Amendment of the United States Constitution, Congress thus created a preference and an aid in favor of conscientious objectors whose conscientious objection is related to, or based upon, a belief in a Supreme Being, as against those conscientious objectors whose objection is related to, or based upon, some other type of religious training or belief. Congress, thus, has abandoned the 'neutral' position in respect of religions placed on government by the First Amendment."[58] The Court effectively answered this by construing the law to include not only Buddhism and other historical religions whose view of supreme being denies the natural-supernatural dichotomy of traditional Christian religion, but all transcendentalists. If this is what the law means, it does not violate the First Amendment. The Respondent's attorney had not argued that the draft law discriminated against non-religious objectors but only that it preferred one form of religion to another. The decision extended the draft law's protection to the furthest reach of transcendental philosophy but no farther.[59]

Not only did *Seeger* not decide the case of the atheist objector; it refused to follow Judge Hand's lead as far as Seeger's attorneys would have liked. ". . . The Constitution [draws no] line between a religious belief compelled, externally, from an assumed divine command and one that is compelled, internally, from the dictates of conscience (Gov. Br. 75,76). The Government (Gov. Br. 66) suggests that 'religion' does not include 'conscience' and that 'conscience' and 'religion' cannot be equated for purposes of the First Amendment. Actually, the two terms were equated in colonial constitutions and in the debates in the Constitutional Convention, and are still being so used today. . . . Judge Hand was entirely right in observing in *Kauten,* . . . (at p. 708), that the response of an individual to conscience is a 'religious impulse.' "[60]

This argument omits several points. While it is certainly right that the authors of the First Amendment assumed that rights of conscience were protected by it, most assumed that both religion and conscience received their content from supernatural sources. The equation of religion and conscience can be maintained even when a different philosophy intervenes. For Seeger, conscience speaks for the transcendent ideal of man; for him this is also the meaning of "religion." For an atheist, conscience is simply man's concrete self engaged in moral affirmation. Judge Hand's exposition in principle would admit both of these. The attorneys for

Seeger actually had no interest in pleading the second of these. This point was caught by the Supreme Court and it refused to embrace both the above classes in its decision. It vindicated Seeger but not sincere proponents of an exclusively phenomenological view of man.

The "test" proposed by the Court neatly draws this line: "Does the claimed belief occupy the same place in the life of the objector as an orthodox belief in God holds in the life of one clearly qualified for exemption?" All the definitions of religion that the Justices quoted express philosophical idealism.[61] "The same place" in the life of an unorthodox objector is a transcendent authority—not transcendent in the same way as supernatural, but transcendent still. We do not think that the compunctions felt by an atheist who repudiates both these philosophies of religion can fall within the purview of the *Seeger* decision.

There can be no question that the *Seeger* decision liberalizes and updates the scope of the draft exemption provisions. The whole line of decisions typified by *Berman* in the Ninth Circuit Court[62] was denied when *Britt* was reversed. The statement that "Congress, in using the expression 'Supreme Being' rather than the designation 'God' was merely clarifying the meaning of religious training and belief so as to embrace all religions and to exclude essentially political, sociological, and philosophical views" included not only Buddhists and Hindus, which the Congress seems to have expressly intended, but also the religious philosophies of Seeger, Jakobson, and Britt. Unmistakably the Court has affirmed the impossibility of distinguishing philosophy from religion for the purposes of the law. Its nearest approach to altering the law lay in its absorption of transcendental philosophy to "religious training and belief" as admissible grounds for objection. It closed no doors, not even to a view of "religion" broadened to include any conscience "which categorically requires the believer to disregard elementary self-interest."

Did the Court give us still another definition of religion? Yes; in that it voted for subjectivity as a regulative principle in determining exemption entitlement under a law that makes "religious training and belief" the hinge. No; in that it moved away from earlier tendencies to define religion in terms of a particular doctrine of God or fundamental religious philosophy, although it did not succeed in wholly renouncing them. Dr. Tillich's view that religion is "what you take seriously without any reservation," quoted approvingly by the Court, wholly evades definition of beliefs. The operative principle of Seeger is not whether the belief held is religion according to a determinate standard, but whether the belief, whatever it is, functions authoritatively for the believer. With religiousness substituted for religion, the focus changes. "While the 'truth' of a belief is not open to question [by the state], there remains the significant question whether it is truly held. This is the threshold question of sincerity which must be resolved in every case. It is, of course, a question of fact—a prime consideration to the validity of every claim for exemption as a conscientious objector." As religiousness has supplanted religion, conscientiousness in the form of sincerity has supplanted moral precepts as the content of conscience. One datum of content remains relevant to conscientious objection: scruple about war. And one datum of content remains to religion: the authority to which the objector responds must in some sense be transcendent. If there is another way the law may bend to personal conscience without permitting every man to become a law to himself, the Congress and the courts have yet to find it.

NOTES

[1] 374 U.S. 203 (1963).
[2] 370 U.S. 421 (1962).
[3] 374 U.S. 398 (1963).
[4] Cf. Philip Kurland, *Religion and the Law of Church and State and the Supreme Court* (Chicago, 1962).

[5] —U.S.—, 85 S. Ct. 850 (1965)

[6] 50 U.S.C. App. 456 (j).

[7] 374 U.S. 306

[8] *Vidal v. Girard's Executors.* 2 Howard 205 (1844).

[9] *Church of the Holy Trinity v. United States* (143 U.S. 226).

[10] R. R. Russell. "Development of Conscientious Objector Recognition in the United States," 20 *George Washington Law Review,* 109.

[11] *The Interpretation of Laws* (2nd ed.) at 141.

[12] F. J. Conklin. "Conscientious Objector Provisions, a View in the Light of *Torcaso v. Watkins,*" 51 Georgetown Law Review, 252.

[13] *Memorial and Remonstrance.*

[14] I Annals of Congress 434 (1789).

[15] H. A. Freeman. "A Remonstrance for Conscience," 106 *Pennsylvania Law Review* 806, 808–13.

[16] Cf., for example, Emile Durkheim. *L'Éducation Morale.* Presse Universitaire de France 1963 (original edition 1934), 20–25.

[17] *The Late Corporation of the Church of Jesus Christ of the Latter-Day Saints v. United States,* 136 U.S. 1.

[18] Cf. 20 Oregon Law Review 301; *Pearson v. Coale* (165 Md. 224), 167 Atl. 54. Also Smith and Bell. "The Conscientious Objector Program: A Search for Sincerity," 19 *Pittsburgh Law Review* 707.

[19] This point was taken up by the government in the *Seeger* case. Cf. *Brief for the United States,* 75; *Reply Brief for the United States, passim.*

[20] *Brief for the United States* at 75.

[21] 293 U.S. 245 (1934).

[22] 310 U.S. 586; 319 U.S. 624.

[23] 283 U.S. 605 (1931).

[24] 42 F 2nd 845; at 846.

[25] *United States v. Kauten* 133 Fed. 2nd. 703; Feb. 8, 1943. Also *U.S. v. Schwimmer* 279 U.S. 644; 27 F 2nd 742. Mrs. Schwimmer declared herself an atheist; 42 F 2nd 845; at 849. Cf. *Bland,* 283 U.S. 636 (1931).

[26] 328 U.S. 61 (1946).

[27] 133 U.S. 333.

[28] Cf. Russell, *op. cit.*

[29] Conklin, *op. cit.* at 264.

[30] A range of exemption cases touching technical legal questions arose in 1944 with *Falbo v. U.S.* (320 U.S. 549). These are not pertinent to this study. Cf. 50 Northwestern University Law Review at 660 for a summary of these. Neither do certain objective grounds of exemption figure in this discussion: for example, ministerial status. *Dickinson v. United States* (346 U.S. 389 (1953)) and preceding cases, many of them relating to the claims of Jehovah's Witnesses, were settled on that ground. A clear difference between such objective criteria and the more subtle problem of conscientious objection was recognized in *United States v. Simmons* (213 Fed. 2nd 901). "The task of probing into and intelligently appraising the conscience of another is a difficult and unhappy one. . . . Whether a registrant is a minister in the statutory sense . . . is a factual question susceptible of exact proof. No search of his conscience is required. . . . The conscientious objector claim admits of no such exact proof. Probing a man's conscience is

at best a speculative venture." (at 903–04) Subsequent reversal of the decision in this case was on technical grounds.

[31] 40 Stat. at 76, 78.

[32] We have quoted the phrase as abbreviated by the Supreme Court in *Seeger.*

[33] 54 Stat. at 889.

[34] 213 Fed. 2nd 901.

[35] At 904.

[36] Cf. 15 *St. John's Law Review* 235.

[37] 112 Fed. Supp. 71; 1953.

[38] At 75. Cf. 19 *Ohio State Law Journal* 352.

[39] 156 Fed. 2nd 377; 1946.

[40] 133 Fed. 2nd 703; 1943.

[41] 133 Fed. 2nd 521; 1943.

[42] 141 Fed. 2nd 845; 1944.

[43] At 382.

[44] At 380. Cf. *Brief for the United States* at 70.

[45] 135 Fed. 2nd 521; 1943.

[46] Both quotes at 523.

[47] 133 Fed. 2nd at 708.

[48] There is a considerable literature on these cases. Cf. 28 *Southern California Law Review* 123; 1955; 31 *Virginia Law Review* 811: 1945; 19 *Pittsburgh Law Review* 695: 1958; 43 *Columbia Law Review* 112: 1943.

[49] Cf. *Seeger* opinion of the Supreme Court.

[50] 375 U.S. 930.

[51] At 854.

[52] 326 Fed. 2nd 853.

[53] 367 U.S. 495.

[54] At 67, 68.

[55] At 76 f.

[56] 2 and 3 Geo. 6 c.81 Relevant here is a view expressed by Judge Manton of the Circuit Court of Appeals in *Macintosh,* reversed by the Supreme Court. "A citizen sharing views which amount to conscientious or religious scruples against bearing arms in what he regards as an unjustified war is akin to one having conscientious scruples against all wars." 42 F 2nd 845, at 848.

[57] Cf. 14 *Catholic University Law Review* at 238. This writer remarks: "By widening the definition of religion under the statute at least to the cosmos the exception provision would seem to have been effectively eliminated." (at 245) With this we cannot agree. The exemption provision still operates under *Seeger* to exclude from exemption those whose objections, being political and sociological, are not supported by some sort of affirmation of transcendent reality.

[58] At 19,21.

[59] The Court accepted the principle of *Speiser v. Randall* (357 U.S. 513; 1958) that even though exemption of conscientious objectors is by legislative grace rather than constitutional right, in conferring exemptions the Congress may not do so in a manner inconsistent with the provisions of the

Constitution. Cf. *Brief for the Respondent,* at pp. 38–60. Cf. *Sherbert v. Verner* (374 U.S. 398; 1963).

[60] At 70 f.

[61] John Haynes Holmes, Paul Tillich, J. A. T. Robinson, the Second Vatican Council, David Muzzey of the Ethical Culture Movement.

[62] Most particularly *Britt v. United States,* at bar in the *Seeger* case.

ABOUT THE AUTHORS

Markus Barth, Presbyterian

Educational Background:

Berne, Switzerland, 1934–35.
Basel, Switzerland, 1935–37.
Berlin, Germany, 1937.
Edinburgh, Scotland, 1938–39.
Doctorate of Theology, University of Goettingen, Germany, 1947, in the field of New Testament.

Publications:

Das Abendmahl, Passamahl, Bundesmahl, und Messiasmahl. Zurich, 1945.
Der Augenzeuge, Eine Untersuchung ueber die Wahrnehmung des Menschensohnes durch die Apostel. Zurich, 1946.
Die Taufe—ein Sakrament? ein exegetischer Beitrag. Zurich, 1951.
The Broken Wall, A Study in Ephesians. Philadelphia, 1959.
Was Christ's Death a Sacrifice? Edinburgh, 1961.
Acquittal by Resurrection (V. Fletcher, co-author). New York, 1963.
Conversation With the Bible. New York, 1964.
"What Can a Jew Believe About Jesus and Still Remain a Jew?" *Journal of Ecumenical Studies,* Fall, 1965.

Other Pertinent Information:

After being the Parish minister of the Evangelical Reformed Church in Bubendorf, Basselland (Switzerland) from 1940–53, Professor Barth became visiting professor of New Testament at the Presbyterian Theological Seminary, Dubuque, Iowa, from 1953–55. From 1956–63 he held the position of Associate Professor of New Testament, Federated Theological Faculty, at the University of Chicago in Chicago, Illinois. In 1963 he became Professor of New

Testament at the Pittsburgh Theological Seminary, Pittsburgh, Pennsylvania. Professor Barth currently serves as an editorial associate of the *Journal of Ecumenical Studies.*

Daniel Callahan, Catholic

Educational Background:

B.A., Yale University.
M.A., Georgetown University.
Ph.D. in philosophy, Harvard University.

Publications:

Co-editor, *Christianity Divided: Protestant and Roman Catholic Theological Issues,* 1961.
The Mind of the Catholic Layman, 1963.
Honesty in the Church, 1965.
Editor, *Federal Aid and Catholic Schools,* 1964.
Editor, *Generation of the Third Eye,* 1965.
Contributed essays to *Looking Toward the Council, The Layman and the Council, Theology and the University,* and *Freedom and Man.*
Contributed to a number of periodicals, including *Commonweal, Cross Currents, Esprit, Christianity and Crisis, Harper's, and Harvard Educational Review.*

Other Pertinent Information:

Dr. Callahan has taught in the Harvard Divinity School, in the Graduate Department of Religion at Temple University, and in the Religious Studies Department at Brown University. He is presently an associate editor of *Commonweal.*

ARTHUR C. COCHRANE, Presbyterian

Educational Background:

B.A., University of Toronto, 1932.
B.D., Knox College, Toronto, 1935.
Ph.D., University of Edinburgh, 1937.

Publications:

The Existentialists and God. Philadelphia, 1956.
Translator, *Karl Barth's Church Dogmatics* by Otto Weber.

The Church's Confession Under Hitler. Philadelphia, 1962.

"The Mystery of the Continuity of the Church," *Journal of Ecumenical Studies,* Winter, 1965.

Editor and translator, *Reformed Confessions of the 16th Century.* Philadelphia, 1966.

Other Pertinent Information:

Dr. Cochrane is Professor of Systematic Theology at the University of Dubuque Theological Seminary. Before coming to the University of Dubuque in 1948 he served two pastorates in Ontario. He spent two years (1955–57) with the Confessional Church in Germany while studying the Reformation Confessions of Protestantism. He received a fellowship from the Sealantic Fund, Inc., under the Rockefeller Foundation, for the 1957–58 academic year and at that time completed his research on the Church in Germany during the Nazi regime. Professor Cochrane spent the year 1963–64 at Yale University as Visiting Professor of Theology. He is a member of the North American Area Council of the World Presbyterian Alliance; and is a past-president of the Trinitarian Theological Society and of the Mid-West Division of the American Theology Society.

ARTHUR GILBERT, Jewish

Educational Background:

B.A., New York University, 1947.

M.H.L. and Rabbinic ordination, Jewish Institute of Religion, New York, 1951.

Graduate studies, National Psychological Association for Psychoanalysis.

Certified, New York State Department of Health, as psychiatric social worker.

Publications:

Co-author, *Neighbor Celebrate.* New York, 1954.

Contributor, *American Catholics: the Protestant-Jewish Viewpoint.* New York, 1961.

Contributor, *Religion and the Public Order* (Villanova University School of Law). Chicago, 1964.

Contributor, *Torah and Gospel.* New York, 1966.

The Jew in Christian America. (Will be published in May, 1966.)
The Vatican Council and the Jews. (Will be published in fall, 1966.)

Other Pertinent Information:

Received Catholic Press Award for best non-fiction article in 1961.
Consultant to Government of Israel in study on Jewish-Christian-Muslim Relations, 1959.
Observer at World Pentecostal Convention, Jerusalem, 1961.
Jewish Consultant to Lutheran World Federation's Consultation on the Church and the Jewish People, held at Logunskloster, Denmark, May 1965.
Participant, White House Conferences for religious leaders on Religion and Race and Religion and Poverty.
Member, editorial board of *Reconstructions* and *Religion and the Public Order* (Villanova University School of Law).
Director, Department of Religious Curriculum Research, Anti-Defamation League of B'Nai B'Rith.
Rabbi Gilbert was recently made an editorial associate of the *Journal of Ecumenical Studies.*

DEAN M. KELLEY, Methodist

Educational Background:

A.B., University of Denver, 1946.
Th.M., Iliff School of Theology, 1949.
Graduate study in sociology at Columbia University on Elizabeth Iliff Warren Fellowship, 1949–1950.

Executive Activities:

Nationwide Study of "Christian Responsibility for Freedom," 1960.
Analysis of House un-American Activities Committee film "Operation Abolition," 1961.
National Study Conference on Church and State, 1962–63.
Opposition to "Becker Amendment" (designed to overturn Supreme Court decisions on prayer in public schools), 1964.
Clarification of church-state aspects of Elementary and Secondary Education Act and of other legislation, 1965.
Opposition to "Dirksen Amendment" (designed to overturn Supreme Court decisions on reapportionment), 1965.

Other Pertinent Information:

The Reverend Dean M. Kelley has served as pastor of Methodist churches for thirteen years, and has been Director of the Commission on Religious Liberty of the National Council of Churches since 1960.

JOHN L. McKENZIE, Catholic

Educational Background:

Entered the Society of Jesus, 1928.
Litt.B., Xavier University, 1932.
M.A., St. Louis University, 1935.
Ordained to the priesthood, 1939.
S.T.D., Weston College, 1946.

Publications:

The Two-Edged Sword. Milwaukee, 1956.
Myths and Realities. Milwaukee, 1963.
The Power and the Wisdom. Milwaukee, 1965.
A Dictionary of the Bible. Milwaukee, 1965.

Other Pertinent Information:

Father McKenzie has been Professor of Old Testament and Hebrew at West Baden College from 1942–1960; Professor of Biblical History at Loyola University, 1960–1965; and is now Visiting Professor of Old Testament at the Divinity School of the University of Chicago.

MICHAEL NOVAK, Catholic

Educational Background:

A.B., Stonehille College, North Easton, Mass., 1956.
B.T., Gregorian University, Rome, Italy, 1958.
Three further semesters in theology, Catholic University, Washington, D.C., 1958–59.

Publications:

A New Generation: American and Catholic. New York, 1964.
The Open Church: Vatican II: Act II. New York, 1964.
The Experience of Marriage. New York, 1964. (editor)
Belief and Unbelief. New York, 1965.

Scholarly publications include: "Newman on Nicaea," *Theological Studies,* 1960; "The Philosophy Implicit in Biblical Studies," *Catholic Biblical Quarterly,* 1960.

Since 1956, Mr. Novak has taken an active part in discussions of philosophy, religion, and American society in *Commonweal, New Republic, Christian Century, Worldview, The Nation, Harper's,* etc. In 1964, he was named Editor-at-large by *Christian Century.*

Other Pertinent Information:

In 1961, Mr. Novak was elected a Kent Fellow and a Teaching Fellow in General Education at Harvard University. In September, 1963, he took a semester's leave of absence from Harvard in order to observe the Second Session of the Vatican Council. In the spring of 1964, he transferred to the Department of Higher Studies in Religion at Harvard, concentrating upon Christian ethics. Mr. Novak is presently Assistant Professor of Religion at Stanford University.

LEO PFEFFER, Jewish

Educational Background:

B.S.S., City College of the City of New York.
Doctor of Jurisprudence, New York University.

Publications:

Liberties of an American. A chronicle of the Supreme Court decisions in civil rights and civil liberties, 1956.

Church, State, and Freedom (included in the White House Library established by President Kennedy).

Creeds in Competition.

Church and State in the United States (with Anson Phelps Stokes).

The Honorable Court. A history of the United States Supreme Court, which was the June, 1965 selection of the Book Find Club.

Numerous articles in many law journals on the subject of civil rights and civil liberties, and contributions to several encyclopedias.

Other Pertinent Information:

Mr. Pfeffer, Special Counsel of the American Jewish Congress and Chairman of the Department of Political Science at Long Island University, is one of the nation's leading constitutional lawyers. He is co-founder and the first president of the Lawyers Constitutional

Defense Committee, which, during the summer of 1964, provided some 150 volunteer lawyers for the defense of civil rights in the South. In the field of civil rights he occupies an unusual position in that he is both a nationally recognized teacher, scholar, and authority, and at the same time an active practitioner in the courts.

ELWYN A. SMITH, Presbyterian

Educational Background:

M.A. and Ph.D., Harvard University, 1942.
B.D., Yale Divinity School, 1943.
Th.M., Princeton Theological Seminary, 1944.

Publications:

The Presbyterian Ministry in American Culture. Philadelphia, 1962.
"The Role of the South in the Presbyterian Schism of 1838," *Church History,* March, 1960.
"The Doctrine of Imputation and the Presbyterian Schism of 1837–1838," *Journal of the Presbyterian Historical Society,* September, 1960.
"The Forming of an American Denomination," *Church History,* March, 1962.
Church and State in Your Community. Philadelphia, 1963.
"Barth Among the Barthians," *Christian Century,* August 10, 1955.
"Foreign Policy for the '60s," *Christian Century,* November 2, 1960.
"Mr. Kennedy's Third Choice," *Christian Century,* March 7, 1962.
"Anti-Americanism: French Style," *Christian Century,* March 10, 1965.
"A New Proposal for Federal Aid to Parochial Schools," *The Catholic World,* June, 1965.

Other Pertinent Information:

Professor Smith has been director of the Westminster Foundation, a student ministry, in Washington, D.C., 1943–45; an editor of education publications, 1945–49; Dean and Professor of Church History, Dubuque Theological Seminary, Dubuque, Iowa, 1950–56; Professor of Church History, Pittsburgh Theological Seminary, 1957–66; and is now under appointment as Professor of Religion at Temple University, Philadelphia. He is co-editor, with Leonard Swidler, of the *Journal of Ecumenical Studies.* He is the chairman of the Commission on Civil and Religious Liberty of the American Area

Council of the World Presbyterian Alliance. He was chairman of the Special Committee of the General Assembly of the United Presbyterian Church on Relations Between Church and State, 1960–63.

MICHAEL W. STRASSER, Catholic

Educational Background:

B.S., St. Louis University, 1947.
M.A., University of Toronto, 1949.
Pontifical Institute of Mediaeval Studies, Toronto, and School of Graduate Studies, University of Toronto, 1947–51.
Ph.D., University of Toronto, 1963.

Publications:

"Liber de Causis (Book of Causes)," *American Encyclopedia of Philosophy,* 1964. *St. Thomas' Theory of the Natural Law.* A series of articles, some to appear in 1966.
Paper on "William of Occam and Platonism," Western Pennsylvania Philosophical Society, December, 1951.

Other Pertinent Information:

Professor Strasser has been Instructor, Assistant Professor, and Associate Professor of Philosophy at Duquesne University from 1951 to the present. He has also taught at Mt. Mercy College, Pittsburgh; Pennsylvania State University and La Roche College, near Pittsburgh. He has held offices in the Western Pennsylvania Philosophical Society, including the presidency in 1964–65; and is active in the American Association of University Professors and the North Hills Association for Racial Equality, Greater Pittsburgh Area. He is also a member of the American Catholic Philosophical Association, the American Philosophical Association, and the Society for Ancient Greek Philosophy.

LEONARD SWIDLER, Catholic

Educational Background:

B.A., St. Norbert's College, 1950.
M.A., Marquette University, 1955.

S.T.L., University of Tübingen, 1959.
Ph.D., University of Wisconsin, 1961.

Publications:

"Ecumenism in Germany," *Commonweal,* January 23, 1960.
"Land of the Reformation: Lutheran Liturgical Revival," *Commonweal,* November 11, 1960.
"The Doktrin and Practis of William C. Talcott," *Indiana Magazine of History,* March, 1961.
"The Catholic Bible Movement in Germany, Report and Analysis," *Interpretation,* 1961.
"An Ecumenical Letter," *American Benedictine Review,* June, 1961.
"German Protestantism and Ecumenism," *Thought,* Spring, 1962.
"Max Josef Metzger, a Witness for Unity," *American Benedictine Review,* June, 1962.
Dialogue for Reunion. New York, 1962.
"Reappraising the Reformation," *Commonweal,* October 30, 1964.
"Freedom and the Catholic Church," *Theology Today,* October, 1964.
Scripture and Ecumenism (editor). Pittsburgh, 1965.
The Ecumenical Vanguard. Pittsburgh, 1965.
Bloodwitness for Peace and Unity. New York, 1965.
Co-editor, *Journal of Ecumenical Studies.*

Other Pertinent Information:

Professor Swidler is a member of the History Department faculty of Duquesne University. He has taught English at Milwaukee School of Engineering; philosophy at Edgewood College; English and history at the University of Wisconsin; history and philosophy at the University of Maryland in Europe; and German at the U.S.A.R. Intelligence School, Fort Sheridan, prior to coming to Duquesne. He is now under appointment as Professor of Religion at Temple University, Philadelphia. Professor Swidler is a member of the executive board of the Pittsburgh Chapter of the National Conference of Christians and Jews; and has been a participant in the Notre Dame Colloquium, January, 1964; the Institute on Religious Pluralism, National Conference of Christians and Jews, Greensboro, North Carolina, July, 1954; and the Institute on Ecumenical Dialogue and Theological Teaching, December, 1964.